Principles of Integral Science of Religion

Religion and Reason 17

Method and Theory
in the Study and Interpretation of Religion

MOUTON PUBLISHERS · THE HAGUE · PARIS · NEW YORK

Principles of Integral Science of Religion

by
GEORG SCHMID
Teachers College,
Chur, Switzerland

MOUTON PUBLISHERS · THE HAGUE · PARIS · NEW YORK

Translated from German by John Wilson

ISBN: 90-279-7864-6

Jacket design by Jurriaan Schrofer

© 1979, Mouton Publishers, The Hague, The Netherlands

Typeset by H Charlesworth & Co Ltd, Huddersfield, England

Printing: Werner Hildebrand oHG., Berlin
Binding: Lüderite & Bauer, Berlin

Preface

I wish to thank, firstly and above all, those who have supported my work with their suggestions, criticisms and interest, especially Prof. F. Buri in Basel, Prof. C. Keller in Lausanne, and Dr. J. D. J. Waardenburg, who is the chief editor of this series, John Wilson, Ph.D. in Möhlin/AG, who translated this book and David Stitt, who made the corrections.

Certainly no less, but only in a different way, do I wish to thank my family, my students and my colleague at the Lehrerseminar in Chur, W. Glücker, all of whom enriched my course of work with patience and understanding. The staff of the Kantonsbibliothek Graubünden deserve special thanks. What would science be without such contributing colleagues?

The reader will discover that this work asks him to follow several new distinctions, and he could have the impression that the author wishes to establish new programs or, indeed, to project a new discipline. That is, however, not the case. Against such misunderstanding I can, to state my goal, use the words of J. Wach in the preface to his methodological studies:

> In all it is a matter neither of programs nor of projections of new disciplines, but of the clear working-out of directions, efforts and tendencies which have always come forward in our science. These should be lifted into methodological awareness and clarified.
> (*Religions Wissenschaft*, 1924:IV).

Although Wach's explanation is now more than fifty years old, it has lost none of its significance. A methodological work exceeds its capabilities if it pretends to give something fundamentally new. It is also superfluous if it does no more than repeat what has already been said. Methodology does not create new ways, but it also does not simply tramp along the old. To employ methodology can only mean to continue along known ways where these ways indicate further work.

This book is no exception to that rule. It will have attained its goal if it succeeds in grasping, clarifying and, here and there developing what science of religion has long carried in itself as beginning point and as possibility.

Chur, 9 June 1978   Georg Schmid

Table of Contents

Introduction

1. METHODOLOGY

If I may begin with a metaphor from the Gospel of Matthew, to employ methodology means to offer the reader a stone instead of bread. However, that in itself is not to be held against methodology. Methodology does, at first, put one's own act above the work one is considering, one's perceiving above what one perceives in the work, one's being under way above arrival. But in doing this, methodology serves the work itself, the perception and the goal far more than an interpretation of the work which, while giving results, says nothing at all about the whence, the how, and the means of the interpretation. In any case, the broad discussion of method in contemporary science of religion[1] has resulted in the conclusion that *we can only be responsible for our perceptions if we are responsible for our method of perceiving*. Methodology may be a sterile undertaking, but it is a sterile necessity.

It is the intention of this work to be a contribution to the methodology of science of religion. But to which methodology? Depending on its point of departure, its understanding of its goals and its procedure, methodology can move in quite different directions (cf. among others G. Sauter, 1973). Therefore, one who employs methodology must tell us what he is talking about. *We name methodology the attempt of science of religion to come to clarity about what it itself does*. What that means may be explained in the following four points.

1. In our view, methodology is more than what G. König means when he says that it is scientific occupation with methods and 'methodics'. It has as its object not only 'individual, definitely given ways of procedure which have to be judged' and systems 'of operationally connected methods which have application in a definite

area' (1973:100). We understand the object of methodology to be nothing more and nothing less than science of religion, and, indeed, science of religion as a theme of science of religion. When science of religion does methodology, it attempts to consider itself critically. It stands, so to speak, before a mirror. Such self-observation leads to narcissism and self-adulation only if it is uncritical and if the science becomes inebriated with its own successes. In this critical reflection on itself science of religion will, in any case, see itself confronted not only with its methods or methodics. Just as fundamentally, it will also have to sight its way of posing tasks and goals, its premises and their consequences.

2. In the attempt to attain clarity about what it does, science of religion can neither proceed only descriptively nor simply establish norms. Certainly the description of its own methodological procedure is of central importance. It is just as important for any methodology that it not only describe what it has done but also, where necessary, prescribe the basic lines of its continuing course. Therefore, methodology proceeds neither only descriptively nor only by laying out norms, but critically: *criticism is constructive description*. Constructive description means giving attention to what is yet possible in what has already been given. It is that description of a course which leads into the prescription of new courses. In its methodology, science of religion makes self-criticism a consequent duty to be assumed.

3. What is the best that can result from such criticism? Methodology cannot attain any sort of eternally valid fundamental laws or complete and self-contained methods of perception in science of religion. Whoever expects the former of methodology confuses methodology with ideology, and whoever expects the latter confuses methodology with an instrument. Apart from signs of wear and tear, an instrument always remains the same before, during and after its application. A method becomes what it is through its execution and not in its abstract formulation. The best that methodology can produce, therefore, are neither immovably basic laws nor complete, self-contained methods but only *principles* or 'beginnings'. We name principles first steps leading to other steps and indicating the basic

direction of these other steps. The further course, these other steps, is the meaning of the first steps, their test, their chance, but also their correction and supplementation. Principles are elements of scientific perception about which science can attain clarity but which science can never hold as unshakable dogmas. The elements of scientific perception become wholly what they are only in the execution of research. On the basis of what has already been said, it is meaningful to speak of 'principles of integral science of religion'.

4. Methodology may not simply be derived from the object of perception of science of religion. Certainly, all perception, including that of science of religion, is largely determined by what is perceived. Nevertheless, it would be false to derive the self-critical knowledge of science of religion from knowledge about religion. That is true because all knowledge about religion, in the case that this knowledge is scientifically representable, is itself a result of science of religion. Not even in its methodology can science of religion proceed from point zero. Wherever it begins, science of religion has to do with previous perception of science of religion. The correlation of religion and science of religion is the central theme of every methodology. We have also emphasized the concept of correlation. That is because science of religion cannot be directly and unilaterally derived from religion.

2. METHODOLOGY AND THE REFLECTION ON, OR THE CONSIDERATION OF (*Be-sinn-ung auf*) THE WHOLE OF RELIGION

Science of religion encounters itself critically, and where this happens we speak of methodology. The necessity of such encounter is to be seen in the critical encounter itself — for example, in science of religion's criticism of its own results. This example is mentioned here as introduction to the problem.

If we ask what modern research of religion in its intensive work — a work which is more than a century old — has actually achieved in insight and knowledge, we are faced with an oddly equivocal answer. *According to one's point of view, the result of modern science of religion is either no less than an enormous sum or no more than nothing at all.*

Knowledge of the religious in science of religion is apparently infinitely multifarious and detailed. By the term religious we mean the religious-historical and religious-ethnological material which has been discovered, collected, reflected on, and interpreted. Every known culture has contributed to the broadening of this knowledge, and often these contributions have been worlds apart in themselves. Numerous forms of society illustrate religious behavior, innumerable persons give witness to their personal religiosity. Whoever tries to gain a knowledge of the religious meets with, as have Roger Caillois and Mircea Eliade, 'a labyrinthine complexity of elements, which yield to no formula or definition whatever. Taboo, ritual, symbol, myth, demon, god — these are some of them; but it would be an outrageous simplification to make such a list tell the whole story. What we have really got to deal with is a diverse and, indeed, chaotic mass of actions, beliefs and systems which go together to make up what one may call the religious phenomenon' (Eliade, 1963:XIV).

The problem lies precisely here. Are we able to find in the chaos of the many any sort of order which binds the many into the one? Do we have in this enormous sum of particulars any sort of presentiment of a whole? Does our boundless knowledge of the religious lead in any way to an understanding of religion? Or, to remain with the image of the labyrinth, will we ever find a way out of this maze and win the over-view or discover the plan which underlies the many in all its enormity?

With regard to this question, an honest and wholesome agnosticism has provisionally come to the fore. It is honest because it corresponds to the situation of modern science of religion. It is wholesome because it is better to persist with a genuine problem than to give oneself to solutions which side-step the problem. That means, with regard to phenomenology of religion:

Instead of claiming to know what religion essentially is, of all investigators the student of religion should rather admit that he, precisely, does not know what religion is. And if he pretends to know it, his phenomenology of religion easily becomes a schematization of religious phenomena (Waardenburg, 1973:117).

Or, with regard to science of religion as science, it means:

> If we consider that we not only have to do with the application of given schemes or the development of a theory of religion generally, then it becomes clear how frightfully little we still know about this object of research. Certainly, in many ways researchers have thought they 'knew' what religiosity or belief is. But this was never a scientific knowledge. Even if the objective forms of religion were empirically investigated, the inner movement of religion generally was by no means comprehended (Waardenburg, 1973b:304).

Today, the same honest agnosticism also largely determines the debates about a definition of religion. Paul W. Pruyser (1972) discusses the whole problem complex in a chapter entitled 'Insolvable Problems' (*Unlösbare Fragen*). After an impressive discussion of 'religion as variety', Kurt Goldammer states:

> The concept of religion is, therefore, *not definable* because religion is an existence- and situation-related irrational phenomenon, a function of man and of our human being which is not found outside the human world and which, therefore, must be regarded as a specific utterance of what is human. But it never appears as unified and univocal (1960:9)
> Especially knowlegeable scientists of religion no longer give any sort of exact definition of religion (1969:113).

As paradoxical as it may sound, the more we know, the less we know. The more extensive and detailed our knowledge is, the greater is the problem and the more reserved are all statements about religion. To use the quite fitting terms of M. Eliade and J. D. J. Waardenburg: we know, on the one hand, a 'chaotic' (Eliade, 1963: XIV)[2] manifold and on the other, 'frightfully little' (Waardenburg, 1973b:304) at all.

What options does science of religion face today in this apparently paradoxical situation? In our opinion there are three possible options.

1. Science of religion may decide that nothing can be done about the situation at all, because the situation is simply necessary. And, indeed, can science of religion seriously occupy itself with something

other than individual religious data? Are not such concepts as religion, *Sinnmitte der Religion*, essence of religion, and basic structure of religion simply pure constructions? According to this view, the object of science of religion is always only the individual concrete religious witness. To search for more, to ask about an orderly coherence in the boundless manifold of the religious — that is no longer science but pure construction.

In our opinion, this option, which is to remain consciously in the chaos, is only possible if science of religion gives itself up and, consciously losing religion in the enormity of the religious, becomes instead a hodgepodge collection of religious data, an arsenal of the history of religion. Such a 'science of religion' would, indeed, have to leave unanswered the question about the principle or criterium of whatever order the collection might have. Without insight into 'religion' there can be no knowledge of any sort of 'characteristics of the religious'.

2. With the ever broadening knowledge of the religious, the question about religion becomes not only ever more difficult but also ever more urgent. The further the research of individual data proceeds, the broader the knowledge of religious-historical and religious-ethnological detail, the more oppressive the chaos and the labyrinth of the known, *all the more urgent becomes the consideration of or the reflection on* (Be-sinn-ung auf) *the whole — even within the enormity of the individual data.* Somehow to risk anew reflection on the whole — that is the second option.

To be sure, questions about such attempts must arise. How is such an attempt to be made? How can science of religion insure that the possibilities of success in this new attempt stand any better than the long chain of attempts to define religion or to determine its essence? It cannot be forgotten that these attempts ended finally in the resignation we mentioned above. The question depends not on the risk of ever new attempts to consider or reflect on the·whole of religion, but on better conditions for this risk.

3. How, then, can science of religion improve the chances for its own work? How can it change the conditions for its question about the whole? The only possible answer to this question is

methodology. Consideration of, or reflection on, the whole of religion must be bound in modern science of religion with this science's consideration of, or reflection on itself. The longer we live with the problem of reflection on the whole of religion, the more clearly it emerges as the urgent task of modern science of religion. But this task can no longer be directly approached; that is, we have to take the indirect course of methodological reflection. If we do not take this course, we have to make up for our inability to be convincing with the usual courage and heuristic; and we must not allow ourselves to be embarrassed for having simply added several links to the long chain of unsatisfactory attempts and, therewith, for having only prepared our end in agnosticism all the more thoroughly. *Reflection on the whole of religion must be combined in modern science of religion with the science's reflection on itself,* with critical consideration of its own task, premises, and methods. If it is possible at all for the science more closely to approach a meaningful and viable answer to the question about the whole of religion, then that must happen through this critical reflection on task, premises, and methods. In our situation today, to choose any other means of approach would be, at best, mere play.

The Task

1. MODERN SCIENCE OF RELIGION

We understand modern science of religion to be *the attempt of modern man to overcome his fundamental dilemma with regard to traditional religion by means of systematic research of religious reality.* That means:

1. Modern science of religion may only in its smallest part be understood as a product of intellectual curiosity or as purely practical desire for understanding. It is certainly true that pure interest in research, in the new, different, and unknown does partially account for the enticement into the infinite breadth of religious reality.[1] Modern science of religion also partially corresponds to an urgent practical need: in the modern period, in which the various peoples are much nearer to one another, awareness of the difference of the other — including his religious difference — is almost forced on everyone, and many feel themselves challenged to understand the difference of the other as well as possible. Both this practical need of the modern world and intellectual curiosity, in its natural desire to leave no stone unturned, have contributed and continue to contribute their part to modern science of religion. It would, however, be very superficial and a degradation of its interest, if modern science of religion were thought to consist only of intellectual curiosity and the practical will to understand. Modern science of religion has never been merely practically meaningful or theoretically interesting. Since its beginnings it has been, above all, existentially necessary. It had its origin as a child of Rationalism (W. Holsten: 1038-1042) and appeared with the beginning of the Enlightenment. (cf. among others E. Herbert v. Cherbury, 1663; John Spencer, 1669 and 1685). That is far more than a coincidence. Science of religion generally becomes necessary at the point where one's own traditional religion

becomes a problem and calls for scientific clarification.

Modern science of religion, therefore, is also based on the relation of modernity to traditional religion.[2] We call this relation a *fundamental dilemma*. That means, first, that in the modern period traditional religion sees itself placed ever more in question. Modern man finds it ever more difficult to assume his traditional religion, as, for example, he assumes his name or his language as a part of himself. Rather, he questions, weighs, tests, and investigates his religion, and it may not be overlooked that a broad perplexity underlies all of his critical activity (P. Meinhold, 1973:381ff).[3]

We also call this dilemma underlying modern science of religion fundamental because it is not limited to merely this or that aspect of traditional religion. Modern man also finds problematic the credibility of a specific religious tradition or the questionable role his traditional religion played at some moment of its history. No aspect of religion is in principle removed from the purview of modern critical questioning. Such questioning began with the most offensive and apparently most unreasonable teachings and customs. It graduated into questioning religion's presuppositions, implications, and consequences, and the result has been that the whole of religion is ever more put into question (K. Goldammer, 1960:6; cf. also P. Meinhold, 1973b:381ff; E. Benz, 1968:8ff).[4]

2. Modern man could simply accept this fundamental dilemma with a resigned shrug of the shoulders. The ground for the necessity of modern science of religion is the fundamental dilemma *with regard to traditional religion*. However one wishes to attain clarity about it, traditional religion is, in any case, an ancient and yet contemporary event. It is extremely problematic, but it is present, and it does not give one the impression that it is about to disappear because there is now a fundamental dilemma. Just the fact that traditional religion was, is, and will be means that it is, if not a vexation, then a challenge for modern critical thought. Somehow modern thought has to explain the strange presence of traditional religion in our time. It has to discover the ground and the justification of its continued life. Even if modern critical thought can no longer gain any value or meaning from traditional religion, it has to ask

itself: how is it at all possible that something so impossible continues to live?

3. *Consideration of, or reflection on (Be-sinnung auf), the whole of religion* follows immediately from the fundamental dilemma. If the whole is questionable, one must question the whole. To question less than the whole would be to deny the ground on which one stands. The fundamental dilemma makes integral research and questioning unavoidable. One cannot be contented with consideration of this or that moment of the religious. The ground and the middle and the whole of religion 'call' us, so to speak, to perceive and consider them.

4. Modern science of religion can see the possibility of an answer to the question about the whole and the essence (*das Eigenste*) of religion only in the *systematic research of religious reality*. The fundamental dilemma with regard to traditional religion leads to an intensity and breadth of religious-historical and religious-ethnological research which has never been equaled in scientific history. In its effort to understand what religion is, modern science of religion rushes through all times and cultures, and all is considered worthy of attention which has to do with sources and observations of traditional religion.

The object of this religious-scientific research is obviously *religious reality*, not the reality of religion. We call *religious reality* the historically demonstrable side of religion. It means, firstly, *the enormously wide field of religious data*, which include holy writings, and other documents, prayer books, theological treatises, the formation of temples, cultic objects, pictures, symbols, songs, church offices and forms of community. We name religious reality, secondly, the whole manifold of religious life and experience which expresses itself or conceals itself in religious data: sacrifice, prayer, meditation, thanksgiving, worship, search, petition, celebration, experience, remembrance, realization, belief, hope, imitation, astonishment, rebellion, enthusiasm, confession, teaching and obedient action.

In what follows, the *reality of religion* means *what is intended in all of this life and experience*, the whence and whereto of all this searching, hoping, believing and worshipping. The reality of religion means the reality for the sake of which all religious reality comes into being. *Religious reality is religion as incontestable appearance. The reality of religion is religion as meaning. Religious reality is religion as datum and event in the life of man. The reality of religion is the reality which the religious event makes present and to which it witnesses.*

As science, science of religion knows of no direct access to the reality of religion. The reality of religion is present to the science only in the witness of the religious reality. Only the religious reality is the immediate object of science of religion, and the science researches this object systematically, that is, in awareness of method and in consistent procedure within the chosen method. If the integral question can be answered, then only through the systematic research of religious reality. Neither speculative philosophy of religion nor pious intuition — both in appearance directly acquainted with the reality of religion — is any longer able to satisfy us. The question about the whole of religion has become radical in such a way that it can only be satisfactorily answered on the basis of clear evidence. Other answers would only cancel the question. They would not overcome the fundamental dilemma with reliable certainty but simply pass over it with uncontrolled assumptions. *In our situation of the fundamental dilemma, certainty may be found only through making the religious reality the object of a science.*

It is self-evident that modern science of religion can never make the claim of being the only effort toward a better knowledge and understanding of religion. The science both knows and acknowledges numerous analogous efforts which have preceded and still accompany its own. Modern science of religion does, however, make the claim of being a very special undertaking among these various efforts. It distinguishes itself in its ground and goal, or in its method, or in both. *The characteristic of modern science of religion is that it always combines an integral interest, that is, a question about the whole of religion, with methods of specific research.* It attempts to approach the whole of religion in real perception through systematic research of the religious reality. It asks, at the same time, about the whole of religion and about religious-historical and religious-ethnological detail. It is this combination of integral interest with methods of specific research which clearly separates the science from its predecessors and from other contemporary effort toward understanding religion.

1. *Research of religion (Religionskunde)* has, since the days of Herodotus, arisen from contact with other religious traditions. Its ground is not so much the fundamental dilemma with regard to one's own religion as simply the experience of difference. Its aim, therefore, is to understand another religion better, to become acquainted with it and to make others acquainted with it. Its aim is not to attain a reliable answer to the radical question about the whole and essence of religion itself. If one wishes to say that this sort of research is science of religion, then qualification must be added that it is science of religion with another ground and, therefore, with another intention. *Research of religion (Religionskunde) is practical science of religion* in which it suffices to do justice to the peculiarity of the religion investigated. It has the intention of promoting a better and more adequate encounter with a different and important culture. It does not research the whole breadth of religious reality, and it does not ask about the whole of religion (G. Rosenkranz, 1951 and 1955).[5]

2. *Philosophy of religion* can be understood as *thinking out the perceptions of specific science of religion to their logical ends.* According to this understanding, philosophy of religion is nothing other than explicit integral science of religion or modern science of religion in its essential intention. However, philosophy of religion can also designate the act *in which science of religion reflects on itself,* on its own premises, methods and perspectives. But with this understanding, too, philosophy of religion is not something outside but a necessary part of modern science of religion. Science of religion loses its scientific character when it no longer reflects on what it itself does. Its results are believable only as long as it can be critically responsible for its process of arriving at those results. But philosophy of religion can also mean the attempt to achieve an idea of the whole of religion apart from specific research. For example, it can attempt to conclude something about religious being on the basis of some

philosophy's analysis of human being. This philosophy of religion is outside the sphere of science of religion. It does ask about the whole of religion on the basis of the experience of the fundamental dilemma, but for its answer it does not need systematic research of religious reality. Philosophical insight into the being of man pushes aside the witness of religious reality. Religion is not asked to speak for itself. One takes one's information about what religion is from another source.[6]

3. *Religious apologetics*, similar to research of religion (*Religionskunde*), is at best science of religion with another intention and ground. It arises from the human, all too human, need to demonstrate the truth of one's own religion in comparison with the half-truths of foreign religion. One has to do with the validity of one's own religion and not with understanding of the whole of religion. In such an approach, in spite of all apparent care and concern for a proper investigation of the other religion, the result is clear from the beginning. With its research apologetics only seeks to cement what it already knows. Its excursuses in specific research seek only the confirmation of the necessary result.

It is here only incidentally mentioned that such religious apologetics has nothing to do with Christian theology and should not appear at all in Christianity. Christian theology confesses, to be sure, the absoluteness of Christ; but just because of that, it should have a clear awareness of the relativity of Christianity. It has no cause to demonstrate the superiority of Christianity or the inferiority of other religions. Christian chauvinism has nothing to do with following Jesus.

4. In its union of integral interest and specific method, modern science of religion distinguishes itself also from its predecessors, *medieval* and *antique science of religion*. Antique science of religion appears, on the one hand, by historians and geographers as research of religion (*Religionskunde*: Herodotus and Strabo), as description of different religious customs and ideas of other peoples. On the other hand, antique science of religion tries to enlighten the whole of religion in a critical-speculative way (critically in Euhemeros, speculatively, for example, in Neoplatonism). Therefore, both the

integral interest and the effort toward religious-ethnological detail are anticipated in antiquity. However, antiquity never convincingly united these two characteristics of modern science of religion into a single process of research. It is, rather, precisely the fact of their separation that characterizes antique science of religion.

The synthesis of the two elements was also not achieved in medieval science of religion. In spite of all its empiricism, it remained finally religious apologetics (Roger Bacon), or, in spite of increasing knowledge of non-Christian religions (Islam and Judaism), it remained finally speculative philosophy of religion (Nicholas Cusanos).

It would be unfair, however, to distinguish modern science of religion from all analogous attempts at a better knowledge and understanding of religion without, at the same time, considering how much it owes to its predecessors and to similar contemporary efforts. Without research of religion (*Religionskunde*), on the one hand, and without speculative and critical philosophy of religion, on the other, modern science of religion could not have come into being at all. The former — on the basis of an exotic interest in the peculiar or on the basis of missionary or culture-historical interests — opens the space in which modern science of religion moves. The latter exposes the ground which causes modern science of religion to enter into the ever broadening world of the religious as it researches, collects, interprets and reflects on itself. In other words, research of religion (*Religionskunde*) anticipates the specific interest of modern science of religion; speculative and critical philosophy of religion anticipate its integral interest. Modern science of religion became possible only in the union of these two.

A thought certain of its own religious truth could not enter into science of religion's questioning. In its view, such fundamental research of the religious is, at best, industrious nonsense and, otherwise, blasphemous perfection. For such certainty, religion is far more an answer to all questions than itself the object of questions. Only where the religious answer begins to totter is religion placed in question. It is the end of religious certainty that marks the beginning of modern science of religion. First came the rationalistic philosophy of religion of the 18th Century and the increasingly speculative and critical philosophy of religion of the 19th Century, which posed ever again the question about the whole of religion and attempted ever again to answer the question. Then, in the second half of the 19th Century, began the systematic questioning about the whole of religion which we call modern science of religion.

On the other hand, the most radical questioning about the whole of religion would be blind without corresponding historical and ethnological breadth. It would not be able to attain any sort of answer on the basis of all the evidence. The broadening culture-historical horizon which unfolded in the 17th and 18th Centuries and at the beginning of the 19th Century first created the presupposition for a judgment about the whole and essence of religion which is more than a nice inspiration, a simple generalization or a lucky shot in the dark. In the second half of the 19th Century we find then not only a consequent questioning about the whole and essence of religion, but also methodological assurance had progressed and the religious world was to such a great degree accessible that one could approach the problem of asking about the whole of religion in the context of systematic research of religious reality. Again, modern science of religion is thinkable only on the basis of the union of these two. We have to bear that in mind especially where we see that modern science of religion is more than research of religion and more than philosophy of religion.

2. THE SPECIFIC AND THE INTEGRAL INTERESTS OF MODERN SCIENCE OF RELIGION

Modern science of religion is characterized by the union of integral reflection and specific research. But what does that mean in the concrete work of the science? Does not this union require an exact definition?

As a rule, 'integral' designates a direction toward the whole, a being ordered in the whole or a belonging to the whole. In accordance with this general use of the word, we use 'integral' to mean 'referred to the whole', 'orientated to the whole'.

'Species' means outer appearance and form, possibly also mental image or presentation. It is what comes into appearance, what shows itself. In religious reality, 'species' is the religious datum in which religious life makes itself evident and behind which it often conceals itself. Therefore, we name 'specific' what orientates itself to individual manifestations of religious life. 'Specific' means 'referred to the individual here and there in which religion makes itself evident', 'attentive to the individual religious datum',[7]

Modern science of religion always includes an integral and a specific interest. The former is its consistent questioning about the essence and the whole of religion in the midst of all research of the religious. The latter is the concern of the science for the individual religious datum and for the individual religious experience in the midst of its restrained passion for the whole. The integral interest means its will to perceive and to understand what religion is in its most inner essence. Its specific interest means its love of religious-historical and religious-ethnological detail, its resolute intention to perceive and understand religion where it actually happens.

It should be self-evident that the integral and specific interests cannot be separated. Rather, they are separable only where one abandons the course of modern science of religion. In modern science of religion, these two condition and supplement one another. *The integral is what is ultimately intended in the specific.* The boundlessly broadening religious-historical and religious-ethnological research has to do ultimately not only with concrete manifestations of religion but also with the question about what occurs in these manifestations as religion. On the other hand, *specific research is the condition of the possibility of the integral.* It is the space in which integral reflection can take place.

Just as it would be nonsense to see the integral and the specific interests as two separable and independent tendencies of modern science of religion, so it is meaningful to distinguish them. It is this distinction which maintains the necessity and the right of each. The distinction prevents the unnoticed absorption and eclipse of the one task by the other. Modern science of religion can abandon neither of its elementary interests. It professes its specific interest, because only the systematic study of religious reality can lead to a reliable answer to the integral question; and it professes its integral interest, because from its ground, the fundamental dilemma, it can do nothing else but ask about the whole of religion. It professes this interest, furthermore, because the boundlessly broadening specific research leads it ever more emphatically to ask about the whole in the many and the various, and, moreover, because science itself requires the most comprehensive knowledge of the matter in question. The first reason, the fundamental dilemma, has already been discussed. The second and third reasons are closely bound with the first and result, in part, from it.

Not only does integral questioning lead into specific research, but broadening specific research leads into more intensive integral reflection. It is clear that integral reflection does not become easier through the boundless breadth of knowledge of the religious. Only he can speak about the whole of religion without hesitation who is hardly acquainted with religious reality. Unilinear and all-encompassing definitions of the essence of religion and all-explaining theories of religion thrive in half-knowledge and in ignorance. Knowledge unmasks them easily as unjustified simplifications. *Religious reality repels unilinear interpretation ever more clearly* — that is, of course, on the supposition that the interpreter is acquainted with it. Nevertheless or precisely because of that, modern science of religion cannot renounce its integral reflection. The fact that simple answers collapse does not cancel the question. On the contrary, *the more difficult it becomes to answer the integral question, the more urgently the question becomes*. It is when known religious reality becomes ever more clearly labyrinthine that science of religion must give itself completely to finding the thread which leads through the enormity of evidence. If the labyrinth becomes chaos itself, the integral question becomes the question about the life and death of modern science of religion itself. In complete chaos nothing is intelligible. Religious reality as no more than a 'chaotic mass' is the end of science of religion. The science is thinkable only as the attempt to discover relations and to find the order which situates the individual in the whole. The more chaotic known religious reality becomes, the more unconditionally does modern science of religion have to understand itself as integral science of religion.

However, the situation of contemporary science of religion, characterized by a boundlessly broadening acquaintance with religious data, is, together with the fundamental dilemma, not the only reason for integral research and questioning. The principle of objectivity demands no less urgently this approach. Science not only tries to present its object of research with the least possible bias, it requires also that its subject matter be presented in the most comprehensive way possible, that is, in its wholeness. It must not neglect whatever has to do with knowledge of its subject matter. Science can limit itself temporarily to treatment of selected individual aspects of its subject matter, but, in so doing, it cannot forget that 'every limitation of scientific research merely corresponds to expediency' (E. Hardy, 1974:2 n. 1). The momentarily helpful and methodically suggested limitation may not become a definitive, fundamental selection. When such a definitive selection is made, science contradicts its principle of objectivity, for it reduces its object for reasons of its own ease and comfort. It no longer seeks to know what is, but to present what it wants to see; and it interprets only the reality which it has made for itself through its neglect and its selection. The intention to recognize only several selected aspects of the subject matter as the object of one's research leads to a contradiction of science in itself. The object of science of religion is no less than religion in the whole of its different aspects and dimensions.

As we consider the togetherness of the integral and specific interests in modern science of religion, it does not suffice to recognize that they condition one another. We have to remember that this togetherness can be meaningfully represented in our science only as long as both the specific and the integral interests are of equal value in being-with-one-another and being-in-one-another. That means that we cannot arrange them in a mere one-sided order in which the one would be anterior and the other posterior. This must be emphasized because modern science of religion stands ever again in a twofold danger. First, it stands in danger of moving from a supposed knowledge of the whole of religion to using specific research simply

as illustration of its supposed idea of the whole. Second, it stands
in danger of pretending that its understanding of the whole is immediately and exclusively derived from specific research. In both
of these instances, science of religion is no longer what it purports
to be; that is, it is no longer the attempt to ask about the whole of
religion within systematic research of religious reality. Rather, it
is in reality a religious-philosophical concept in search of a fitting
religious-historical alibi and only in its pretension a researched collection of material with a systematic consequence. Neither in reality
nor in pretense is such a science of religion just toward its integral
or its specific interest. The pretense is shattered by the fact
that integral insight never simply results directly from specific knowledge. *Integral reflection cannot be only an excercise supplementary
to specific research.* If science of religion makes this mistake, it de-
ceives itself. *In all specific research, a guiding understanding of the
whole and essence of religion is already operating.* If that were
not true, specific research would not be able to understand any sort
of datum or experience as religious. As insight into the whole is
always a product of the knowledge of specifics, so, on the other
hand, research of specifics is the consequence of a guiding insight
into the whole. This circle cannot be dissolved into unilinear process of before and after.

It hardly matters what sort of unilinear process modern science
might prefer. By means of unconcealed generalization, it can attempt
to move from specific knowledge to integral insight according to the
motto: what shows itself here as religious is all that religion is. It
can also attempt, by means of a process of reduction, to lead the
manifold of the religious back to a constitutive 'one', which is held
to be the religious function in the soul of man and which is the
source and root of religion in experience or, indeed, the origin of
religion in prehistoric times. It can also take the simplest course of
pure abstraction and, in the religious manifold, leave all that aside
which distinguishes the individual datum or experience. What remains after this abstraction is taken to be typically and essentially religious or the essence and concept of religion. Other possibilities
include the attempt — made on the basis of conscious selection and

isolation, and by means of a gift for empathizing — to fathom the essence and typical of religion in the plenitude of the religious. It can be the attempt simply to compile large amounts of specific knowledge of the religious, thereby hoping that insight into the whole of religion will automatically drop into one's lap. These are only several among the many possible attempts to correspond to the integral interest by means of an excercise supplementary to specific research.[8] As unilinear, none is trustworthy, because none takes into account the fact that all research of the specific already includes a knowledge of the whole.

This mistake also in reverse, contradicts the being-with-one-another and being-in-one-another of specific research and integral reflection. As an attempt at pure deduction, it breaks the circular relation of the two just as surely as the attempts at immediate induction. Proceeding from a supposed concept of religion, it seeks corresponding proof in religious reality, and, as a rule, it will usually find such proof. Religious reality is so boundlessly broad and manifold that even the strangest concept of religion can, with a bit of circumspection, find a proof.

The error lies simply in the assumption that guiding ideas need proofs. It is clear that science of religion must proceed from a guiding idea of what it has to research. But such an idea or such a conception (*Vor-stellung*), this attempt to catch sight of the object in a first approximation, should not be misunderstood as a true concept of religion which, at most, only needs confirmation. Every guiding presentation or idea of the whole and essence of religion is, at most, an approximation to the whole and, therefore, does not in the first place need confirmation but testing, supplementation and correction (cf. below, Chapter 4.1). Real integral reflection would mean to move from a limited and one-sided insight into the whole of religion, in constant encounter with religious reality, to new and better integral insight. In this movement one would not fall to the illusion that one, even in the best of insights, has encompassingly grasped the whole of religion. The better insight that can be won never corresponds fully to the whole, but it does enable one to win a still better insight, because it is truer to the subject matter. Integral reflection and specific research can only be carried forward with one another in mutual correction and help. Neither can be dispatched by an exercise subsequent to the other without violating what is taken to be the before or the after. *The integral and the specific interests come into their right only with one another and in one another or, otherwise, not at all.*

EXCURSUS I. ON THE DIFFERENCE BETWEEN HISTORY OF RELIGION AND SYSTEMATIC SCIENCE OF RELIGION

Modern science of religion has ever again felt itself pressed to distinguish the different interests within its range of work, and sometimes these distinctions closely approximate what we mean to distinguish with our concepts integral and specific. Goblet d'Alviella, for example, makes a distinction between *hierography* and *hierology*:

L'Histoire général des religions comprend l'hiérographie et l'hiérologie. L'Hiérographie, ou histoire des religions proprement dite, a pour objet de décrire succesivement toutes les religions particuliéres et d'en retracer le développement respectif. L'hiérologie ou histoire comparée des religions a pour objet de découvrir, par la comparaison de phénomènes religieux, les lois suivant lesquelles ils se produisent et se modifient (G. d'Alviella, 1887:38).

Hierography and hierology were later supplemented by a third, hierosophy (Transactions, 1908:377).

C. P. Tiele places *'morphological investigation'* beside *ontological investigation*, and he divides the latter into a phenomenological-analytic part and a psychological-synthetic part:

The method of science of religion is...not the one-sided empirical method, which is contented with the mere collection and ordering of facts and which reaches its high point in the positivistic method. Just as little, however, is it the one-sided speculative method, which establishes a system a priori without attention to what is determined by observation, insofar as this is incompatible with its system, and which, therefore, lacks any sort of sure ground. (C. P. Tiele, 1904:2 and 1897:18).

Rather, science of religion asks, on the one hand, about 'self-renewing and changing' forms or about the development of these forms and the corresponding laws of development. On the other hand, it divides and 'dismembers' the phenomenon religion (phenomenological-analytic investigation) and addresses itself finally to the questions, for example, about the essence, the origin, the significance in spiritual life, the possible decadence of religion (psychological-synthetic investigation) (C. P. Tiele, 1904:5).

P. D. Chatepie de la Saussaye distinguished between *history of religion* and *philosophy of religion*:

The object of the science of religion is the study of religion, of its essence and its manifestations. It divides itself naturally into the philosophy and the history of religion. These two divisions are most closely connected. The philosophy of religion would be useless and empty if, whilst defining the idea of religion, it disregarded the actual facts that lie before us; and the history of religion cannot prosper without the philosophy of religion. Not only the order and the criticism of religious phenomena, but even the determining whether such phenomena are of a religious nature, depends on some, if only a preliminary definition of religion (1891 as quoted by J. Waardenburg, 1973c:108).

In a similar way, science of religion is divided by Th. Achelis into a historical and a philosophical part (1904.5). W. B. Kristensen recognizes a third division besides history of religion and philosophy of religion, namely phenomenology or typology:

Thus we see that anticipated concepts and principles are used in all the provinces of the general science of religion: history, typology and philosophy. We are continually anticipating the results of the later research. That typifies the character and the 'authority' of each of the three subdivisions of the science of religion. None of the three is independent; the value and the accuracy of the results of one of them depend on the value and accuracy of the results of the other two. The place which the research of phenomenology occupies between history and philosophy makes it extraordinarily interesting and important. The particular and the universal interpenetrate again and again; Phenomenology is at once systematic History of Religion and applied Philosophy of Religion (W. B. Kristensen, 1960, as quoted by J. Waardenburg, 1973c: 393).

Joachim Wach distinguishes between *history of religion* and *systematic science of religion*. These two are the essential parts of what, in summary, can be called science of religion. Beyond this empirical science of religion, Wach recognizes philosophy of religion, a non-empirical discipline:

> Science and philosophy are different, in spite of all entwining of the two; therefore, it is recommendable to perceive as clearly as possible the fundamental difference between the task of science of religion and the task of philosophy of religion (J. Wach, 1954).

But how are history of religion and systematic science of religion to be distinguished? Wach writes:

> The object of science of religion is formed by the diversity of the empirical religions. It has to research this object, to understand and present it. And it has to do that from two sides: according to the object's development and according to its being, both 'longitudinally' and 'latitudinally'. Therefore, an *historical* and a *systematic* investigation is the task of general science of religion (J. Wach, 1924:21).

Wach's historical and systematic investigations lead, finally, to a common goal.

> The task of science of religion is the comprehension, working and interpretation of the 'historical' data. All methods and procedures serve this task which have been formed within it and reach the point of application. Historical and systematic endeavors go together in order to approach more closely the goal of science of religion, and that goal is *to understand the religious* (J. Wach, 1924:21).

H. Frick understands *history of religion* and *psychology of religion* to be the research of the 'reality of religion'. He distinguishes this research from *typology of religion* and *philosophy of religion*, which asks about the essence of religion.

> The research of religion has to do, on the one hand, with its *reality* and, on the other, with its essence. The reality of religion

has to be studied under two points of view. One has, first, to ask about its historical appearance, the emergence and change of the individual religions. The conclusion of this *special* history of religion is summarizing *general* history of religion, which, for example, has to present the origin of belief in God.

Just as important as the emergence of religion as a great historical power is its realization in individuals and in the life of groups. That is the business of psychology of religion, which is easily partitioned into the individual and the collective.

Second, with the presupposition that both the historical and the psychological emergence of religion are under investigation, the *essence* of religion may be critically worked out. One has to ask about the lawful forms of appearance within which religion emerges. Here an answer is possible only on the basis of a comparative consideration of the different historical and psychological facts. This is the work of *comparative science of religion or typology.* What it can work out as the essence of religion is empirical.

Different from that is the metaphysical essence. *Philosophy of religion* occupies itself with this problem as it asks about the essence and truth of religion in its normative meaning (Heinrich Frick, 1928:9).

In H. J. Schoeps the integral interest appears as systematic and comparative.

Science of religion falls into general history of religion and comparative research of religion (*Religionskunde*) as a systematic branch of science. *General science* of religion has to do with concrete historical forms and follows their origin and development. ...Here the emphasis lies on the facts. Different from that is *comparative science of religion*, which builds on the results of general history of religion. As a systematic branch of science, it attempts, by comparison, of the religions as whole appearances and with all their various colors and manifold forms, to perceive typical developments, characteristic peculiarities and constant laws (H. J. Schoeps, 1970:14).

As 'secondary branches' of science of religion, Schoeps mentions sociology of religion, psychology of religion and philosophy of

religion (H. J. Schoeps, 1970:15). In a way very similar to Schoeps',
Gustav Mensching distinguishes general and special history of religion
from comparative science of religion (Gustav Mensching, 1938:25;
see also W. Baetke, 1974:139f).

C. H. Ratschow distinguishes between *methodical orientation* and
understanding, which is the *methodical basic principle of science of
religion*.

> Therefore, 'methodical orientation' of research in science of re-
> ligion to the sciences which science of religion needs can be
> distinguished from a methodical basic principle of science of
> religion, which we would characterize as 'understanding'. The
> 'methodical orientation' of science of religion can be historical,
> philological, psychological or sociological. It means, therefore,
> that science of religion can and must enter into different sorts of
> procedure in order to do justice to the different forms of ex-
> pression of the religious. Science of religion can just as little
> do without sociology as it can do without psychology. It needs
> the historical method just as much as it needs, for example, phil-
> ology. The whole of the work of science of religion as 'understand-
> ing' of the religions as wholes stands over-against this methodical
> orientation of the science of religion to the individual sciences
> (C. H. Ratschow, 1973a:367f).

The methodical orientations and the methodical basic principle
condition and influence one another:

> Here we are dealing with science of religion…as a science whose
> method consists in the circle between the plurality of method-
> ical orientations and the methodical basic principle. Science of
> religion has its own peculiarity in the togetherness of the two
> (!) methodical beginning points (C. H. Ratschow, 1973a:369).

If we ask now about the common elements in all these schemes
(and we have not tried to be complete in our presentation of them),
the result is a series of characteristic observations.

1. In all work in science of religion, at least two phases are to be
distinguished.

2. The first phase presents material which the second phase reflects on.

3. This reflection is the deepening or supplementation of the scientific view of the subject matter won in the first phase.

4. The whole of religion first comes to satisfactory presentation in the cooperation of and in the successive engagement in the two phases. The successive engagement stands in the foreground as a working model. At first, the work of presentation is engaged, then the work of more intensive reflection on the material.

5. The tendency exists to bring the two phases into connection with the individual disciplines of science of religion or to identify the phases with individual disciplines of the science. (This tendency probably exists because the individual phases are different in their methods.)

3. Specific and Integral Science of Religion

If it is clear that modern science of religion, on the basis of its initial problem (the fundamental dilemma with regard to traditional religion), can do nothing other than ask specifically and integrally about religion, there arises a second question. This question is, how can and how should modern science of religion unite its specific and its integral interests? Our answer to this question has three parts.

1. It takes both interests equally seriously.

2. It does not subsume the one interest under the other.

3. It unites both interests in such a way that now the first is united with the second and now the second is united with the first. And it unites both of these procedures with methodologicsl reflection.

ad 1. As systematic research of religious reality, modern science of religion is also immediately specific science of religion. As a rule, it represents its specific interest with methodological discipline and critical reflection. The same may not always be said of the integral interest. Even if modern science of religion is inconceivable without a guiding insight into the whole of religion and without the attempt to gain a deeper integral insight through what is won in specific research, so modern science of religion can be tempted to dispatch its integral interest in the quickest and most shortsighted way. In committing such a mistake, it can be guided by the thought that insight into the whole may be directly derived from knowledge of individual data, that the integral interest, therefore, may be quickly and without problem dispatched by a simple appendage to specific research. Or, on the other hand, it is afraid that its integral interest leads all too easily into speculative flights of fantasy and tries to deal with this interest in the easiest way possible. It limits itself to a few introductory remarks on the integral problem or to a summarizing conclusion adjoined to the presentation of specific research.

Modern science of religion, with this emphasis, does, in effect, just what it does not want to do, for it is not the consciously treated and at every stage of research reflected relation to the whole of religion that shows itself to be arbitrary and speculative. Rather, a concept of the whole is arbitrary and speculative which is imposed uncritically on religious data or derived uncritically directly from it. That integral insight is arbitrary and speculative which is simply produced without consideration of the conditions and circumstances of its production.

On the other hand, it would be just as false for modern science of religion to pursue only its integral interest with scientific, critical care. In this case, due to the lack of careful research of religious data, it would obviously be only speculation. The specific and the integral interests deserve to be taken seriously in exactly the same way. *Modern science of religion cannot afford to follow the one interest with critical acumen and the other with nonchalance.*

ad 2. If the specific and the integral interests are divided into different disciplines, the necessary concomitance of the two interests is lost. A construed separation or sequential relation replaces their necessary continuing and lively togetherness. The specific interest is absorbed into so-called history of religion, psychology of religion or sociology of religion. The integral interest is absorbed into so-called comparative, typological or systematic science of religion or in philosophy of religion. This means a construction which, in two ways, is far from reality.

First, purely specific research or purely integral questioning is an illusion. One cannot do history of religion, for example, without a guiding insight into what characterizes religious data as such; that is, without a guiding understanding of religion. Without such a guiding idea, history of religion is, at best, an arbitrary series of data. Just as little is systematic science of religion exhausted by a mere questioning about the whole. This interest may be successfully followed only as long as it is bound with interest in individual religious data. A purely integral systematic science of religion would be scientifically worthless.

Second, the separation of different disciplines is completely different from the concomitance of integral and specific science of religion. In the separation of different disciplines, relations are equated which are not equal. Each discipline corresponds to a definite perspective combined with methods corresponding to this perspective. The various disciplines supplement one another, because each describes religious reality out of its own perspective. Integral and specific science of religion, however, are not simply perspectives which need supplementation. They are, rather, basic orientations in all perception in science of religion, orientation to the specific and to the whole, research of the religious and questioning about religion. These basic orientations are never to be separated in science of religion, whether systematically, historically, psychologically or however. *In every individual discipline concomitantly present, neither specific nor integral science of religion is ever a separate discipline.* When we speak of integral science of religion, we do not mean, therefore, a new occupation beside or apart from specific research in addition to history of religion and psychology of religion. Rather, we mean by integral science of religion simply that we consciously take the question about religion seriously; that is, the question through which all specific research is consciously or unconsciously characterized. Integral science of religion is consequent questioning about religion in the midst of all research of the religious, but it is not a separate undertaking, neither an addition nor an appendage to something else.

The attempt, on the basis of certain similarities, to associate the integral and the specific interests chiefly, if not exclusively, with this or that discipline is understandable. But even this association cannot be accepted. At first sight, history of religion seems mainly to be specific research, and systematic science of religion seems mainly to be an integral questioning. This appearance is due, however, to the fact that each discipline often all too quickly dispatches the other − hidden − interest. One discipline is entrusted with one interest, another discipline with the other interest. We do not see why such simplification should in any way be declared a duty or, indeed, a virtue.

ad 3. We always have to reckon with the possibility that modern science of religion not only opens access to the whole of religion and to the individual religious datum, but also that, in its conditions, methods and consequences, it closes access in many ways. A guiding idea of religion can, for example, not only lead to optimal openness to the religious datum. It can also make openness almost impossible. In fact, the guiding question of integral science of religion is the question about to what extent science of religion, in its beginning point, methods and perspectives, misses, changes or opens the subject matter it has to research. If one does not reflect on this question, it can happen that science of religion will find access to a whole of religion, but a whole of a religion which it has finally invented and not the whole of actual religion. *Modern science of religion has to find the way to itself, if it wants to find the way to the whole of religion*. It has to attempt to gain clarity about the hidden premises and ideas which determine its access to the subject matter; which determine its methods, perspectives and, finally, also its results. It has, in the encounter with religious reality, ever again to realize its responsibility for these guiding ideas, premises, methods and results.

This finding-its-way-to-itself cannot, however, be considered a precondition for the encounter with the subject matter. Indeed how is science of religion at all to perceive the narrowness and one-sidedness of its ideas before engagement with the whole range of subject matter leads it into such reflection? On the other hand, how is the science to sight the whole range of its subject matter, if it largely covers the access to it by its own too narrow ideas? *Re-*

flection on the whole of religion and reflection on the conditions of one's own scientific perception can only proceed hand in hand, if either is to proceed at all.

This mutual dependence also determines the procedure in this work. We cannot simply take our point of departure in a critical reflection on the premises, methods and results of modern science of religion in order, then, to seek an insight into the whole of religion. Nor can we take our point of departure in a preconceived knowledge of the whole in order, then, to discover the too-narrow conditions of modern science of religion. We can reflect on the guiding understanding of religion in the premises, methods and consequences of our science only as we address ourelves to what we perceive in religious reality and as religious reality.

If, with these premises, methods and consequences of modern science of religion, we are attentive to what they imply and open for integral understanding, then we may meaningfully begin with the premises, that is, with the conditions which the science assumes in its beginnings, whether consciously or unconsciously, whether freely or not — the conditions which, then, largely determine the further course of the science.

2

The Premises

1. RELIGIOUS REALITY AND THE REALITY OF RELIGION

As the attempt to overcome the fundamental dilemma with regard to traditional religion in systematic research of religious reality, modern science of religion admits religious reality (*religiöse Wirklichkeit*) as the only practical object of its consideration and research. It is the theme of the endeavors of the science; it holds the entire interest of the science.

That has led, for example, through the principle of the exclusion of transcendence (Th. Flournoy, 1911 and 1919) to the conclusion that, ideally, the reality of religion (*Wirklichkeit der Religion*) is excluded from scientific research. The objects of the science of religion are the demonstrable religious data and the religious experience which expresses itself or conceals itself in the data. The reality to which all religious life refers and from which it understands itself — the reality of religion — is not a demonstrable datum and can, therefore, not be an object of scientific consideration.

Modern science of religion establishes, with this limitation to the demonstrable or at least with this concentration on the religious datum, a very definite accent in the area of religion. It turns its subject matter upside down. *It allows itself as the only valid object of its interest something which is completely secondary for religion.* Of secondary interest for religion is its own thanksgiving, experience, hope, prayer, sensitivity, teaching and behavior as well as all the material in which this religious experience expresses itself. These are interesting for religion only in their relation to the reality to which all religious experience refers. One who prays does not regard his formulations and his religious feelings as objects for his attention — unless he understands prayer as self-reflection, which is not actually prayer at all. For one who truly prays, not his own religious reality is the center of his undivided attention but the reality before which he stands in prayer, which is the ground of his entire hope, supplication, thanksgiving, feeling, his stuttering search for words or his sacred recitation. The same is to be said of every man who religiously acts, perceives, expresses himself and experiences. The foremost interest of one who makes a sacrifice is not the sacrifice itself or the way in which he presents it. This way is, indeed, often decisive for the validity of the sacrifice. Even in his concern for the correctness of his sacrifice and the propriety of its presentation, his foremost interest is in him to whom it is made. In a religious celebration one does not celebrate, first of all, one's sense of rhythm and color but the reality which gives cause for the celebration. The possibility certainly exists that this reality might move into the background and the celebration be initiated by enchantment with its own pomp and circumstance. Therewith, the celebration degenerates into pure folklore. A religious reality which celebrates no more than itself is a contradiction. The same may be said of all religious data. The center of interest in myth is, for one who experiences the life of the myth, the superb reality which expresses itself in the myth, which makes itself present and audible in the believer. The importance and center of the symbol is not the bare facticity of the sign but the reality in which the symbol shares and which it signals.

One can go on and on making such distinctions. In every case the point would be that first and central interest of religion in religious reality is not the religious reality itself but the reality to which the religious reality refers and from which it lives. Science of religion reverses that order and makes the secondary primary, places the relative in the center, consciously limits its concentration to that which regards itself as secondary. Religious reality sees itself as reference to what it witnesses to in its belief, celebration, search, experience, behavior. What happens actually when modern science of religion limits itself on principle to religious data not as referring beyond but as interesting in themselves? What actually happens when this science, on the basis of an exclusion of transcendence, refuses to be referred to what religious reality intends?

If the undemonstrable reality of religion is the meaning, center ground and goal of all religious reality, and if science of religion brackets out everything undemonstrable from its consideration, then science of religion questions religious reality only while altering it. Instead of letting itself be directed by the data to the reality beyond the data, it becomes intensely interested in the director and the act of directing. Such truncated religious reality may fit well into the scheme of so-called empirical research, and it may be that science of religion maintains its claim to be a real science only by means of such truncation. But the fact is that its subject matter is no longer what comes to appearance in the religious data and occurs as religious experience. It is, rather, a decapitated religious reality, a religious reality devoid of its meaning. That means, in short, that the subject matter of such a science is, finally, a construction of the science. And moreover, as religious reality is limited to the demonstrable, it is not only deprived of its actual meaning, but it also stands as a meaningless manifold which requires from the science some sort of meaning. To be understood, it must somehow be meaningful. One understands something only insofar as it is meaningful, not insofar as it is a meaningless manifold.

Among the attempts in the science to find a ground and meaning for the data the science decapitates, the most successful is the postulation of a religious a priori, which recommends itself through its empathy with important aspects of the emotional side of religious experience. It is, so to speak, the *via regia* of all misunderstanding in the science of religion. In the following discussion, only the basic interest of this postulate will be treated.

Beyond a mere objectively correct interpretation, understanding is indispensable for a meaningful activation of science of religion. The researcher is so brought in the direction of what Rudolf Otto called the 'religious a priori'. This is a concept won through religious philosophical questioning, but it is, nevertheless, not a religious predisposition of man, not perhaps and therewith (sic) something historical.

This religious a priori is rightly understood as the indifferent situations differently unfolding religious predisposition of man and not as the divine itself. This is what, in the manifold of its formations, can finally be understood in concepts by the scientist of religion. Only here is the object of his science, religion, in its final depth to be found. On the other hand, the *object of religion* itself, the holy or the divine, is his task only insofar as he investigates it in the historical utterances and reflexes which appear in religious persons, religious institutions, organizations and events in history. Its metaphysical essence does not allow the researcher investigation of itself, ever as it remains true that the object of religion and the object of science of religion continually touch one another tangentially. The divine and the analysis of its reality is, rather, the object of theologians. *The object of science of religion is always only man himself as one who carries and gives form to religion.* 'Whoever means history of religion means the history of a *Geist* qualified for religion,' said Rudolf Otto (K. Goldammer, 1967a:32).

According to this idea, science of religion stands in the following dilemma. (1) The object of the science can only be religious reality and not the reality of religion, not the object of its object. The reality of religion is the occupation of theology. (2) Nevertheless, religious reality and the reality of religion cannot be separated. These 'touch one another tangentially', Religious reality witnesses to and makes present the reality of religion. The dilemma is that the object of the science refers to another object which can never be the object of a science. Through this dilemma there arises a third term to which the immediate object of the science, the religious reality, evidently also refers: 'religion in its last depths', the predisposition of man, the religious a priori. And it is this which, in its manifold forms, can finally be understood conceptually by the scientist of religion. The factor is, however, that orientation to this third term does not present a legitimate way out of the mentioned dilemma. If religious reality is essentially referred to the reality of religion, why is it 'finally' referred to a third term? Is it because of devotion to the principle of 'exclusion' and the fear that science of religion could become theology? This danger is not significant as long as science of religion does not abandon its primary insight, that is, the perception that its immediate object can only be religious reality. For the science, the reality of religion is, in fact, only present in the witness of religious reality. And it is truly present there and cannot be cut away without a very arbitrary surgery. The whence and whereto of all religious reality may not be disregarded simply for the sake of a principle, nor may it be replaced by the postulate of a religious a priori. If religious reality is essentially referred to the reality of religion, then the science of religion must either constantly be referred to the reality of religion or fail to recognize the reality of religion for what it is. The previously mentioned real dilemma can be avoided only at the cost of abandoning the actual intention of its subject matter. To be really meaningful, the science does not avoid the dilemma but endures within it. It is constantly referred by the religious reality to the reality of religion, and it knows that the reality of religion can never directly become the object of modern science. Within the dilemma the science finds itself repeatedly placed at the very limits of its own possibilities as science. If, however, it refuses to be placed at these limits, it deprives itself of ever having an understanding of the witness of religious reality as witness. *Whoever wishes to understand religion will, at one point or another, reach his own limits.* And that is necessary for the science of religion. The science may not fear the situation of being at its limits and the dilemma of this situation and it may not flee the situation until it has experienced it. *Science of religion is not only a task but also the boundary at which science and religion enter into relation and the place where science attempts to come so near to religion that it succeeds in understanding it.*

The task and limits of modern science of religion can probably be best understood through a conscious distinction of three *dimensions of religion*. The first dimension is that with which science of religion is immediately occupied; from its point of view, its scientific observation, the foreground or *first dimension* appears clearly as *the broad field of religious data* such as holy writings, documents, cultic objects, the facilities in a temple, symbols etc. This foreground or first dimension of religious reality is the only direct object of scientific observation; only this dimension is immediately accessible for scientific observatiọn. The *second dimension* never comes directly before the eyes of the scientific observer because it gives only indications of its presence and conceals itself again. This second dimension of religious reality is known as *religious experience*. Customs, rites and texts may be immediately observed, not, however, what happens within a person who practices rites and customs or who writes or uses texts. Science of religion never looks directly into the religious experience of an individual or community. What science of religion can say about religious experience is based only on its research of religious data and their interpretation. That is true also of psychology of religion. It has no direct access to religious experience but bases its conclusions on the interpretation of data which give evidence of religious experience. If modern science of religion wished to be purely 'empirical' research, to hold itself to the immediately demonstrable and be nothing more than a science of facts, it would have to refuse to speak of religious experience. What happens in the soul of religious persons is never directly observable, is not a datum of 'empirical' research. It is an event to which the religious datum refers.

The *third dimension* of religion does not lie within the area of religious reality. It is the intended in all religious reality, *the reality of religion*. This third dimension is, in a far more radical sense than the second dimension, removed from direct scientific observation. For the science of religion, this dimension is only present in the religious reality, but it is not part of that reality. Rather, the religious reality refers beyond itself to this dimension. More precisely: the third dimension is present only in the second dimension, which is indicated in the first dimension, the religious reality.[1] The question is, may science of religion, because of this difficulty of perception exclude the third dimension of religion as 'transcendence' from its consideration altogether? It may, only insofar as it is no more than pure consideration of data; it may not, insofar as it wishes to have some sort of understanding of the data. As interpretation of religious data leads to insight into religious experience, so the attempt to understand religious experience leads necessarily to reflection on what religious experience thinks as the reality of religion, what it hopes, conceives, makes present and has in its life. It is clear that science of religion can never risk unmediated statements about the reality of religion. If it were to make such an attempt, it would no longer be science of religion but theosophy. And yet the science must express itself about what in religious life is thought, felt, witnessed to and made present as the reality of religion. It must reflect on this if it is to understand religious experience.

As integral science of religion, as science of religion which makes the whole of religion its task (E. Troeltsch, 1906:4887), it cannot, on principle, exclude any of the three dimensions from its range of thought. It cannot assume that what is not obviously present does not belong within its range of understanding. It cannot bracket out even a twice mediated reality, if that reality shows itself to be the actual and deepest meaning of the immediate reality. Need it be mentioned that an integral science of religion would be in complete contradiction with itself if it cut away from this whole of religion its deepest meaning and ground? What would the whole of religion be without the reality to which and from which all religion lives and for whose sake it is? It would be a periphery without a center, an event without meaning. Integral science of religion will not only investigate, observe and describe religious data, it will also through interpretation find the way to religious experience, and, in the attempt to understand religious experience, it will reflect on what this experience knows as the reality of religion.

It may be here incidentally noted, that theology and science of religion are probably not so different from one another as the above quoted passage leads one to think.

The clear distinction between the object of religion and the object of science of religion is an indispensable presupposition for a theoretical and methodological statement about science of religion. Such distinction is also the real and only point of departure for a distinction between science of religion and theology (K. Goldammer, 1967a:32).

It is our opinion that not even theology, at least not Christian theology, stands in immediate relation to the reality of religion. It does not have immediate access to this reality. Theology is in the

same position of knowing the reality of religion only through the
witness of religious reality. Theosophy may claim to be a divine
science, theology knows God only through the word which witnesses
to him.

2. RELIGION IN QUESTION

The fact that out of the dilemma with regard to traditional religion,
modern science of religion became necessary has a further very significant consequence for this science's understanding of religion.
For modern science of religion, religion has meant and still means,
exclusively or above all, traditional religion, that is, the religion
which tradition names religion and which names itself religion. This
traditional so-called religion is the point of departure and the object
of modern science of religion. The fact that, more exactly considered, religion not only occurs in or is to be found in these traditionally so-called religions (such as Christianity, Judaism, Islam, etc.)
is hardly of importance for the science and is mentioned, if it is
mentioned, only marginally. That seems to mean that modern
science of religion is so absorbed with certain problems that it is
blind to others. Its occupation with traditionally so-called religion is
so intense that it makes every effort to insure that even in the most
ancient past no stone is left unturned which might yield additional
knowledge. But the science seems to occupy itself only slowly and
with displeasure with the thought that, with progressive secularization, religion occurs more and more clearly beyond or outside
the bounds of all traditional religion. It occurs more and more
clearly in the midst of the so-called secular, in the passion of the
researcher, in the fascination of art, in the absolute dedication of
the athlete to his sport, in the ritual of mass sports events, in enthusiasm for one's own nation, in the adoration of a great star, in
nature mysticism, in the mysterium of drugs, in the celebration
of science, in participation in the more-than-scientific mysteries
of parapsychology, in the unconditioned claim of a political ideology, in undivided devotion to one's career, in the mystery of love
which dissolves meaninglessness.

That is *secular religion*, and only in the past few decades can one find the slow, almost foot-dragging beginnings of occupation with it in science of religion. Kurt Goldammer, for example, acknowledges not only 'the group religions of primitive peoples', 'national culture-religions' and the 'universal religions', but also 'modern individual religiosity' which has developed out of the last two. This modern individual religiosity is named the fourth 'fundamental structure' (*Gestaltstruktur*) of religion. It is religious experience outside of all organized religions:

It is only natural if such subjectively experiencing modern individuals no longer wish to feel themselves bound to the forms and contents of religion which have been historically passed down in the tradition. The personal experiential core of an individual religiosity, which was always basic to the world religions and to the finest appearances in the national culture religions, is beginning to unfold and make itself independent. The religious individual seeks and finds his experience in the most different areas of nature, in the values of art, in the perceptions of science and in all good things in life. He can be encountered by divinity just as well in the aesthetic values of music and poetry, in philosophical reflection, in a mathematical proposition as in appreciation of a landscape or of the heavens. He draws from these his conclusions, and usually he does not order his conclusions in a strictly structured system. He also does not refer them (*e.g. the religious experience of nature*) to the experiences of a group. He distances himself from history. Whatever consciousness of history he might have diminishes or is suppressed, as we experience today in Europe. Occasionally he discusses his experiences with congenial persons and joins with them in a freely chosen and non-obligatory fellowship. Such groups arise more out of coincidence than anything else. In the main, the individual religious person lives in solitude, and, in that, he is similar to the mystic and contemplator of older stages of religious development (Kurt Goldammer, 1960:18f).

As important as this reference to modern individual religiosity is, one should not be misled into thinking that secular religion is the same thing as individual world-piety. Just as traditional religion, secular religion has different forms. If, with regard to traditional religion, one speaks of tribal, national and universal religion – and each of these elementary forms is different from the other – so, with regard to the formally different appearances of secular religion, one should at least distinguish between *individual world-piety* and *secular-religious mass movements*. If, in the former, one joins a group only 'coincidentally', in the latter one has to do with the organization of half a nation, with grasping the masses, with the official teaching of a movement, with the model of a *Führer* or a 'glorious chairman', with struggle against heresies, with secular-religious cult celebrations of the movement, with the celebration of predecessors and martyrs of the movement, with oaths of allegiance to what is absolutely valid for every member and with the ordering of everything in terms of the final aim of a group's secular eschatology.

Paul Tillich has very urgently and impressively made us attentive to the religious character of these secular-religious mass movements. He calls them 'quasi-religions', and he sees a major feature of the religious situation of our time in the struggle between traditional religion and quasi-religion.

I dare to make the seemingly paradoxical statement, that the main characteristic of the present encounter of the world religions is their encounter with the quasi-religions of our time. Even the mutual relations of the religions proper are decisively influenced by the encounter of each of them with secularism, and one or more of the quasi-religions which are based upon secularism.

Sometimes what I call quasi-religions are called pseudo-religions, but this is as imprecise as it is unfair. 'Pseudo' indicates an intended but deceptive similarity; 'quasi' indicates a genuine similarity, not intended, but based on points of identity, and this, certainly, is the situation in cases like Fascism and Communism, the most extreme examples of quasi-religions today. They are radicalizations and transformations of nationalism and socialism, respectively, both of which have a potential, though not always an actual religious character. In Fascism and Communism the national and social concerns are elevated to unlimited ultimacy (Paul Tillich, 1963:5f).

In view of such references and in view of the age of the visible parallels between the dogmatic forms of traditional religion and the ideological forms of modern secular religion, one has to ask why science of religion has waited so long to take up secular religion in its individual and collective forms into the whole of its consideration. One reason is the urgently felt questionableness of one's own traditional religion. But the following circumstances have also played an essential role.

1. *Secular religion is unusual by virtue of its place.* It does not occur where one expects to find religious experience, that is, in connection with traditional religious worship and custom, but in the midst of the so-called secular. It happens, for example, as enthusiasm for sports (cf. M. Hörmann, 1968 and S. von Kortzfleisch, 1967). Seen from the standpoint of traditional religion and, at the same time, from the standpoint of a science of religions orientated to traditional religion, secular religion is non-religious religion[2] and, therefore, a paradox, an absurdity. One needs a good measure of freedom from the usual idea of religion in order even seriously to consider this new and unexpected appearance as religion at all.

2. *Secular religion is largely anonymous religion*, that is, it is religion which does not designate itself religion. It does not wish to place itself together with what calls itself religion — perhaps precisely because traditional religion occurs in areas which are foreign to real life. That does not mean secular religion cannot use means made ready by traditional religious thought in order to speak of its own experience. It is characteristic that it never names itself religion. Secular religion is, as a rule, the religion of one who is convinced he has no religion. On superficial observation, therefore, secular-religious experience gives no cause at all for being taken for and considered as religion. It shows itself as religion not on its labels, but in its unconditional concern, its complete devotion, its orientation to highest truth and untouchable value, its belief in redemption, its eagerness for mission, etc. Not in its self-designations — which are, for example, 'world-view', 'science', 'movement', 'society' — but in its reality does it designate itself as religion. Certainly it is not simple for the scientist of religion to see through the labels and press through,

with observation and understanding, to what really happens.

3. *Secular religion is often 'modern individual religiosity'*, that is, religion in its beginning — immediate religious experience which is neither unfolded nor organized. As religion *in nuce*, it does not lead to teachable fixation, to organization similar to a church or to a broad pedagogically relevant tradition. In the form mass movement, secular religion (e.g. a political doctrine of salvation) can, naturally, make the claim of unconditional truth; and, if it is successful, it can lead to structures similar to a religious order, to a hierarchic system, to political dogmas and to detailed traditions. As broad secular-religious tradition and as developed system it has to be recognized sooner or later by the scientist of religion. But as religion *in nuce* it can easily go unnoticed simply because it is of itself hardly noticeable. There is need, so to speak, for a Herman Hesse to make perceptible what happens in a person as he listens to a concert:

> It was at a concert of lovely old music. After two or three notes of the piano the door was opened all of a sudden to the other world. I sped through heaven and saw God at work. I suffered holy pains. I dropped all my defences and was afraid of nothing in the world. I accepted all things and to all things I gave up my heart (H. Hesse, 1963:38).

If modern individual religiosity finds itself almost only coincidentally in a group, we must feel it to be a seldom exception when this individual religiosity communicates itself clearly enough for one standing outside to perceive it as a deeply felt experience. It belongs obviously to the individual character of this individual religiosity that it usually conceals itself in the person. The happy 'coincidence' of an ability to communicate and a willingness to communicate is needed in order to make it visible at all. Nothing is easier, therefore, than to overlook the manifold and the intensity of individual world-piety.

4. Alongside all that has been mentioned before, last but not least, it is to be considered that *secular religion, just as traditional so-called religion, becomes the object of science of religion at the moment it is felt to be questionable.* Science of religion can ask only about what is questionable, that is, about what has really been placed radi-

cally in question and is worthy and deserving of radical questioning. In the case of traditional religion, both presuppositions of real questionableness are clearly given with the beginnings of modern science of religion. Traditional religion found itself not only in all its essential aspects ever more clearly placed in question, but at the same time, with knowledge of its manifold and history, there grew up the awareness that, in all its questionableness, traditional so-called religion is a strangely respectable appearance, a fascinating mixture of error and truth, humanity and inhumanity, highest truth and most trivial failure. In short, there grew up the awareness that traditional so-called religion is a reality which very much deserves to be questioned.

The matter is different with secular religion. Modern science of religion stood for a long time *both too near and too far from* secular religion. It stood too near insofar as it itself, on into the beginnings of our century, unmistakably indulged in a secular-religious attitude, namely scientism (belief in science). On the whole, the congresses of science of religion at the beginning of our century were celebrations of scientism. They were happily emphatic where it was not really a question of the subject matter, traditional religions, at all, but of the achieved successes and the possibilities of science in general and of science of religion in particular (cf. Proceedings, 1900). The religion these congresses found questionable was traditional religion. The religious attitude in which one moved and thought was one of boundless trust in science. One was convinced that the pure truth was to be encountered in science, and pure truth was what, in many regards, the traditional religions in their 'muddy waters' failed to give. One placed one's hope and trust in science. But how could one perceive a secular-religious attitude, when one had no critical distance from it? Whoever devotes himself completely to scientism confuses science and scientism, and he does not feel himself at all obliged to question his scientism critically. He stands too close to science to put it seriously in question. Therefore, one cannot be surprised that those at the congresses at the beginning of the century intensively discussed the religions of the most distant times and cultures, but were unable to see the religion present in their own gatherings and meetings.

In order to question in the sense of science of religion, real questionableness is needed, that is, 'engaged distance'. If, in the case of belief in science, distance was lacking, so in many other cases, at first, the feeling for engagement was lacking. That may be seen in the fact that, with regard to secular-religious behavior, scientists of religion have spoken disdainfully of pseudo-religion of *'Ersatzreligion'* or *'Religionsersatz'*. Even when such phenomenon as exaggerated nationalism, political doctrines of salvation, and totalitarian world-views with their dogmas, rites, hierarchies and models were recognized; even when religions of drugs and enthusiasm for sports were recognized, no cause was recognized by scientists of religion to enter into these matters with questions, research, and a search for understanding, because one could not recognize their religious-historical significance. Pseudo-religion was the business of sociology or psychology or, as in most cases, of psychopathology. For the science of religion, the whole matter was a secondary derailment of the history of religion.

Fascism, national socialism and communism had to make their impact felt before the science could, with Tillich, perceive that secular religion as mass movement was anything but of secondary importance for the history of religion; before it could perceive that modern history of religion decides what it itself is, above all in the struggle of traditional religion with these forms of secular religion; before it could perceive that political doctrines of salvation and totalitarian world-views are not secondary pseudo-religion, but eminently significant secular religion. Secular religion becomes an object of the reflection of history of religion only in the experience of 'pressing' distance, that is, in the experience of unavoidable questionableness.

In view of this pressing distance the main argument against the acknowledgement of secular religion as religion, as Joachim Wach expresses this argument, appears in a new light. Wach acknowledges four criteria for determining whether an experience is religious or not. Mainly by the measure of his first criterion, secular religion is seen to be pseudo-religion and, therefore, not real religion at all.

"The first criterion of religious experience is a response to what is experienced as Ultimate Reality. By Ultimate Reality we mean that which conditions and undergirds all, that which, in the words of Dorothy Emmett, 'impresses and challenges us.' (D. Emmett, 17) Thus we can say that the experience of anything finite cannot be a religious but only a pseudoreligious experience. (Symbols, as long as they are understood as such, may point to the infinite and hence do not necessarily fall under the category of the merely finite.) (J. Wach, 1961:30).

Pseudo religion may exhibit features of genuine religion, but in it man relates himself not to ultimate but to some finite reality. There are four major types of pseudo religion today. The first is Marxism. Of the two major elements in Marxism, chiliasm and economic theory, it is the first which gives it the semblance of religion. It is well known that communism is at least a pseudo religion since it transcends a mere materialistic creed with its sacred books, dogmas, rituals, and its fellowship, its insistence on the creation of a 'new man', its possession of an impressive sense of justice and willingness to sacrifice. Yet not only its methods but also its principles show that it is not a genuine religion. The basic difference is the lack of a satisfactory solution to the three kinds of quest central to genuine religion — the theological, the cosmological, and the anthropological. Because man is central, there is no acknowledgment of his numinous unworth (sin) and of the necessity for more than an economic liberation of man and society. The second type of pseudo religion is biologism — the cult of life as such or of the sexual drive — of which Nietzsche, D. H. Lawrence, and Huysmans were the prophets. The third is populism or racism in which divine character is attributed to an ethnic, political, or cultural group instead of to its creator. Examples of racism can be found in Europe, America, Africa, and Asia. Finally there is statism, the glorification of the state, be it the German, American, Russian, Japanese, Chinese, or Indian version. Indeed, physical or economic well-being either of individuals or groups is a good. But it is a finite good which must be seen in perspective and not equated with an ultimate reality. All four are instances of what is known as secularism. It is secularism which represents the gravest danger in both the West and, increasingly, in the East "(J. Wach, 1961:37-38).

The distinction between final and finite reality immediately calls forth the following critical question: How does the researcher of religion know that in all explicit religion (that is, in religion which calls itself religion) and exclusively in explicit religion, final reality is encountered? What does such an assertion mean? What does it intend? Four possibilities are to to be considered.

1. It could be a matter of a theological judgment. In this case, however, it would be a strange sort of theology. It would, against every Biblical witness (consider, for example, the statements about the idols in Deutero-Isaiah), make the blanket judgment that all explicit religion is relation to ultimate reality and all implicit religion is merely relation to finite reality.

2. The judgment is, perhaps, to be interpreted in terms of psychology of religion. Perhaps it tries only to repeat what those directly engaged experience, think and feel from case to case. But, in this interpretation, only the first half of the judgment is correct. One engaged in explicit religion knows that he faces final reality. But as secular religion makes its infinite claim one engaged in it does not consider the claim more provisional, of less value, and less binding. The secular-religious cults of life which Wach mentions certainly experience ultimate and highest reality no less than the explicitly religious cults of ever newly awakening, insuppressible life.

3. Wach's judgment could be metaphysical — born out of a knowledge of the essence of all, therefore, knowledgeable of the place where ultimate and penultimate reality meet. But another metaphysics could be proposed which would judge the matter entirely differently.

4. Most probably Wach's assertation is an unadmitted moral and, therefore, apologetic judgment — conscious *apologia religiosa*. Explicit and secular religion simply cannot be of the same kind, on the same level. One resists even considering the possibility. They have to be at different levels, different in kind. One is pseudo, the other is genuine. One is ultimate, the other is finite. One knows, in any case,

the bizarre and demonic manifestations of secular religion: the Hitler cult and similar personality cults, sports hysteria, pathologically exaggerated patriotism or scientism, drugs mysticism, adventure addiction. Who wants to risk putting such a list in a series including early Buddhism, Islamic mysticism, earliest Christianity? Wach's judgment is, as unconscious moral qualification or disqualification and therefore as *apologia religiosa*, quite understandable, and yet it is an illusion. Explicit religion itself knows not only high points but also crass and ugly forms, trivial 'magic' and inhuman fanaticism, just as secular religion. And secular religion is not by any means simply a group of pathological forms. Excesses are, indeed, always more apparent than personal conviction and a concealed but no less deeply felt individual experience. But precisely where religion does not consciously call itself religion (consider individual or, indeed individualistic uncommunicative world-piety), it shows itself again and again in such impressive restraint and concealment. Secular religion is not simply through and through excessive, offensive stupidity and error. Traditional, explicit, religion is not simply through and through spiritually sublime or a flight in the heights. Morally and aesthetically judged, men experience in both, exemplary high points and abysses, the most beautiful possibilities and the most fanatic forms of human culture. *It would be unfair to compare only the excesses of secular religion with the high points of explicit religion.*

With all of that, it is necessary again to emphasize that, today, religion in all of its forms, traditional as well as secular, lies within the area of the questionable for science of religion. Science of religion may no longer overlook the fact religious reality does not cease to be at the outer boundary of what one traditionally calls religion. It must recognize that religion continues to be beyond these boundaries in new ways and forms, in individualistic world-piety and in secular mass movements. Religious reality is not limited to data and experience which labels itself religious. In that which does not name itself religion, which occasionally even claims to be anti-religion, religion often occurs with exemplary consistency and dedication of self. A modern science of religion which asks about the whole of religion and intends to occupy itself with systematic research of the whole of religious reality — such a science can no longer overlook the secular forms of religion which are so (almost fatefully) significant for contemporary history of religion.[3] *Openness for the whole of the elementary forms of religion belongs necessarily to the question about the whole of religion.* Just as a modern and, therefore, an integral science of religion, in its understanding of each religion, tries to correspond to all dimensions and, therewith, to all depths of each religion, so it searches for openness to the whole of religious reality, openness to the entire breadth of religious experience, whether within or without what explicitly names itself religious. It must try to be so open in order not to lose all proportions. As much as it belongs to its research to reconstruct religions out of the most distant past from fragments and ruins, all this work has to appear rather bizarre if it simply passes by the religion which occurs under its very nose and through which the present history of religion, for the most part, is decided.

3. INTEGRAL AND INTEGRATING SCIENCE OF RELIGION

The questionableness of what has traditionally been called religion belongs not only to those conditions of modern science of religion which may gradually, with the increasing questionableness also of secular religion, be overcome in the direction of an integral understanding of religion. If this questionableness of traditional religion is understood in a certain way, it is part of those conditions and perspectives with which modern science of religion impedes the view of the whole of religion.

Compared with the believability of a modern science, traditional religion can be understood as a very uncertain and unbelievable matter. The scientism mentioned before clearly confesses such a view of traditional religion. In this case, one is inclined to speak of a *partial questionableness* or, more clearly, of a *self-secure insecurity*. The fundamental dilemma with regard to traditional religion has here gone so far that the scientist regards all statements and intentions of

religious reality with extreme caution, and he treats these with extremely critical investigation and interpretation in his attempt to deal
with them. But when the limits of traditional religion are reached,
the insecurity disappears and the integral question expires. The scientist enters onto the secure ground of scientific results and the modern world-view, and here nothing is put radically into question.
Rather, whatever one has to have for this security is simply assumed
– without examination, without question, thankfully. Often one can
almost hear the sigh of relief over the fact that one has again the sure
ground of modern knowledge under one's feet, after having found
the way through religious ideas and feelings. One has the idea the
scientist has experienced something like a walk on the Sea of
Galilee.[4]

But one cannot reproach modern science of religion for having the
feeling it is walking on water. The radical questionableness of traditional religion is part of the historical situation in which modern
thought finds itself. Self-defeating is only the feeling that it reaches
unshakably firm ground when it arrives back at the modern world-
view. This assumption is an illusion, and one full of consequences.
Modern science of religion seems to question the whole of religion,
and it really wants to perceive and understand the whole. But in its
questioning about what religion is, it has already largely decided
what religion is and is not on the basis of its so-called modern certainties and especially on the basis of its modern understanding of
man. The questionableness of traditional religion runs up against
unquestioned modern axioms and supposedly sure knowledge. The
insecurity of traditional religion meets with the certainty of the
modern. What can happen in such an encounter is, in the individual
case generally astonishingly predictable.[5] In this situation, *the
question about the whole of religion – limited by unquestioned
modern assumptions – has to find an answer which, without resistance, also fits within these limits.* The integral question is open,
but all ways of answering the question are, from the beginning, pre-
determined. Scrutinizing consideration of this point must lead to
the conclusion that the integral question cannot be consistently
asked under conditions of only partial questionableness. *Integral*

science of religion slips easily into *integrating* science of religion. The attempt of the science to perceive and understand its object as comprehensively as possible slips into being an attempt to deal exhaustively with the questionable and dubious fact of traditional religion from the standpoint of the modern world-view, to explain as much as possible from a basis in this standpoint. Under the conditions of partial questionableness, the dilemma with regard to traditional religion may only be overcome through a more or less successful integration of the phenomenon 'traditional religion' into the modern understanding of reality. That is, the place has to be found and assigned to traditional religion which, given certain limits, is still allowable in the modern understanding of man and the world. Certainly modern science of religion discovers new certainty and understanding through such a process, but only with regard to religion which somehow yet harmonizes with the modern world-view. Integrating science of religion forces traditional religion into the procrustean bed of unquestioned assumptions and is not satisfied until it has amputated enough to make its victim fit nicely into that bed.[6]

Integral questionableness handles the matter otherwise. Integral science of religion requires the possibility and right to question integrally. It does not bow reverently before these unquestioned modern assumptions or before the supposedly certain results derived from them. Just as religion is questioned by integral science of religion, so this science can be given nothing which cannot be placed in question. It can hold consistently and consequently to its integral interest only if it can keep itself open to every insight which results from encounter with the subject matter — even the insight which fits poorly or not at all into momentary modern basic understanding. This science tries to understand religion as it is and not as it must be and as it can yet be accepted under given conditions. Integral science of religion takes the freedom not only to ask about the whole of religion, but also to ask about the whole of itself and even about certainties that almost every scientist of religion accepts as self-evident. Only through such integral questioning is access to the whole of religion possible.

It would be a strange metaphysics, indeed, which distinguished between the fundamentally questionable and the fundamentally unquestionable in the whole of reality and never perceived that, for a truly consistent thought, everything is questionable! What a hybrid interpretation of that naive metaphysics it would be which identified its own modern perception and interpretation with what is unquestionable, and which, on the other hand, identified traditional — and now foreign — perception and interpretation with the questionable!

4. THE WHOLE OF RELIGION

As an example of a premise of modern science of religion, we mentioned its *guiding idea (Vor-stellung)* of religion (see above, pp. 21f). Science of religion could not ask about the whole of religion or attempt to come nearer to the whole in perception, research and understanding, if it did not try to make at least the suggestion of this whole and essence of religion real to itself.

Again, in this process, it is not to be ruled out that the *Vor-stellung* of the whole not only opens access to the whole but in many ways and at the same time obstructs this access. On closer consideration, such guiding ideas can show themselves to be very limited and, therefore, to be only supposed ideas of the whole. Hence, it is commendable that these guiding ideas of the whole be made conscious. It is in the fact that the different projections of ideas of the whole stand beside one another, that the possibility of the limitation of each is evident. What is perhaps unseen in one projection may be consciously emphasized in another.

1. For a long while in the *Vor-stellung* of modern science of religion, the whole of religion coincided with the *origin of religion* and the development of its later stages from this origin. Whoever wished to be clear about the whole of religion and to know what religion really was needed only to ask about an 'historical' or 'psychological' origin. One discovered the key to the whole of religion in an original religion of earliest man, in a prereligious magic or early religious animistic, preanimistic or urmonotheistic

stage. And then again one discovered the key to the whole of religion, in Rudolf Otto's words, in the *'fundus animae'*, the 'bottom' or 'ground of the soul' (*Seelengrund*), in a predisposition' (*Anlage*), a 'seed of potentiality' (*eine Keimen vergleichbare Veranlagtheit*), even in a 'religious impulsion' or a 'driving impulsion' in the soul of man (Rudolf Otto, 1923:116ff. and 1963:139ff.). Rudolf Otto refers to the 'fundamental biogenetic law' which 'uses the stages and phases of the growth of the individual to throw light upon the corresponding stages in the growth of his species' (Rudolf Otto, 1923:120). Predisposition to religion in the soul of the individual is generally the cause of religion and its development in the history of humanity.

> The *predisposition* which the human reason brought with it when the species Man entered history became long ago, not merely for individuals but for the species as a whole, a *religious impulsion*, to which incitements from without and pressure from within the mind both contributed. It begins in undirected, groping emotion, a seeking and shaping of representations, and goes on, by a continual onward striving, to generate ideas, till its nature is self-illumed and made clear by an explication of the obscure *a priori* foundation of thought itself, out of which it originated. And this emotion, this searching, this generation and explication of ideas, gives the warp of the fabric of religious evolution (Rudolf Otto, 1923:120).

Where do the evident and clearly stated[7] weaknesses and failures of this *Vor-stellung* in our time, this guiding idea of the whole of religion as origin of religion lie? Certainly first of all in the assump- that one can discover an historical or psychological origin of religion. As far as an historical or, more exactly, prehistorical origin of religion is concerned, the most contradictory results have shown with sufficient clarity what one must think about such an 'origin hunt' (G. Widengren, 1974a:104). Theories of a religious predisposition in individual persons are uncontested only as long as they remain nothing more than vague indications. As soon as they take on definite contours and univocally state what this origin of religion is, they are immediately contradicted (K. Leese, 1954:147ff).

On the basis of principle, there is a second objection to be made. By what right does one assume that the whole of religion may be explained by means of knowledge of the origin of religion and of its development out of this origin? By what right does one assume that religion in its essence is nothing other than an origin and its unfolding? Even if this origin could be investigated, in the investigation one would not have simply discovered, and not at all have understood, the whole of religion. Religion is a multifarious process and, therewith, living history. As living history, it is far more than only a theoretical point of departure and a subsequent unfolding. In light of this objection, it is also not at all clear why, above all, an alleged beginning phase of religion is supposed to open up the whole of religion. This could only be true if religion, together with its whole history, never was and can never be other than what it basically already was in its beginning. History of religion would be basically already only an 'unwinding' of an always self-identical one. One does not need a great deal of fantasy to see how this simple scheme contradicts the incalculable manifold of religious life and its history, a life and history which does not allow itself to be fitted into schemes.[8]

2. A second guiding idea of the whole — the *abstract essence of religion* — has already been briefly mentioned. In the many-sidedness of the individual one searches for what unites all religion. It is abstracted from what characteristizes only the individual as such. With this abstraction one attains the concept of religion or of the essence of religion.

This guiding idea of the whole of religion also cannot be suitable for integral science of religion. Firstly, concepts of religion are *either not real concepts or they are not concepts of religion*, they are either not encompassing enough or they are so encompassing that they are no longer concepts but 'flourishes' which say everything and nothing. Concepts of religion either hit their mark and are valueless or they are helpful and false. Religion still shows itself to be far more and unexpectedly different than that definite and content-full idea and expectation of it which science of religion has. F. Max Müller has already made us attentive to that as he, after examining 'a few of the more recent definitions of religion' comes to the conclusion that 'almost every one is met by another, which takes the very opposite view of what religion is or ought to be.... Thus we see that each definition of religion, as soon as it is stated, seems at once to provoke another which meets it by a flat denial'.[9] Every concept of religion shows itself to be too narrow where it consciously defines and delimits and has to be supplemented and corrected with a new definition. That suggests that science of religion can, at best, define its *Vorstellung* and expectation but never religion itself.

Secondly, an abstract defined essence cannot be identical with the whole of religion, because the wholeness of an essence is the identity with itself. A pure essence is unchangeable, eternally identical with itself, without tension or contradiction in itself. But religion is neither non-historical nor unchangeable, nor ever exactly identical with itself and never without contradiction. A questioning about the whole of religion which finally establishes an essence of religion and its definitions abandons, in fact, just what it seemingly grasps – the whole of religion. Integral science of religion can only ask about the whole which corresponds, in its living and incalculable manifold, to religious reality.

3. The whole of religion can be thought as the *sum of everything religious*, as complete surveyal of the history of religions or as comprehensive collection of the phenomenology of religions. This guiding idea of the whole is also unconvincing. A sum becomes a whole through the presence of all its parts, that is, through the addition of its last member. But where is such a last member in history of religions or in phenomenology of religions to be found? Whoever imagines he is calculating the sums of history of religion or of the phenomenology of religion does not know what he is doing. Compared with the whole of religious reality, even the most comprehensive so-called sum is a helpless fragment.

In addition, even if we were able to grasp and describe the sum, the whole of religion need not thereby be understood. The sum of the religious would, at best, be identical with the total of religious data. Little would actually be said about the whole of religious experience and probably almost nothing at all about the ground and meaning of all religion. The sum grasps only the most evident dimension of religion. The whole of religion can only be understood in the togetherness of all its dimensions.

4. Friedrich Heiler tries to think the whole of religion in the *image of concentric circles*.

This method treats the religion of mankind as a whole, and views the lower and higher forms of religion together. Every single manifestation is traced from its most primitive to its most spiritual form. In concentric circles we penetrate from the outer manifestations to the inner ones, to the experiences, and finally to the intended object. It is the method of the κυκλικὴ εἴσοδος ἀπο τῶν ἔξω, an expression derived from Dionysios Arcopagita's mysticism... ...Three rings are penetrated in the following order:

I) The world of outer manifestations (*sinnliche Erscheinungswelt*) i.e. the institutional element of religion.

II) The world of spiritual imagination (*geistige Vorstellungswelt*) i.e. The world of ideas, the rational element.

III) The world of psychic experience (*psychische Erlebniswelt*), i.e., the dimension of values, the mystical element of religion.

The center forms the objective world (*Gegenstandswelt*), i.e., the object of religion, Divine Reality (F. Heiler, 1961:19).

In the 'object-world' of religion, the further distinction is made between the inmost center, which is the divine mystery and the *deus absconditus*, and the circle next to the inmost center, the circle of the *deus revelatus*, of the God who turns himself toward man. Also the outer circles are further distinguished. The correlation of the various circles is decisive:

...the physical forms of expression, thoughts, feelings, correspond finally to divine reality. Although that reality can never be completely expressed in human forms of expression, thoughts, and experiences, there is a cerain correspondence to the divine, the *analogia entis*: the created being corresponds to the non-created divine being. The most perfect religion would be one in which the institutionalized ritual, the rational and the mystical elements would be unified, resulting in the closest possible relationship between finite being and infinite mystery (F. Heiler, 1961:21).

It is clear that this rather detailed projection avoids the problem of the one-sidedness of a pure search for an origin, essence or mere total of everything religious. Thought does not remain with the dimension of religious reality, in the 'area of the physical-perceptible, visible, audible, touchable' (F. Heiler, 1961:20). In other words, thought does not get 'stuck' in the dimension of religious data, but searches, in and with the data, to recognize the religious thought and life to which the data refer. In the attempt to understand religious thought and life, it turns also to what this religious thought and life experience as its ground and its aim, as the reality of religion.

Nevertheless, Friedrich Heiler's projection as *Vor-stellung* of the whole of religion is only half convincing, precisely because he goes so much further than the previously mentioned guiding ideas of the whole and already orders into a system what the others do not yet even mention. As a religious-scientific model for the question about the whole of religion, Heiler's concept, in a threefold regard, says too much:

a) The reality of religion is only present to the science of religion in the witness of religious reality. From this witness one cannot take the unequivocal idea that all religious reality is directed toward the same reality. To say that a *deus absconditus et revelatus* is the middle of all spheres of religious thought and life does not correspond to an insight of science of religion but to a theological postulate. For example, the Biblical witness to one God who is the opponent of idolatry does not allow that this one God be thought so easily as the center of all religious endeavor.

b) A theological postulate or a nearly ecumenical program tries to order harmonically in the same circle the contradictory manifold of religious reality. Before religious reality can appear in such a harmonious order, one would have to inquire about its attitude toward other religious reality. It may be assumed not only that this inquiry leads to the thought of concentric circles, but also, if the religious reality in its expression is left unquestioned, that such an order does not correspond to an insight in science of religion.

c) Friedrich Heiler's order becomes altogether theology of religion where it postulates an *analogia entis*, a correlation to the one God for all religious reality generally, and where it, then, understands itself as the measure for the judgement of the perfection of a religion. It cannot be the task of science of religion to make general judgments about the relation to God of everything religious. The task of science of religion is to recognize what every religious reality experiences as its own reality of religion. Just as little can science of religion use its guiding idea, *Vor-stellung*, of the whole of religion as a measure for the judgment of the perfection of a religion. Its guiding idea of the whole is, at best, an aid to understanding, but never a norm by which religious reality must be measured. On its ways toward greater understanding, science of religion can find no norms. It can discover them, at the most, in its own religious conviction or in religious-philosophical speculation.

5. The whole of religion can, in the *Vor-stellung* of modern science of religion, also fall together with one or more of the *significances* (*Bedeutungen*) of religion. We name a 'significance' the position and effect of religion in an outlined area of human reality. Each religion has significance in the art, society and even economy of its time.[10] Without doubt, these and other significances may be partly investigated. A most comprehensive research of religion will certainly also try to become acquainted with religion in the greatest possible number of its significances. It only remains questionable whether the whole of religion is recognized and understood with one or with the greatest possible number of its own significances.

We take as example the beginning point for different works of the 'Groningen Working-Group for the Study of Fundamental Problems and Methods of Science of Religion' (Th. P. van Baaren and H. J. W. Drijvers, 1973). Here religion is seen primarily as a function of culture. In connection with what we have already said, we assume the right to speak of the significance of religion for and in its culture. This point of departure, religion as a function of culture, is, in fact, able to make us again attentive to aspects of religion that are elsewhere too quickly passed over. It is to be especially mentioned that religion must be considered in its connection with other functions of culture; that in comparisons between different religions we have to be aware of the uniqueness of each individual religion and its comparability; that the question about correct terminology in science of religion is again newly under way, and that religious behavior has moved anew into the center of interest of science of religion (Th. P. van Baaren and H. J. W. Drijvers, 1973:162ff., summary). The question about the effect and position of religion in the frame of its culture certainly contributes to the question about the whole of religion, but is the whole of religion grasped in the significance of religion for and in its culture? We think not, unless one defines the term culture so broadly that it corresponds with the whole of human reality, for example also with its personal and individual dimensions, and unless one defines the concept of function or of significance so broadly that the concept of *meaning* is included; therefore, unless one defines the concept so that all is included *which religion immediately says to one who lives it.* Therewith, the question about a significance of religion would be broadened into the integral question about the whole of religion. And the usually rather non-participatory attitude of considering the significance — it is the outsider who asks, above all, about the significance, that is, about what something effects or does — would be supplemented through reflection on or through a conscious taking-up of what religion says to one who knows himself claimed by the reality of religion. In itself, the view of one standing consciously outside religion can never be knowledge of the whole but, at best, a necessary and helpful contribution to the whole.

We refer only briefly to two basic problems of all questioning about significance. A not yet ended or never ending task — also in the case of the mentioned studies of the Groningen Working-Group — becomes evident when it is a matter of defining the frame of human reality in which religion is to be shown significant. (Th. P. van Baaren and H. J. W. Drijvers, 1973:36, 136f.) Secondly, further clarification is needed in the question about the relation of what is significant to its place in the discussion. What is significant and its significance, what is effective and its effect, can often be almost imperceptibly confused (H. H. Penner, 1971, 91-97).

6. Closely related to the attempt to identify religion with one of its significances is the guiding idea of *an essential characteristic of*

7. It seems to be the case, therefore, that science of religion limits its integral interest from the beginning, when it, in its question about the whole of religion, allows itself to be led by the guiding idea (*Vor-stellung*) of an origin, essence, system, significance, essential characteristic or a sum of all religious data. To ask in any of these ways about the whole would be, from the beginning, to exclude essential moments of religion, to force the whole into a scheme that doesn't fit it, and, in all that, to miss the *integrum*, the whole of religion.

How is our attempt any better? We take our point of departure from what is common to all these mentioned attempts:

(a) In all of the mentioned guiding ideas of religion, the whole of religion is thought as the (in one case more provisional, in another more definitive) product of a process of perception. Science of religion finds the way to the whole through adding up the sum, systematizing, comparing, ordering, reducing, holding firmly to a characteristic, considering a significance. But, under critical scrutiny, may this presupposition be held in every case? Is the whole of religion comparable to the solution of a riddle or to the result of a calculus? Considered as a whole, is religion not much closer to mystery than to riddle or calculus? And if that is the case, can we find the way to the mystery other than as the mystery, at the same time, finds the way to us? Is insight into the whole perhaps at most a result or yield (*Er-gebnis*), but never a product of our perception — therefore, an insight that 'yields itself' (*sich ergibt*).

(b) A second common feature of the mentioned *Vor-stellungen* of the whole lies in the fact that the product of the various procedures may, as a rule, be formulated. Frequently, the product is a relatively short formula which, in the course of further research, shows itself to be as much a hindrance as a help. But is integral science of religion dependent on such formulas? May the whole of religion be at all concentrated into a formula? Considered as a whole, is religion a condition or existence (*Befindlichkeit*) that can be fixed? Considered as a whole, is religion not a process which is never ended in time?

It seems to us that integral science of religion, if it finds the way to formulas, has not exactly found its way to the whole of religion.

The formula is a momentarily helpful construction which later becomes a hindrance. It is sometimes necessary in that it indicates direction, but only in this function. Ordinarily, the guiding idea of the whole should not become a formula. At the most, it should be an orientation and an expectation. But what orientation and what expectation?

In the following, we state as a working hypothesis: *the whole of religion discloses itself in its meaning (erschliesst sich in ihrem Sinn).* As a first approximate definition,[12] we name 'meaning' what religion says to one who lives it. Meaning encounters us in the reflection of religious thought on its own religious experience, that is, in the self-understanding of religion. But meaning opens itself not simply where the religious man can reflect on and state what moves him and what he experiences. Meaning encounters us as indication in every religious datum and every religious life, even in the unreflected religious life. Integral science of religion will reflect on the stated meaning and elevate the indicated meaning, if it wishes, with understanding, to come nearer to the whole of religion.

Our guiding idea of the whole does not lead to a fixed formula. It does not say what the whole is. Our working hypothesis is an orientation and an expectation. It refers to the place or, rather, to the process in which we expect the whole to disclose itself. That is, it refers itself to the meaning of religion. We do not state as a working hypothesis that the whole is the meaning of religion. We simply state: In the meaning the whole discloses itself (*erschliesst sich*). The whole does not, therefore, limit itself to what religion says immediately to one living it. Our expectation is simply: only when we understand what religion says to one living it, will we find the way to the whole of religion. Therefore, we do not need to create order in the confusing manifold of religious reality with reductions and systems, exclusive characteristics and singly decisive significances. Our expectation is: from the meaning of religion, religious reality orders itself ever anew — not into system, not into a complete sum, but into the meaningful, living whole. The better we understand the meaning of religious reality, the more clearly do we find the way — not to the origin, the abstract essence, the only essential characteristic, but — to the living middle, to the central essence of religion. Also the significancies of religion appear, considered under the aspect of their meaning, in a new light. They are now seen no longer to state the whole, which is never identical with a significance. Every significance is a meaningful contribution to insight into the whole. Every guiding idea previously, in its immediate aspiration, showed itself in its consequence as simply meaningless. Now, however, it mediately contributes its own to insight into the whole. Mediate means: accompanied by reflection on (*Be-sinnung auf*) the whole.

Perhaps the image of the circle which F. Heiler uses[13] is, apart from all systematization, a helpful comparision. Religious reality may be compared with a circle. The meaning of religious reality would be the middle of the circle. This middle is not the whole. But the whole opens itself from the middle and only from the middle may the circle be drawn. The whole of religion opens itself from the meaning of religion.

3

The Methods

1. INTEGRAL AND HERETICAL SCIENCE OF RELIGION

At first we would like to warn against all judgments which say something like 'you have to do it this way' or 'you cannot do it that way'. The old byword is, if at all, only in its formulation old-fashioned, which says: 'it seems to us to be a duty of research to leave no means untried which, when rightly used, brings hope for a more basic knowledge of its object'.[1] Every means and every method which furthers the perception of individual aspects of religion is, thereby, also a contribution to better perception of the whole of religion. That different means and methods further only perception of a part and not of the whole, does not reduce their significance for perception of the whole — *presupposed* (if we may personalize these terms) *that they do not hold the part they perceive to be the whole* and that they remain open for the contribution of other supplementing methods. If means and methods recognize their relativity and understand themselves only as valid for research of individual aspects, they are, within their own frameworks, valuable contributions to the perception of the whole and, indeed, necessary means and methods of integral science of religion.

Where they do not recognize their relativity, where they mistake their part for the whole, they are heresies. *'Hairesis'* designates the selectivity which believes it has the whole in its selected part. As heresy, they are of highly equivocal value for integral research and questioning, for what they open for perception is of small significance when compared with the obstruction of perception which occurs in their absolutizing of their own views.

2. RELIGIOUS REALITY AND THE METHOD OF SCIENCE OF RELIGION

We take it as a *fundamental principle* for all discussion of method in contemporary science of religion — for all so-called methodology —that *responsible method in science of religion can only be, where our perception is confronted by at least one aspect of religious reality.* Method in science of religion is, therefore, not a process which is independent of all religious reality. It is not developed out of purely theoretical presuppositions. Method in science of religion can only be a path. It is grounded only in the fact that at least one moment of the datum requires it. Exact consideration of the matter reveals that not the scientist of religion chooses his methods, but the religious datum forces methods on the scientist. Method in science of religion is not basically ways and means which help us to gain insight into religious reality, but chances which we have to concede to religious reality where we recognize that the religious reality 'wishes' to bring itself to expression in this or that aspect. To approach religion with assumed modern means of perception is, by far, not yet scientific method, but, at best, a form of intellectual occupation with religion. It is a sad fact that intellectual occupation with religion and science of religion are often confused. That confusion is impossible, if we are clear about the fact that methods are not our means for working over religion, but religion's own possibilities — possibilities which we only perceive, or the unfolding of those moments in which religious reality offers itself to us. Therefore, a responsible method in science of religion is more *comparable to a space which holds our perception free for religious reality in the area of scientific perception.* It is more comparable to a space which religious reality is able to present and explain itself than with a tool which we develop and apply to our object. If method in science of religion were comparable with our own previously developed and subsequently applied tool, it would not present and understand religion in the first place, but handle and revise religion. Such a false method leads to the religion one wants to have and does not allow the religion to be and to speak what actually happens.

What are, then, the elementary methods of perception in science of religion — elementary, because they correspond to and are required by a fundamental moment of religious reality? We think these elementary methods are essentially three: *description, comprehension and understanding*. All others which may be required seem to us to be variations of these three.

3. DESCRIPTION

Knowledge and perception in science of religion have to do with what is given for the science, and what is given is, exactly considered, only religious data, (see above, pp. 67ff.) that is, what the science perceives as religious data according to its guiding idea of religion. Earlier we named religious data the immediately visible, perceptible aspects of religious reality, such as texts, symbols, cultic objects, temples, songs, offices, pictures, etc. First of all, these religious data are to be recognized as religous data and be taken as they are given.

Descriptive science of religion tries to correspond to this requirement. It has no other purpose than to become acquainted with individual religious data, to observe, present and, therefore, perceive each datum as it is. To the greatest possible degree apart from every judgment, interpretation, ordering and systematization, descriptive science of religion attempts to take stock of the obvious dimension of religious reality in the most encompassing and detailed way possible. Practiced in all consequence, it leads to the boundless plenitude of all known religious data.

One could think that such acquaintance and description is the most simple thing in the world. The broad discussion about so-called phenomenology of religion — together with many differences in the application of concepts such as 'phenomenon', 'epoch', 'essence', and with the differences in the understanding of the relation of phenomenology to history[2] has produced an immediate positive result in the demonstration that, as in all human efforts to perceive, nothing is more difficult in science of religion than perception and simple description.

Why is that the case? I. M. Bochenski has referred to two essential difficulties which can never be fully overcome.

(1) Man is such that he has an almost insurmountable inclination to 'see' or imagine elements into things which are foreign to those things. We do that either through our subjective emotional attitudes (a coward sees the power of his enemy double), or through knowledge we have gotten elsewhere, that is, we project our hypotheses, theories and ideas into the given object. In eidetic reduction,[3] however, it is a matter of sighting only what is given. To attain such a sight, it is necessary to apply a carefully worked out and practiced method. (2) No object is simple, rather, every object is infinitely complex, and, indeed, every object consists of different components and aspects which are not equally important. One cannot grasp all the moments at once, one must observe them one at a time. This, too, requires a well thought out and practiced method (I. M. Bochenski, 1971:24f.).

The difficulties mentioned seem to recommend the establishment of positive rules for pure vision:

(1) As far as possible, one should try to see *all* that is given. In itself clear enough, this simple rule has to be expressly formulated and consciously applied because man is such that he has a strong inclination to see only some aspects of the given. Uexküll   has shown that animals grasp only what is vitally important for them; man has much in common with animals. Yet he has more ability than animals, which is evident, among other things, in his ability for theoretical, non-practical knowledge and perception. Nevertheless, we are all too inclined to remain blind to certain elements of the given. The first task of phenomenological research is, therefore, the uncovering of overlooked phenomena. (2) Furthermore, phenomenological vision should be *descriptive*. That means the object should be taken apart and described according to its parts, analyzed. Every object is infinitely complex. The clearer the vision is, all the better can the elements be distinguished and held apart (I. M. Bochenski, 1971:30).

Pure vision is, therefore, anything but child's play. We do not simply always project 'non-arbitrarily our earlier acquired knowledge into the object' (I. M. Bochenski, 1971:29). Phenomenology of religion, that is, pure description of what shows itself as a religious given, cannot be without a guiding idea of what it means to describe something as a religious given and to ignore something else as a non-religious datum. This pre-decision is already interpretation, and, strictly taken, it makes pure vision impossible. Nevertheless, the effort to attain pure perception is the enduring basis of all science of religion. If science of religion fails to continually make this effort, it is in danger of asking only about the religion which it conceives itself and wants to have, but not the religion which really exists. As guidelines for pure vision, the phenomenological postulates are for every science of religion practically indispensable, even if, in theory strictly considered, they are impossible.

There are three limits set to such a phenomenology of religion developing out of the application of phenomenological postulates. To ignore any one of the three limits can cause the phenomenology of religion to harm the science of religion instead of being a service to it.

1. As the attempt at pure vision, phenomenology is *one method among others*. It cannot be the only process in religious-scientific perception. 'He who proceeds phenomenologically does not renounce application of other procedures at a later time' (I. M. Bochenski, 1971:24). In a pure description of numerous religious givens, religion is not yet understood. Pure description needs insight, conception and understanding as supplementary methods.

2. The understanding of phenomenology which completely pursues aims other than pure perception and description of what is given cannot serve phenomenology's best and actual interest, which is pure vision. The phenomenological *epoché* is reserve toward everything subjective, the attempt of the researcher to exclude 'everything that comes from himself, from the subject, above all his feelings, wishes, personal attitudes, etc.' (I. M. Bochenski, 1971:26). But if this *epoché* is compared with 'the loving look of the lover at the loved object' (G. van der Leeuw, 1956:783) and unites itself programatically with the 'inclusion of the phenomenon in one's own life', with feeling oneself and sinking oneself into foreign life and experience, with the interpretation and experience of what shows itself (G. van der Leeuw, 1956:783), then it has a great deal to do

with the interest of interpreting and understanding science of religion, but hardly anything at all to do with the phenomenology of religion. All this inclusion of the given in one's own feeling and experience is the opposite of the phenomenological *epoché*. The accomplishments of Gerhard van der Leeuw's phenomenology of religion are in no way contested by this objection. They remain obvious accomplishments just because they are far more than only those of a phenomenology of religion. But one should not use the concept 'phenomenology' for such programmed projecting oneself into a foreign experience. According to the root meaning of the word, 'phenomenology' means a *'legein'*, a reading of phenomena and, therefore, of what shows itself. Phenomenology is and should remain the method of pure description of the given. *The task of pure description is only made more difficult, if one brings into it completely different interests, such as lovingly feeling-oneself-into foreign experience and arranging different phenomena systematically.* Where experience and feeling are mixed with the attempt at pure observation, how can one be at all certain that his perception is not simply what he himself thinks and feels into the given object of observation?

It seems to us just as problematic and obstructive for the interest of pure observation, when Friedrich Heiler attempts, under the title 'The Phenomenological Method', to unfold his concept of the whole religion, which has its parts in the five concentric circles mentioned earlier (F. Heiler, 1961:18-21). What does pure observation of the given have to do with religious-theological projections and discussions of concepts as burdened by the weight of theological tradition, such as *'analogia entis'*, *'deus absconditus'* and *'revelatus'*? Does not phenomenology require the exclusion of such previously given theories and conclusions simply in order to see the phenomenon as it discloses itself? One has the impression that, now and again, quite the opposite of phenomenology clothes itself in the title 'phenomenology of religion'; that 'phenomenology of religion' is not always the pure vision and description to which the title refers. Such a *mixture* of different, in themselves legitimate interests of science of religion finally *serves none of the different procedures*.

3. Not everything that was brought forward in the philosophical

discussion on the theme of phenomenology may be self-evidently included in the pure description of religious data. Phenomenology of religion cannot disregard the existence of what is given. It is of decisive importance for phenomenology of religion that it *regard the religiously real and not simply the thinkable*. Here the *epoché* would be in the wrong place, even if phenomenology of religion tries otherwise, with good reason, to realize the three-fold *epoché* from everything subjective, theoretical and hypothetical, and from all about the object in the tradition. It also seems to us that the *epoché* from all that is inessential in what is given is problematic. How may such a reduction be united with the requirement 'to see, as well as possible, all that is given'? (I. M. Bochenski, 1971:30).

We have seen that science of religion, above all as phenomenology of religion, tries to attain a descriptive presentation of what discloses itself (*des sich Zeigenden*), even if it conceals completely different interests under the title 'phenomenology of religion'. Constructive criticism of phenomenology of religion is, therefore, certainly able to contribute much that is essential toward approximating the postulate of a descriptive science of religion, even if this postulate shows itself as already fulfilled in none of the phenomenologies of religion published to date.

The other way to a descriptive science of religion which we also have to consider is that of immediate reflection. This becomes possible when we ask the question: what must happen in and with science of religion in order that it be capable of pure description? What hinders the science from seeing a religious datum as what it is in all its aspects? The difficulties of pure description, as the discussion of phenomenology of religion has clearly shown, lie not so much in the object to be described as in the one who intends to describe it. The central problem of phenomenology of religion is the phenomenologist himself.

We have already mentioned two answers from I. M. Bochenski to the questions we have just raised. Now, especially with regard to interest in a descriptive science of religion, we wish to clarify and supplement these answers.

1. If pure description tries 'to the greatest possible degree to see

all that is given' (I. M. Bochenski, 1971:30) and, at the same time, if the one describing has already, in his guiding ideas and expectations, projected his picture or idea of what is described into what is described, so the following is certainly a first fundamental rule for all description: *one must make oneself as conscious as possible of the guiding ideas (Vor-stellungen) and expectations with which one, in observation, approaches what is given.* It would be illusion to think that we could ever describe a religious datum without guiding ideas and expectations. Such freedom and total openness is beyond human possibility. It is possible and recommendable, however, to ask about the conditions under which our observation is made. Only if we are conscious of the limits of these conditions, can we, if need be, overcome them in favor of new and better guiding ideas and expectations. All pure vision begins with the question, "What do I expect to see?"

2. 'To see, to the greatest degree possible, all that is given' is, at best, an ability of one who finds his way to a rather paradoxical attitude. We would like to designate this attitude as the '*expectation of the unexpected*'. We mean by that the readiness to let oneself be suprised, the openness for what clearly lies beyond the limits of one's own expectation. After the first question, "What do I expect?", follows immediately the second question, "Am I ready to grant what lies beyond my expectations or which perhaps even contradicts my expectations? Is my expectation for me simply a rather clumsy guideline, or is it a blind norm?"

3. To perceive and describe what is given to the greatest degree possible in all its aspects, calls necessarily for another basic attitude of the one perceiving. He must be attentive to those aspects of the given which he, through his guiding *Vor-stellungen* or ideas, is disposed to overlook as uninteresting or inessential — something he usually does even before he is really acquainted with the given. Nothing in the given is uninteresting for pure description, even if something might seem, at first, rather unimportant. On the contrary, it is precisely the apparently completely unimportant aspect which, as a rule, refers especially clearly to the limits of our own guiding ideas and expectations. It is in reflection on what is unimportant

that the too-narrow confines of one's own perception may be overcome. Not to consider what is unimportant would mean to disregard the best chance for correction of one's guiding ideas. Consequent description will not disregard such a chance. Rather, it will ever again attend especially to what is apparently unimportant and ask why this aspect seems to be so insignificant. Real phenomenology knows about the wholly *special dignity of what is unimportant*, about the special help and special value which enter into description from what is apparently without significance.

4. Pure description of what is, is thinkable only when it is bound with the greatest *reserve toward all hasty designations and comparisons*. How is the given to show itself as what it is, if the observer, as soon as he is barely acquainted with the datum, begins to stamp it with concepts such as 'myth', 'mysticism', 'God', 'hierophany', 'symbol', 'sacrament', etc., and if he places the datum at once within a series with hundreds of others from completely different cultures and times? In this sort of framework, can a datum yet speak for itself? Where is there room for its own peculiarity and particularity? Pure description has to distance itself consciously from all general designations. Such designations are no more its business than are comparisons. Designation and comparison on the basis of pure description lead, at best, to labels and prejudices. *Only what has been understood may be meaningfully compared and designated.* That is true because understanding first unveils the whole problem of such comparisons, general categories and schemata. Prior to understanding, purely on the basis of initial description, both comparison and the application of categories can indeed easily be done. What is hardly known can always be made to fit nicely into a schema. But it is just in the schema that all thorough description expires. One no longer perceives the datum in all its peculiarities and aspects, but as a single case in the frame of a general appearance. Comparison and general designation are, at best, tasks of understanding. Prior to understanding, they are a mere labeling of the datum and a drawing of parallels resembling the datum. Mere description hinders meaningful comparison and designation just as hasty comparison and designation hinder an encompassing description. Considering the fre-

quence in which modern science of religion designates and compares data that have hardly been described — the offense has often been almost a sport, we cannot more emphatically state the fact that comparison and designation cannot be the business of pure description. Pure description, in its perception, intends to make room for the religious datum in all its aspects. This is only possible, if we do not, with hasty clichés, obliterate this space. We have to provide this space, not take it away.

5. If pure description does not enter into general designations and comparisons, so we have, now, to ask about the order of what is merely described. Must not purely descriptive science of religion somehow find a system of the data described; perhaps such that, when comparisons are made, like be placed with like? It seems to us that the order or, indeed, the system of religious data is not to be considered a task of pure description. Such order either remains a mere construction which forces individual datum into a scheme and stands in the way of its comprehensive description, or it is not derived from the attempt at a mere description, but from the attempt to comprehend religious reality in concepts and to understand religious reality. Pure description will always be united with the *courage to disorder and to non-systematize*. It cannot and does not wish to clarify, where only the subject matter can clarify itself to the one making the effort to comprehend and understand it. Supposed order hinders real insight, and hasty clarity hinders better understanding.

4. COMPREHENSION

The consequent next step and the unavoidable supplement to pure description is comprehension. We name comprehension (*Begreifen*) the attempt to perceive the relations in which a described datum stands and, in that attempt, the effort to supplement and deepen acquaintance with the datum.

Every religious datum stands in a manifold of relations, and only in these relations does it become what it is. For example, it stands in relation to the historical circumstances which play a large part in forming it and which are probably, in part, formed by the religious datum. It owes its being the way it is, perhaps, to the cultural, economic or political conditions of its time, and in some essential characteristics the datum refers to other, similar data of its time which were not without influence on it. It may refer very clearly to definite events in the biography of a man whom we encounter in the mentioned datum, to his personal dispositions, abilities or problems. Or perhaps the datum is formed through the community which expresses itself in this man through the language in which the datum transmits itself to us. All of these and similar relations must be perceived and considered, for the insight into such relations has consequences for the acquaintance with what is given. No religious datum is isolated. Therefore, pure description, which considers a religious datum as isolated can only be a first step on the way of perception in science of religion.

Let us briefly consider what would be lost by such comprehension. It would be impossible to write any sort of history of religion. Just as impossible would be the attempt to write a sociology of religion. The relation of the religious witness to the economic conditions of its time would remain outside every consideration in science of religion. It would be impossible to see the function of certain religious data within the social and cultural life of their time. It would be just as impossible to write a biography of a religious individual or to recognize the manifold and mutual relations between different religious currents. In short, comprehension, the perception of religious data in the relations in which they stand, belongs to the most necessary and incontestable methods in the effort of science of religion to perceive. The fact that the science comprehends is hardly questionable.

Questionable is simply the *how* of comprehension. Here begins the contention of different opinions, for the way one comprehends is practically always different from the way another comprehends. Modern science of religion cannot avoid thinking about how it is to comprehend what is given in a religious reality. It seems to us that this question calls for a fourfold answer:

1. A fundamental law of human perception is that perception,

if at all possible, simply adds what it has little knowledge of to what it knows more about and, thereby, makes the former into something which is better known. This procedure, perception of what is not well known by way of ordering it with what is better known, conceals itself in the expression 'comprehension' (*begreifen*). To 'prehend' (as *'greifen'* in the German word *'Begreifen'*) means to 'grasp'. *From ones standpoint, from what one has or knows, one 'grasps' that which one does not yet have or know and so makes it ones own.* Therefore, how religion is comprehended, that is, in which relations religious reality is thought, is to a great degree determined by the state of perception of one who tries to comprehend or, better, by the definite perception one thinks one has. Therefore, a certain accidental character is unmistakably in all comprehension. *Religious reality is chiefly or exclusively transposed from its own setting into one with which we are familiar.* One who thinks he is acquainted with the life of a definite form of society will see religious reality chiefly or exclusively in relation to this social reality. Another researcher is convinced that he, as historian of religion, has a good grasp of certain religious-historical connections, and he will, quite naturally and immediately, put a new religious datum into the order of historical connections which he knows. Such comprehension, that is, the setting of a datum in relation to that with which one is already familiar (in case these relations are real and not imaginary, i.e. if these relations really co-determine the way of being of a religious datum) — such comprehension contributes much that is essential to acquaintance with a religious datum. But this essential contribution is always only a fragment, an essentially accidental contribution, Each considers the relation of the datum to what is familiar to him, and he hardly considers other relations at all.

How may this always more or less obvious accidental character of comprehension be overcome? It seems to us that a certain degree of it is impossible to overcome, because no one can be familiar with everything which influences and forms religious reality. Because of that, this accidental character of all comprehension is not to be overlooked and not to be undervalued. No comprehension of religions presents a truly encompassing picture of the whole of religious reality and the relations in which this reality stands. All comprehension is a meaningful and necessary contribution to perception of the whole — nothing less and nothing more.

2. *Accordingly, all attempts are completely wrong which explain religious reality* on the basis of one of the relations determining it. *We name 'explanation' that comprehension which, in its ordering of the datum in a definite relation, finds in the relation not only a condition for the way of being of the datum, but also the sufficient and, usually, the only ground for the being and way of being of religious reality.* For example: comprehension sees the relations between the economic conditions of a specific time and corresponding religious data; explanation absolutizes these relations into an all-encompassing theory. Explanation says, because the economy at that time was of such a kind, the religious reality of the time was brought into being.

3. Since comprehension thinks relations, it always stands in danger of one-sidedness or one-directionedness. Every living relation — and religious reality is human life — is seen by careful observation to be a *mutual relation.* An A does not determine a B without, in its determination of B, being itself determined by B. It is just this mutuality that really makes comprehension interesting, but it also makes it more complicated and more difficult. Much simpler would be a one-sided or one-directioned scheme: A determines B, or, indeed: A, therefore, B. For example, how simple it is to reduce the multiplicity of relations between religious and economic life to the following one-directioned scheme: economic life determines religion. Conception will inhibit rather than further better acquaintance with religious reality, if it does not protect relations from such one-directionedness, and if it cannot escape fascination with over-clarity. What it discovers as genuine relation should not be a burial of other living relations. *Comprehension may not become a simple derivation.* And science of religion is not to be reproached for defending itself ever again against simple derivation.[4]

4. We have defined comprehension as the addition of the less known to the better known. We also find this procedure practiced in the form of a certain important variation. One does not add the little

known with the better known, but the unknown or hardly known to that which one unquestionably knows. One sets not merely an X in relation to a Y in the hope of arriving, through the relation, at a better perception of both. One sets an X beside an A. The former needs clarification, the latter is known without question. Conception has lost its deepest meaning when it makes that with which it is familiar into a *fundamentum inconcussum*, into a knowledge lifted above all doubt. For where does the actual meaning and the best aim of all conception lie? It is not in simply putting them in the proper relationship to one another, or in clarification, or in the explanation of one datum, but in the fact that, in reflection on a living relation, what is hardly known and what is familiar become clearer, more differentiated and detailed. Therefore, in the comprehension of a newly discovered religious datum on the basis of already known developments in the history of religion, it can only partially enlighten the mentioned datum through prior knowledge of the respective religious history. The other — just as valuable — aspect of comprehension is also to be considered: how much can the newly discovered datum enlighten, confirm, supplement, correct or contradict what is already known? Only that comprehension which falls neither into simple catagorizing and arranging nor into linear derivation fulfills its potential and has its place in an integral science of religion.

Excursus II. On the Theory of Understanding in Science of Religion

Those occupied with understanding as a method in science of religion leave us in no doubt about its significance: ' "Understanding" is the business of the comparative religionist to the extent that he desires to do more than merely collect archaeological, historical and philological facts' (R. J. Werblowsky, 1959:32). Understanding makes science of religion what it actually is: 'A work is not actually science of religion, if its intention does not lie in the "understanding" of religion in the context of the religions'(C.H.Ratschow,1973a:369).

All endeavor in science of religion flows into understanding: 'Historical and systematic interests go together in order to bring the scientist closer to the goal of science of religion, which is to understand
religion' (J. Wach, 1924:132). Corresponding to the significance
it attributes to understanding, science of religion tries to clarify this
method to the greatest possible extent. This clarification has hardly
reached its conclusion. Indeed, it is, in many ways, only in its beginnings. At the elementary level, to be sure, certain basic lines can be
discerned.

1. The Goal

There is a relative degree of clarity about the goal of understanding,
even if it is not so widely defined as in Ratschow and R. J. Zwi
Werblowsky. Somewhere along the lines of their projections lies
the goal that almost all understanding seeks: 'Roughly, the claim
is that to understand human beings and their actions we must put
ourselves in their position, e.g. think their thoughts, feel their feelings' (Jane R. Martin, 1969:53). Understanding, therefore,
does not ask, what is religion? Nor does it ask, how does it come
to be? Rather, its question is, what does religion mean for one
who lives it? 'Science of religion wants to "understand" what
religion in the religions is, what religion means for one and how one
lives before his God. ... The rites and myths are first understood
when we see why this or that is meaningful from the perspective of
the "believer"' (C. H. Ratschow, 1973a:392, 394). R. J. Zwi
Werblowsky once compared understanding with slipping one's
feet into another's shoes.

> This scholarly pursuit is as far removed from mere fact-collecting
> as it is from mere 'empathy', undisciplined intuition and the like.
> It is an attempt to look first at the other fellow's shoes and then
> at his feet, continuing to do so until we somehow 'see' how he
> stands in his shoes and how they fit his feet — and perhaps also
> where they pinch. This demands a fair amount of disciplined imag-
> ination, the capacity, as it were, to step ourselves into the other
> fellow's shoes; and this again, as everyone realizes, also implies

the capacity to take our own shoes off first (1959:33).

Understanding is, therefore, an entry into the point of view of another. Or, in other words: if description and comprehension open up the outer view (*Ansicht*) of things and, therefore correspond to the position of the observer, understanding has the goal of *insight* (*Einsicht*) into the position of the other. Understanding intends to open itself to this position. Understanding may be defined as the *attempt to move from outer vision (Ansicht) to insight (Einsicht)*.

2. The Ways

How do we, however, move from outer vision to insight? What are the ways in which genuine understanding moves? It seems to us that this central question needs clarification. All that science of religion has given as answer is partly nebulous and partly fragmentary.

Two models seem to be offered. First, entry into the other can mean a sinking oneself into his existence. Second, the other can be drawn into one's own existence. In the first, understanding seeks participation (*ein Teil-Nehmen*). In the second, understanding seeks to concede the other a place (*ein Anteil-Geben*). Both models are bound with each other in manifold ways.

With regard to the first, K. Goldammer writes:

Understanding is the sinking of oneself into another existence together with the temporary, partial or hypothetical renunciation of one's own existence. In any case, understanding is the encounter of existences which seek contact, and at least one of these existences has the will to press into the other. Understanding is a stepping out of the attitude of an observer, an abandonment of distance, an inner participation. (K. Goldammer, 1960:XXV).

So we have to evaluate understanding as a breaking through one's own existence, insofar as it must go beyond one's own existence in order to draw near another existence; as an intersection of existences, insofar as it crosses itself with a foreign existence; as a heightening of one's own existence, insofar as it leads to an increase in one's own (Christian) feeling for life in encounter with foreign religions, which can mean confirmation and, at the same time, excite feelings of superiority. (K. Goldammer, 1954: 238).

The difficulty with the idea of going beyond one's own existence and sinking oneself in another, clearly lies precisely where the question arises (to remain with Werblowsky's image): can I step out of my own shoes in order to slip into those of another? Kees W. Bolle thinks that it is impossible to move outside of one's own tradition.

> To advocate such a suspension in order to enable oneself to 'get at' another religious tradition is like saying that the best way to get acquainted with another person is to divest oneself of one's own personal presence (Kees W. Bolle, 1967a:103-104).

The experiences and observations of E. Benz seem to confirm this criticism: 'Even in the serious effort to deal with other religions, we are stamped, into our deepest being, by our own tradition' (E. Benz, 1959:11-39; cf. also K. Klostermaier, 1965:13-25). K. Goldammer is himself well aware of the problematic of moving beyond one's own tradition. In the same article quoted above, Goldammer postulates: the scientist of religion will have more success at following the original meaning of religious life 'the more he can, for this purpose, temporarily loosen himself from his own religious habits, convictions and insights, for this renunciation of self — heuristic renunciation of self or of intelllectual and experiential self-assertian — is the basic presupposition of understanding' (K. Goldammer, 1967a:27). However, in conclusion Goldammer states:

> This will to understand another is limited by the boundaries of the human spirit and by the fact that a person is always referred to his own historical space and his own continuum of tradition. That is a fact which we may ever again feel as tragic, but it simply hangs together with the limits of our human being (K. Goldammer, 1967a:34).

Postulate and reality stand sharply contrasted in the idea of moving beyond one's own existence and sinking oneself into the existence of another.

With regard to the second model mentioned above (drawing the other into one's own existence), we may look to statements by G.

van der Leeuw and G. Mensching. The interpolation of the phenomenon into our own lives belongs essentially to phenomenology.

This introduction, however, is no capricious act, we can do no-
otherwise. 'Reality' is always *my* reality, history *my* history,
'the retrogressive prolongation of man now living' (Spranger)
(G. van der Leeuw, 1963:674). But that means to understand:
to 'plug' (*einschalten*) the historical fact into one's own life in
order to grasp its inner life and, through the mediation of the concept, to bring this inner life to feeling and consciousness (G.
Mensching, 1959:14).

In conjunction with that, G. van der Leeuw unites his idea of 'plugging in' with the postulate of living-oneself-into foreign life (G. van
der Leeuw, 1963:773). C. H. Ratschow sees understanding as mutual
communication:

Understanding intends what is concretely over-against it, that is,
these religions 'as what' they are for their 'believers', namely as
religion. In this understanding, the one who understands and the
one who is understood are bound in a process, and both are
through one another: it is a matter of religion in the religions.
Religion is the with-one-another and through-one-another of the
understanding researcher and the understood specific religions
(C. H. Ratschow, 1973a:391).

In view of this with-one-another and through-one-another and in
view of the mentioned 'plugging' the phenomenon into one's own
life, it has, of course, to be asked to what extent what is to be understood is changed in the process of understanding. If the idea of sinking oneself into the existence of the other cannot convince us that
we can move beyond ourselves, so also the guiding idea of drawing
what is to be understood into our own existence cannot convince us
that adequate understanding, rather than an essential alteration of
what is to be understood, can be the result (J. Wach, RGG^2/V:
1572).

3. The Preconditions

Not everyone can move in the same way on the course from outer
vision to insight, and circumstances further or hinder understand-

ing. J. Wach refers to the necessary equipment for understanding, especially knowledge of languages.

There is no hope of understanding a religion or a religious phenomenon without the most extensive information possible. We owe a great debt of gratitude to the painstaking work of the past one hundred and fifty years which has so increased the depth and degree of our knowledge of other religions. The most comprehensive survey of this development has been given by the French Jesuit scholar, Pinard de la Boullaye, in the first volume of his *Étude comparée des religions* (1922). The student of religions is never well enough equipped linguistically. It is now desirable to know many languages and families of languages which were barely known by name fifty years ago. This is especially true with regard to the ancient Near East, Africa, Central Asia, and South America. Yet we agree with Webb when he says: 'I do not indeed suppose that it is necessary, in order to enter into the spirit of a religion, that one should be able to read its scriptures and its doctrines in their original languages. A man may be a very good Christian without Greek or Hebrew, and a very bad Christian with both'. It may not be necessary, but the chances of an adequate understanding are infinitely better where the interpreter is in a position to at least check on the translation of key terms, if he is not actually competent to read the foreign tongue. Yet this competence in and by itself does bot guarantee positive results in the study of religion.

Secondly, a successful venture in understanding a religion different from our own requires an adequate emotional condition. What is required is not indifference, as positivism in its heyday believed — 'Grey cold eyes do not know the value of things.' objected Nietzsche — but rather an engagement of feeling, interest, *metexis*, or participation. This is not an endorsement of the widespread notion that religion as such is an exclusively emotional affair (a notion held by Schleiermacher and Otto). As we shall see in greater detail, religion is a concern of the total person, engaging intellect, emotion, and will.

The realms of the human personality and human values are often invaded by a scientism which insists upon only one method of knowing and one type of knowledge. One of the weightiest arguments for those who want to preserve the human personality and its values against the imperatives of science is the demonstration that any form of reduction falls short of the aim of a student of religion which is to do justice to that religions's true nature.

A third form of equipment, the equipment of volition, is therefore required for anyone who wishes to deal adequately with the religion of his fellow man. The will must be directed and oriented toward a constructive purpose. Neither idle curiosity nor a passion for annihilating whatever differs from one's own position is an appropriate motive for this task. Ignorance, uncontrolled passion, and lack of direction are enemies of that state of mind which alone promises success in the venture of understanding. There will never be a lack of those differences (difference of temperament is one example) which make it difficult even for the student of broad concerns and deep sympathies to comprehend various kinds of religiosity, types of religious thought, or devotional practices which differ sharply from his own.

But there is still something else that is essential equipment for the study of religion, and that is experience. We use this term here in a wide sense, leaving the analysis of the nature of religious experience for the next chapter. We should like to define experience in the broadest sense, thus opposing all narrow concepts which separate and even isolate it as a province of life into which only the specialized professional can enter. In all likelihood there is no contact with any aspect of life which would not bear upon the problem of understanding another's religion. As the psychologists and sociologists of religion have told us, there are not only different reliigous temperaments (beginning with William James's 'healthy-minded' and 'sick-minded') but also different types of religious institutions. Whoever has had wide experience with human character possesses one more qualification for understanding an alien religion, for such a person has thereby contacted the minds of people in the variety of their acting, feeling, and ways of thinking. (J. Wach, 1961:11-13).

Besides these various presuppositions, a certain affinity for the subject matter is and remains the basic condition for all understanding:

Beyond the essential preconditions, an affinity for the object seems required, which, in general hermeneutic, is often expressed as spiritual relationship, congeniality, and, theological hermeneutic, as spiritual determination (*Geistesbestimmtheit*), (J. Wach, RGG[2], V:1573).

Is it to be derived from this principle of affinity that the scientist of religion, in the case that he wishes to understand another religion, must himself be religious? K. Goldammer gives an affirmative answer.

Only he can write about religion in a way that is true to the subject matter who himself has a religion and, therefore, knows approximately what the other religion is about (K. Goldammer, 1960:XXV).

C. H. Ratschow goes even further and emphasizes

that this significance of the religions as religion only opens itself to one who himself knows what religion can mean and, therefore, who can be impressed with the power and inner truthfulness of the religions he researches. It is...a conviction common to all scientists of religion that the 'understanding' of religion is based on the researcher's own possession religion (C. H. Ratschow, 1973a:392ff).

J. D. J. Waardenburg is of a different opinion.

Our task is to research religion where it appears, therein taking our point of departure in the assumption that researchers whether they are religious or not, can enter into communication by virtue of their being human (J. D. J. Waardenburg, 1973b:305).

4. The Limits

To what extent can we gain insight into what religion means to one who practices it? The greater the demands made on understanding, the more sober is its result. As has been seen, K. Goldammer requires of understanding 'the heuristic renunciation of oneself' as basic presupposition of all understanding (K. Goldammer, 1967a:27).

This renunciation

> places far greater demands on the spiritual capacity for work
> and on readiness to engage the material than do abstract opera-
> tions with collected facts. As van der Leeuw has rightly seen, it
> requires love. And this means not only the claim of love to hear
> or to fulfill, but, just as much, the loving readiness to renounce.
> It is a separate question as to what extent an identification of
> experience with the observed object is attained. Existential under-
> standing among men can, according to its essence, always only
> mean the attempt at the greatest possible approach to the other,
> that is, approximation. Such an approximation can become a
> fateful (*schicksalhaft*) continuing condition of the researcher
> (K. Goldammer, 1967a:27).

C. H. Ratschow sees an 'absolute limit' for all understanding.

> The God of a religion is the point of reference according to which
> all in this religion has to be interpreted, because all that happens
> in this religion as religion is derived from him. That is what is
> meant in the concept of God and its equivalents. But this God
> remains eternally closed off to one who does not worship him. . .
> With the question about God in the different religions, therefore,
> we stand at the limit of work in science of religion! ...This limit
> does not mean, however, that science of religion may renounce
> having to do with divinity as the last and actual goal of its work.
> The central work of interpretation in science of religion consists
> in leading up to this limit (C. H. Ratshow, 1973a:395).

Wholly apart from the fact that God often conceals himself from his
worshipper — and this experience in religious life is as shaking as it
is widely spread — the reality of religion places an absolute limit to
all endeavor in science of religion. Only the reference of religious
life to this reality, and not the reality of religion itself, can be the
object of understanding.

Joachim Wach seeks, in the question about the limits and possibilities of understanding, a realistic mean:

> Theoreticians of understanding have, in all that, to hold to a mid-
> dle line between a too-broad optimism and a too-broad scepti-
> cism in relation to the possibility and range of understanding. A

central question is where the limits of understanding are qualitatively and quantitatively to be drawn (J. Wach, RGG^2/V:1572).

As we also, in the following chapter, must occupy ourselves with understanding as method in science of religion, we have to make the clarification that we will deal with only one aspect of the whole problem — with that aspect which, in our opinion, today deserves the most attention. We mean by that, the fact that *the religious datum leads us toward understanding*. 'The phenomena themselves give our hermeneutic certain rules' (K. W. Bolle, 1967a:47). The religious datum itself invites and leads our understanding. If at present, in spite of all discussion about understanding, there is no real clarity about the way to insight or about the corresponding presuppositions in understanding, understanding in science of religion can perhaps gain further clarification from what is to be understood, for religious reality itself leads us to understanding.

5. UNDERSTANDING

Without comprehension, description leads to a hodge-podge of more or less accidentally similar data. Without understanding, comprehension leads to a setting-in-relation of religious data without interest in the meaning of the data. Both description without comprehension and comprehension without understanding, measured by the task of an integral science of religion, miss the whole and are therefore of little promise. Only understanding asks about the meaning of religious data — not only about the relations *in* which religious data stand but also about *the relations* which these data are *according to their own intention.*[5]

Accordingly, understanding is something like both the crown and the abyss of all efforts to perceive in science of religion. Nowhere does researching insight come so close to the whole and the essence of religious reality. And yet in no other way can science of religion so lose control of its subject matter and, instead of leading to understanding, issue into the presentation of one's own favorite concept and conviction. The possibility of such failure exists because understanding, more than all other attempts to know, seeks insight and not only the most possibly encompassing and careful registration and description, not only an acquaintance and consideration of the relations in which a religious witness stands. Understanding is a deepening oneself in the given witness through questioning, researching and perceiving; a respect for and consideration of the witness' inner life. It is a respect for and a consideration of its inner relation and no longer merely of its outer relations. Such insight and deepening is only possible when bound with a living-oneself-into (*sich Einleben*) the object. What guarantees that the one understanding, in the act of living himself into his object, does not, above all, bring his own life into the understanding? Who or what protects him who understands against the danger that, in his understanding, he only interprets himself, that his living-himself-into becomes finally a well-meaning but completely uncontrolled feeling-oneself-into (*Sich-Einfühlen*) the object?[6]

This question, decisive for all understanding, can only be answered if we succeed in seeing what really happens in the process of understanding. Thereby, it has to be our foremost interest to reflect on the relations which the religious datum itself is according to its own intention. No religious datum is isolated and closed in itself. In itself, every religious datum is relation and event, living relation.

One has referred to the fact that different etymologies of the word 'religion' yield little for the understanding of what religion is. Considering the uncertainty of these derivations, that may be the case. The proposed variations of the definition are fear (*Scheu*), exact observation (*genaues Beachten – religere*) and being bound (*Verbindung – religare*). It cannot be an accident that these proposed variations, as well as equivalents of western 'religion' in other cultures (way, vehicle, Dharma), refer to an eventful relation (*ereignishafte Beziehung*) or to a much related event (*beziehungsvolles Geschehen*). However one derives the meaning of the word (M. Kobbert, 1910), 'religion' means living relation.

But how is this living relation, encountered in every religious datum, to be transcribed? What sort of relation is it? We think it is possible to distinguish a twofold relation in every religious datum:

(1) the datum's being referred to the thought and experience of the person (persons) who expresses himself in it, and (2) the reference of this thought and experience to the reality of religion, that is, to the reality which is meant in all religious encounter, questioning, flight, search, turning-toward, love, confession and belief. Therefore, the inner relations of religious data, that is, the relations which correspond to the data's own intention, may be diagramed as follows.

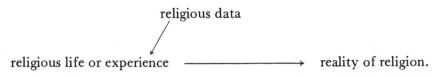

religious data

religious life or experience ⟶ reality of religion.

The religious datum refers to a definite religious thought and life or experience, and these refer to the whereto of the datum, the reality of religion. However, the religious datum does not simply refer to thought and experience which correspond to it. Because this experience expresses itself in the datum, becomes visible and audible in the datum, it lies in the sense of the subject matter itself to understand the relation of datum and experience as mutual, as affecting both ends of the relation. One refers to the other, and the other expresses itself in the one. Something similar is valid for the relation of religious experience to the reality of religion. The religious person so relates himself to the reality of religion that this reality is, at the same time, the whereto and the whence of all his religious thought and experience. It is not only the aim of his hope, his search and desire, but also the ground of his certainty, of his joy, of his encounter. The religious person does not experience his relation to the reality of religion only as a from-himself-to the reality, but just as much as a from-the-reality-into the center of his own life. The so modified sketch may, therefore, take the altered form:

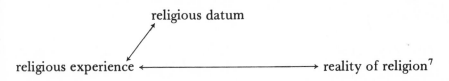

religious datum

religious experience ⟷ reality of religion[7]

In the corrected sketch, an illusion is suggested which springs more from wishful thinking than from the matter itself: for the understanding, the relation of religious life to the reality of religion is never as immediately present as the relation of religious data to religious life. We know actually nothing directly and immediately about how a religious person behaves toward the reality intended in all his religious thought and experience. Only as religious life speaks in the religious datum and, in the religious datum, confesses the reality, witnesses to it, refers to it or, indeed makes it present in the symbol — only as that happens is the relation to the reality of religion relevant for the science of religion. Prior to that and without it, the reality of religion remains the secret of the person who gives no sign or expression which might cause us to move toward understanding his religiosity. We assume that such silent, nowhere really expressed religiosity can occur, and it probably does occur far more often than the religiosity witnessed in religious data. Nevertheless, we cannot occupy ourselves with it at all. Only *that* relation of the religious person to the reality of religion can be an object of understanding *which is witnessed and made visible in a religious datum*. In the above diagram, therefore, in consideration of the possibilities of understanding, the horizontal relation should be set in parentheses in order to show that it can never be the immediate object of understanding science of religion. The relation is not dropped, but taken back into the religious datum. The datum not only gives expression to religious life but, at the same time, refers to the reality of religion.

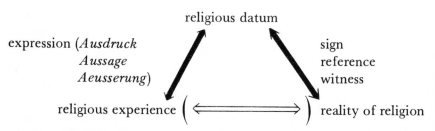

For understanding, every religious datum shows itself to be twofold, corresponding to its twofold relationship or, in other words, its twofold intention. It is both *expression* (*Ausdruck, Aussage, Aeusserung*) *and sign*, reference, witness. One moment may be dominant in one religious datum, the other moment in another religious datum. There are strongly expressive (*ausdrucksstarke, aussagekräftige*) religious data — for example, a personal story of conversion, a religious autobiography. On the other hand, we also know of data where sign and witness dominate — for example, a song of praise, which almost totally disregards personal experience and turns itself fully to what is intended by the praise. Therefore, one moment may almost completely obscure the other. Nevertheless, every religious datum necessarily includes both moments, if it is the expression of a real religious life and, just in that, always a *religious* datum, that is, a datum referred to the infinitely decisive thing, to the great *Hauptsache*, the reality of religion.

We defined understanding as giving attention to the meaning of religious data. But what does such attention, such consideration, seek? Should it register the expression or interpret the sign? Where does understanding find the meaning of religion in the intentions of the religious datum? Certainly not in just the expression of religious thought and experience. If that were the case, the meaning of religious life would, again, only be religious life in itself. It is basic to all religious life and experience that it not remain standing by itself, but that it go beyond itself. The meaning of a religious datum is also not simply its reference, the fact that it witnesses to the reality of religion. The reality of religion in itself cannot yet be understood as the meaning of religious reality. Only as the reality of religion comes into relation to the religious reality is the former the meaning of the latter. We *name meaning the presence of the reality of religion in religious experience, searching, presentiment, celebration, confession and memory*. The meaning of all religious data opens itself only in the relation of religious life to the reality of religion. (See diagram on following page.)

That means:

1. In itself, a religious datum has no meaning. It is *meaningful* only as *expression* and *sign*, in its being referred to religious life and the reality of religion.

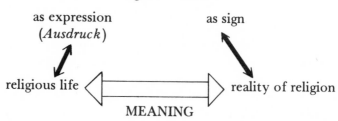

religious datum

as expression   as sign
(*Ausdruck*)

religious life ⟨⟹⟩ reality of religion

MEANING

2. All understanding remains vague interpretation (*Deutung*) as long as it holds only to the expression or only to the reference in the religious datum. Thereby we name *Deutung* the result of an understanding which *considers only one intention of the religious datum.* One-sided interpretation cannot attain the meaning of religion. Only if understanding does both — both registers the religious expression and thinks the sign, both attends to the expressive statement and lets itself be referred through the witness — can it attain an awareness of meaning (*Besinnung*) and insight into the relation of the religious experience to the reality of religion.

3. The meaning of religion opens itself exactly in the relation we previously, in our diagram, put in parentheses because no scientific perception ever finds immediate access to it. Therefore, the meaning which understanding, at best, attains is never an evident datum but the *result of reflection.*

4. Meaning is, indeed, always bound with intention — J. D. J. Waardenburg has emphasized this point.[8] Without consideration of the intention of the religous datum, one never finds the way to the meaning of religion. But the meaning of the religious datum never opens itself simply in one of its intentions, but in the place where *both of its most essential intentions, expression and witness, are together,* where consideration of the witness lets itself be referred to the reality of religion, where attention to the expression finds its way to the religious experience, where the reality of religion becomes visible in the religious life.

5. In distinction from one-sided interpretation, which lacks all control, *understanding carries a certain evidence in itself.* One-sided

interpretation may come very close to the religious experience or adequately interpret the reality of religion in the sign of the religious data, but it can also completely fail at both of these. The tragedy of one-sided interpretation does not lie actually in these frequent failures but in the condition that, in one-sided interpretation, understanding and misunderstanding cannot be distinguished. One-sided interpretation remains a sort of lottery in which the lots are never drawn. The special danger of a bare interpretation of the expression lies in uncontrolled living-oneself and feeling-oneself-into the expression. Because uncontrolled, all those moments which characterize, above all, one's own religious or profane experience may easily be brought into the religious experience expressed by the datum. The danger of bare interpretation of the sign, on the other hand, is, similarly, that of thinking-oneself-into the sign. Here the possibility is that one interprets one's own ideas, intentions and perspectives into the religious witness of the reality of religion. Even if, in the course of a bare interpretation of the sign, one speak emphatically of that which its object intends as the reality of religion, it remains true that one who interprets one-sidedly has essentially thought only the ground and the center of his own conviction. If one perceives this danger and wishes to avoid it, but does not abandon the course of a one-sided interpretation of the sign, one falls only all the more easily into the opposite danger of exoticism — the inclination toward what is most different and unusual without regard for what, in the religious experience expressed by the data, is perhaps all too familiar. One distances oneself from one's own conviction; however, one does not arrive at the thought expressed in the data but at what was never thought, at a most foreign and abstruse construction. An understanding does not fall into that danger which abandons the course of one-sided interpretation and finds its way to consideration of the data as expression and as sign. Precisely in the fact that the meaning (*Sinn*) of the religious datum only appears where both elementary intentions — expression and sign — are together, does reflection (*Besinnung*) gain a certain evidence in itself. The hearing of the expression and the reflection on the sign have each in the other their confirmation of their correction. If they are together — that is, if the researcher succeeds at attaining an insight which, uniting these elements, is insight into the relation of the religious life to the reality of religion — then it is, with a certain right, to be assumed that the uniting insight also corresponds to that uniting insight which was responsible for the religious datum itself. But, to be sure, only with a certain right, for the hearing of the expression and the reflection on the witness can both very well also lead the researcher astray in analagous fashion. They can be in harmonious error.

But are there other guarantees for the success of reflection (*Besinnung*) purely within the process of understanding? (It is presupposed that description and comprehension are of guiding (*wegleitender*) significance for all understanding.) We cannot overlook the fact that hardly a single religious datum stands for itself alone in historical reality. As a rule, every datum, whether visible action, confessional statement, cultic object, etc., is accompanied by other data which belong to it in the historical context. Comprehension can define this context and investigate it. It is important to recognize that the historical context is a very essential guideline for all understanding. Reflection on (*Besinnung auf*) a religious datum has its test in reflection on other data which obviously belong with the given datum. The meaning of an individual religious datum has its confirmation or its correction in the *meaning of the wider connection (Zusammenhang)*, the meaning of a definite time and of a definite community. If one-sided interpretation of an individual religious datum becomes a pure game of chance, so *Besinnung*, that is, attention to both essential intentions and consideration of the historical context, leads to a certain evidence of understanding. It is clear that in such *Besinnung* all possibility of misunderstanding is not excluded. But if science of religion only wants to deal with tasks that do not include the possibility of failure, then it should rather also immediately leave all description and comprehension alone. In science of religion, just as in any human undertaking, certain success is never guaranteed.

6. INTEGRAL SCIENCE OF RELIGION AS DESCRIPTION, COMPREHEN-
SION, AND UNDERSTANDING

We summarize: we can, as an expedience, distinguish three dimensions and three aspects of religion.

The three dimensions of religion are: *religious data, religious life* and the *reality of religion*. We named religious reality the religious datum in its relation to religious thought, life and experience. The immediate, i.e. visible and audible, object of science of religion is the dimension of the data alone. Religious life (thought, feeling, will, experience) expresses itself in the data, and, as sign, the data refer to the reality of religion. Religious life itself, however, is available to science of religion only in the expression of religious data, and it is understandable only in the course of interpretation. On the other hand, science of religion encounters the reality of religion only as reference and sign in the religious datum and only as meaning in religious life. That is, the best possible encounter of the science with the reality of religion is twice mediated (C. H. Ratschow, 1973a: 353): the datum speaks of the life, and the life makes present, seeks, has presentiment of, experiences, thinks, confesses and hopes for the reality of religion. In itself, religious life is not exposed to science of religion, and the reality of religion in itself cannot at all be an object of scientific perception. The reality of religion is twice removed from consideration. Science of religion knows itself referred to the reality of religion only in its reflection on the religious sign and on the actualization of the reality of religion in religious life. That is to say, science of religion knows itself referred to the reality of religion in the question about the meaning of religion.

As *aspects* of religion we have named the three moments in religious data which are visible for perception. First is the existence of the datum, that is, *the datum, unique in its being given as it is*. Science of religion tries to correspond to this aspect in description. Second is the *complex of relations in which the datum stands*; the involvement of the datum with social, economic and cultural reality and with other religious data. Science of religion occupies itself with this setting-in-relation in comprehension. The third aspect of the religious datum is its *inner relations* or its *elementary intentions*: as expression, the relation to religious life; as sign, the relation to the reality of religion. Science of religion tries to think these intentions in understanding.

Integral science of religion is distinguished from all other forms of work in science of religion through its attempt consciously to have as its task the whole of religion. That is, it attempts to do justice to religion in all its aspects and dimensions. In this form of science of religion, the question about the meaning of religion has special significance. Only in the meaning (*Sinn*) of religion are all dimensions of religion thought together and understood together, and only in Besinnung (reflection) does attention to the different aspects of religion lead to the one and the whole.

This last point — the unity and togetherness of description, comprehension and understanding in *Besinnung* — is now to be considered more closely. Consideration of the progress in perception in science of religion results in the judgment that, apart from the guiding idea of what a religious datum is, description is primary and basic. How should what is inaccurately observed be subsequently comprehended and understood? All scientific perception begins with the circumspect and cautious questioning about what is. It can only be of service to this perception when description does not flow immediately into comprehension and understanding, but when interest remains, at first, with doing a thorough job of pure description. Only so can perception do justice to the many-sided datum. It is the first task of science of religion to have a clear and accurate description of what is to be comprehended and understood. When this task is accomplished, the attempt at comprehension and understanding may begin.

It also seems to us that comprehension, as description, must precede understanding. Closer examination of comprehension reveals that it is itself a kind of attempt to perceive what is given in the most encompassing way possible. In comprehension, the given no longer speaks for itself, but is clarified, for example, in its historical, economic and wider cultural contexts, and just in these does the given show itself for what it is. The contribution of comprehension, therefore, is unconditionally necessary. We cannot imagine a responsible science of religion which would simply move from a description which ignores these contexts into understanding.

However, a merely descriptive and comprehensive science of religion is not yet integral science of religion. Understanding must follow description and comprehension, if the inner relations, the essential intentions and, with these, the meaning of the religious datum is not to be lost, and if the simple explanation is not to triumph. Mere description and comprehension finally leave religious reality meaninglessness. A 'meaningless' science of religion also lacks a meaning for the whole. Only with understanding does perception become integral science of religion, for only in understanding does it find the way to the essence and whole of religion.

But not only is understanding dependent on description and comprehension. These are also dependent on understanding. That is true because only understanding, even if in a very fragmentary way, leads to a pre-understanding (*Vor-verständnis*), a guiding idea, of what is to be attended to, described and comprehended as a religious datum. Therefore, neither understanding, comprehension nor description can function without the other two. Only in their *togetherness* and in their *sequence* can integral science of religion come into being.

How decisive the togetherness of these three is, is to be seen especially clearly in historical comparison. Only a superficial heuristic can draw parallels in the world of the religions on the basis of mere description. For such comparison, even something completely foreign in meaning becomes, by virtue of the presence of outer similarities, a correspondence. No less superficial are comparisons made on the basis of the relations in which the different data stand. For example, a comprehension which, simply on the basis of similar functions within different societies, stamps religious data as correspondence, can, under certain circumstances, give cause to the most significant misunderstandings. What in meaning are not at all correspondents are placed suddenly together. Religious data may be meaningfully compared only if science of religion first makes the effort to describe them, to comprehend them, and to understand them.

Comparisons made without this effort have never contributed to the progress of the science, although there have always been such methodologically one-sided comparisons precisely in comparative science of religion.[9]

7. NON-IDENTICAL CORRESPONDENCE AND CATEGORY

It is the question about comparison that leads into a fundamental problem of modern science of religion. Science of religion constantly makes statements about more than only a single religious datum. Often it even discusses at the same time religious data from very different times and cultures. It has always asked about its right to do this, and it has given the answer by referring to various sorts of identities, similarities, analogies, homologies or parallels.

Precisely considered, one can never speak of identity (*Gleichheit*) in religious data, for no datum is identical with another such as two numbers can be. Every religious datum is a part of human reality and, as such, not interchangeable with another, nor is it in its whole being repeatable.

On the other hand, it also does not do justice to the peculiarity of each religious datum, when science of religion only distinguishes between *the similar* and *the different*. It is clear that we do, ever again, meet with data which are similar, that is, which remind us of each other. One prayer reminds us of countless similar prayers, etc. The alternative to a science of religion based on such similarities (*allgemeine Religionswissenschaft, die das in allem Gemeinsame betont*) is not, however, a science of religion which, to balance things out, emphasizes the point of difference as well. Such balance is, to be sure, necessary as a provisional correction. But an integral, that is, an understanding science of religion cannot simply end with the determination of similarities and differences. Rather, it will, in its research of religious data, seek *that which does correspond*, that is, that which speaks at the same time not only for a single datum but for others, that which at the same time enlightens and clarifies the statements of other data. *We name correspondence that phenomenon in which religious data, without being identical, are able to clarify each other and to come near to each other in meaning.* An understanding of science of religion is only possible if the science — apart from all identification and beyond the mere determination of similarity and difference — recognizes correspondences, reflects on them, and allows itself to be led through this mutual interpretation and deepening.

But how may what is only similar be distinguished from what corresponds? First, what is similar is always separable from what is dissimilar. In dissimilarity, one datum does not remind one of another. Correspondence shows again and again how much of it does not exclude but includes contradiction, even open contradiction. Two religious confessions can make one another more understandable even where they contradict each other literally. Second, similarity is a once-made determination. Correspondence may not be simply thus determined. In the course of understanding, it is a *continual process*. It is the event in which religious data contribute to the better understanding of each side of the correspondence. Third, similarity, as once-made determination, is often seen already in descriptions. Correspondence is, rather, an event in the course of understanding. And, therefore, fourth, attention to the similar leads, at best, to a loose outer order, whereas attention to what corresponds leads to a mutually deepened interpretation of the data found in correspondence. We name similar what can result from a comparison of outer appearances. We name correspondence the possibility that the data of religious reality, in the course of understanding, are mutually enlightening.[10]

Through observation of similarities among different religious data, science of religion has developed what we would like to call 'categories'. These are closely connected with the mentioned possibility or impossibility of comparison. We name category those scientific general concepts which chiefly serve for the division and grouping of the infinitely wide world of religious data. On the basis of categories, science of religion speaks, for example, of cult, myth, mana, totem, mysticism, prophesy, power, God, holy — all used in a very encompassing sense.

But what is really grasped with these categories? Which realities are really designated with them?

On the basis of a category, one can make the impression of talking about identical things, but there are no identities in religious reality.

Categories can refer to similarities, and in this way they serve to arrange the material. They place what is similar into groups. And, as one always has seen the category as somehow based on similarities, one has been able to use it as the principle of order for the presentation of a general science of religion (*einer allgemeinen Religionswissenschaft*).

However, category can also be understood as correspondence, mutually contribute to their better understanding.[11] It is our opinion that only in this third sense of the word category can one responsibly use the word in an understanding of integral science of religion. This is true because every category which is based merely on similarities does not finally serve *Be-sinn-ung*, reflection on the whole of religion, but impedes it. An integral science of religion, a science of religion which does not simply divide and order but wishes to understand religious reality, will accept categories only insofar as they mean correspondence which actually help understanding. Because, however, with most currect categories it is not determined whether they generalize (*verallgemeinern*) what is similar or whether they have to do with genuine correspondence, it is to be recommended that integral science of religion use these current categories only seldom and, when they are used, with reserve. With this renunciation or this poverty of categories, religious reality and its understanding are not impoverished. Rather, the contrary is the case. Categories have not outlived their use, but no understanding can assume them uncritically. Understanding must first be clear about whether a real correspondence is expressed in them or not.

8. THE WAY TO THE WHOLE AS SUPPLEMENTATION OF THE INDIVIDUAL

Only an encompassing regard for all aspects and dimensions of religion can open an understanding of the whole of religion. But how can research which is never completed move nearer to such an encompassing view? That is possible only by way of the supplementation of the individual. In every phase of research it is valid to pursue especially the method which, at the moment, is neglected and to move those aspects of religious reality into the light which, at the present time, are easily forgotten. The movement toward the whole is always a conscious movement beyond a one-sidedness or perhaps even an heretical narrowness of contemporary science of religion. We name integral that research which succeeds in seeing not only familiar but also hardly regarded or all too easily forgotten aspects of religion.

But what does 'the way to the whole as supplementation of the individual' mean in the practice of an integral science of religion? Its meaning is at least twofold:

1. Supplementation of the individual can mean the supplementation of known data through additional new data which leads to a new, more encompassing understanding of religious reality. However, after having recognized, collected, described, comprehended and interpreted a vast plenitude of religious data, it is not to be expected that the whole view of religious reality can be essentially supplemented and understood in a more encompassing sense through the addition of a few previously unrecognized data. Rather, the supplementation of the already known world of religious data will, when measured by the enormous sum of what is known, probably at best contribute only a valuable addition.

2. The more clearly the supplementation of known religious data becomes a mere addition, all the more urgent becomes the *supplementation of individual perspectives and methods*. The vastness of the known data challenges too one-sided or general interpretation. To be sure, myriad data have already been described in certain of their aspects, but where has a description ever recognized all the aspects of a religious datum? Or where has a comprehension ever comprehended a religious datum in all its relations? Or, even more poignantly, where may it be asserted that a religious datum has been understood in its whole expression and in its whole witness? Integral science of religion happens today less through the discovery of new

data than through research which is more encompassing of the already given, because it goes beyond the one-sidedness of every individual perspective and method.

Supplementation of perspectives and methods means, first of all, *supplementation through consideration of the whole.* In large parts of scientific work, this consideration is pushed completely into the background by description and comprehension. Yet how can science of religion come perceptively nearer to the whole of religion, if it omits asking about the meaning of religious data?

4

The Verification

1. EXECUTION, APPLICATION AND VERIFICATION

Science of religion has been named integral when it makes its task the whole of religion. It has been seen that modern science of religion cannot be understood without this integral goal, and the conditions have been sought which promote or impede interest in the integrum of religion. In part, such conditions are those pertaining to the beginning point (*Ansatz*) and, therefore with the preconditions or premises. In part such conditions are those of the course of work, of already used or postulated methods.

But does what one perceives or envisages verify (*bewähren*) itself in the course of research? As long as this question is not asked of methodology, methodology remains a fruitless play, theory as an end in itself. Methodology always needs practical verification (*Bewährung*).

Verification has however, a much broader meaning than can be presented in the frame of this work. In what follows, verification is limited to the following meaning.

1. Verification of methodology in science of religion is not a mere listing of results, for every result is what it is only in relation to the intentions, premises and methods which produced it.

2. Verification does not attempt to execute or apply what is stated in the methodology, for what methodology states is neither a recipe nor a law nor a program which can be so applied or executed. We have understood methodology to be the *Besinnung* (reflection) of science of religion on what it itself does. The result of such reflection is, accordingly, not simply a rule, program or recipe, but, at best, *a clearer self-understanding, a clearer knowledge of the possibilities and limits of the science and, therefore, a clearer knowledge of its course of work.* It is hoped that this knowledge, in the execution of

practical research, will not only be simply emphasized but confirmed, deepened, corrected, and supplemented. If practical research does not lead ever again to renewed change and deepening of the self-understanding of the science, then it must be assumed that both theory and practice will fail their subject matter. Theory will mistake the possibilities and limits of its research, practice will mistake the religious reality it pretends to research. That is true because reality, including religious reality, is never a simple confirmation of what one had perceived or has a presentiment of. Rather, reality is the ever new and incalculable encounter of one's idea with the claim of the subject matter, of one's pre-understanding with the call to new understanding, of one's expectation with the resistance which adheres to everything concrete when the concrete is supposed to correspond easily to expectation. A theory which seeks in practice only the confirmation of itself contradicts itself most clearly at the point where it apparently finds full confirmation, for it would involuntarily show that, just as it confirms all its theses, it has mistaken reality.

3. Verification of methodology in science of religion consists not only in weighing and thinking the course perceived in methodological reflection, but also in moving onto this course. To assume to be able to cover the whole course of integral science of religion would only again demonstrate that one has mistaken this course. With regard to integral science of religion, verification can only be a stage of this course.

But which stage of the course is it? Is it the one which seeks a new, most encompassing description of religious data? Or does previous insufficiency in research press us toward a most possibly encompassing comprehension of the outer relations of religious data?

We shall, in a first section below, attempt to describe, comprehend and understand a particular religious datum in the most encompassing way possible.

We would like, at least once, to pursue all the basic possibilities of perception in science of religion. To be sure, it cannot be avoided, considering the brevity of our treatment, that our attempt presuppose some detailed knowledge of the subject matter.

After this attempted description, comprehension and understanding, we would like — true to the principle of supplementation — to occupy ourselves with a single stage on the way to an integral science of religion. We mean the question about the meaning of religious data. We have stated that this meaning is not to be found in one of the intentions, in the sign or the expression of the data, but in the relation of religious life to the reality of religion. We have named meaning (*Sinn*) the reality of religion in religious search, presentiment, celebration, confession, hope and memory. All question about the meaning of (*alle Be-sinn-ung auf*) religious data leads, therefore, finally to the question: what happens in the relation of religious life to the reality of religion?

In what follows, this question will be pursued in consideration of religious signs and expressions. This consideration is the beginning of all *Besinnung* (reflection) on the whole of religion.

It is clear that only a limited selection of signs and expressions can be our object here. But what selection can show us what occurs in the relation of religious life to the reality of religion? The selection largely determines the result. Therefore, we must responsibly answer the question about the 'how' of our selection.

1. We select data from different times and cultures. No single religious tradition is to refer us to the meaning of the data, for that would give free course to generalizations and unjustified schemes. What is perceived would too rapidly become generally binding and not what may be found in a non-identical correspondence. We encounter non-identical correspondence only in reflection on (*Besinnung auf*) data from different times and cultures. Naturally, no interpretation can completely avoid the fundamental mistake of all modern science of religion, which is the attempt to draw conclusions about the whole of religion from knowledge of an individual case of religion. That is both limitation of the base and generalization of the result. We shall attempt to avoid running directly into the arms of this mistake by, from the beginning, not limiting ourselves to a single religious tradition.

2. The religious data which will be considered are almost exclusively texts. That is not to say that texts are the only form of religious

data. However, in a book such as ours, a text is the form which speaks the most immediately for itself. Religious practices must first be thoroughly reported; pictorial signs require mediating representation.

3. We limit ourselves to texts which do not need long introductory commentaries, which the reader versed in science of religion can immediately localize and place in the larger context. This also makes easier our attempt to reflect on (*Besinnung*) the whole of religion, for we do not have to lose ourselves in the indispensable work of comprehension.

In the following attempt, again, it cannot be the aim of our work, in reflection on the sign and the expression, to find the way to a more encompassing equation for all that the reality of religion means in religious reality, or to find a common term for all forms of religious life as this life is expressed in the data. Rather, the result of our *Besinnung* will be, at best, the discovery of *non-identical correspondence* in which one sign or expression enlightens the other.

2. As an Example: Yasna 32:8

Before we turn to this section from the *Gathas*, we ask about the conditions under which the perception of science of religion in this case occurs.[1] What does the researcher find as he turns to the *Gathas*? He finds himself facing texts which confront him with a measure of uncertainty, ambiguity, questions and problems which are rather unusual.[2] Whoever sets about to interpret strophes of the *Gathas* is well advised to struggle through that attitude which can be named *programmatic scepticism*, because the most of what we, as a rule, know about other texts is in these texts uncertain and contested.

We know neither the time nor the place of origin of these songs. References (or speculations) in medieval literature place them in the 6th Century before Christ.[3] But certain considerations make an earlier date probable, among them: the language stands close to the *Rigveda*; the archaic picture of society visible in the *Gathas* suggests nothing of later Iranian empires; the younger Avesta has difficulty doing justice to the message of the *Gathas*, also when the Gathas refer to Zarathustra as authority. Among others, the following dates have been proposed: 714 B.C. (H. Lommel, 1930: 6), at least around 900 B.C. (Chr. Bartholomae, 1970:10), in the period from the 9th to the 8th Century B.C. (K. Rudolph, 1970:278; B. Schlerath, 1970:354), essentially not later than 1000 B.C. (H. H. Schaeder, 1970:117), perhaps between 1000 and 600 B.C. but certainly significantly earlier than the great archeminid kings (G. Widengren, 1965:61), between 1400 and 1000 B.C. (M. Boyce, 1975:190f). All of these are no more than assumptions.

The exact geographic place of origin of the *Gathas* is just as difficult to determine. Perhaps the culture that produced the *Gathas* had only just changed from a nomadic into a settled one and is therefore difficult to localize (M. Boyce, 1975:189). Linguistic arguments suggest northeastern Iran.[4]

What may be said about the singer and the poet of these songs? According to tradition, we hold Zarathustra to be the composer. The great authority he had in later tradition, the clearly autobiographical reminiscences heard in the *Gathas*, the indissoluble connection of the *Gathas* — texts with his name, and, in spite of all difficulties of interpretation, the still obvious originality of a passionate thinker and great singer visible in the *Gathas* (cf. J. Duchesne-Guillemin, 1951: 15-38) — all of these are reasons for our trust in the tradition.[5] But what reliable knowledge do we have of Zarathustra? We may draw on the later legend about Zarathustra only with great caution. Essentially, the *Gathas* must speak for themselves. They show us a Zarathustra who, in one person, was priest,[6] singer and prophet; who, with his message, met with the greatest resistance but also found influential followers; who once saw himself in the role of an outcast and a poor fugitive[7] and once in a desperate situation — the midst of winter — found no one who would shelter him and his animals.[8] This very sketchy picture is supplemented by names of relatives, followers and opponents.[9]

We think we know a little more about the *Sitz im Leben* of the *Gathas* than we know about the time and place of their origin. They later served and still serve as liturgical pieces. Probably Zarathustra sang these songs at sacrifice. Parallels to the ancient vedic priests (cf. H. Lommel, 1970a:199-207) and formal correspondencies to songs in the *Arthavaveda* and in the *Voluspa* suggest, indeed, the idea that Zarathustra, as priest and singer, stands in the oldest indogermanic tradition of priest and singer (H. H. Schaeder, 1940:399-408; H. Humbach, 1959/I:74). Yet the exact intention of these songs is unknown. Are they only hymns of sacrifice sung to *Ahura*?[10] Do they not also proclaim a new message to the people taking part in the sacrifice? And how do the clearly autobiographical reminiscences fit with the pure function of hymns of sacrifice and of almost magically effective words?

Furthermore, another decisive question for the understanding of the *Gathas* is still open. To what extent and for what reasons would not the later followers of Zarathustra understand the *Gathas* — in spite of or because of the fact they constantly referred to him as authority? Was the reason a great distance from Zarathustra in time? Was it the archaic dialect of these songs, a dialect which later disappeared? Was it the intentional ambiguity of these texts (H. Humbach, 1959/I:42ff.) — and ambiguity which, till today, resists clear understanding? Were these strophes, from the beginning, not at all intended to serve any sort of understanding? Did they originate in a mysteries celebration not accessible to the general public? (M. Moré, 1970:335; cf. also M. Boyce, 1975:9) Are they a priori magically effective formulas or ecstatic-drunken stammer? (cf. also H. S. Nyberg, 1970:53-96) Or does an essential difficulty lie in the fact that, in these songs, form and content hardly fit one another, that a revolutionary message clothes itself in the 'traditional forms of an already overdeveloped sacred poetry, a poetry which has lost its originality and become artificial' (H. H. Schaeder, 1940:405), that, therefore, the prophet in Zarathustra cannot be at one with the priest and singer in him? Does a difficulty lie in the fact that we do not have these songs in their original order but that they have been arranged according to their meter, and that even with the greatest effort (cf. J. Duchesne-Guillemin, 1948:163-289; 1953:31-37) the original order cannot be reconstructed? (M. Boyce, 1975:181n.1) Are the *Gathas* so difficult to understand because we simply know too little about the author and the time and place of their composition? Or were they so difficult to understand by his followers so soon after Zarathustra, because of their strikingly limited use of mythological tradition? Or does a chief difficulty lie in a peculiarity of the singer: his use, with odd regularity, of those so-called 'problem words' (H. Humbach, 1959/I:54f.; W. Hinz, 1961:60ff.) in which the *aməša spənta* were seen? (M. Boyce, 1975:196ff.) Or were later centuries simply unable to continue with Zarathustra's radical message? Could the later followers, who united their loyalty to Zarathustra with renewed worship of the *Daēvas*, understand the *Gathas* at all? Did they not have to transform and restyle these songs into harmless formulas of celebration. If we know in what measure and why the younger *Avesta* no longer understood the *Gathas* but, instead, misinterpreted them; if we knew why the songs still give us such unusual difficulties in interpretation; if we could find the exact reason for these difficulties, only then could we go about the business of overcoming these difficulties with the probablility of success.

After these remarks on the conditions under which scientific research of the *Gathas* must proceed, we now seek acquaintance with the statement and the reference of a single stroph on the basis of the language of the text. Description seeks to deal with the text — only this. In our example, we have a text and, therefore, also a statement. (Our guiding assumption is that this text wishes to state and to designate something, that it not only orders magically effective and otherwise nonsensical syllables and that, in it, not only ecstatic stuttering is expressed. This guiding assumption seems correct because nothing else explains why, for centuries, the *Gathas* were passed orally and in written form with such respect and precision. If the actual meaning of the songs was no longer understood, then these many generations must have had a sense of a powerful meaning lying in them.)

After we have attempted to analyse the language of the text, we will confront what we have perceived with texts on the same theme from later or earlier times; that is, we will attempt, to the greatest possible degree, to comprehend (*begreifen*) this statement in its tradition.

Finally, we will ask about the meaning of this statement — a meaning which, probably as in all parts of the *Gathas*, is always sensed but seldom understood. If the modern interpreter wants to come closer to this meaning, and this is his right and his duty, he will attempt also to understand difficult data. But he cannot do that in the belief that he has grasped the meaning of the *Gathas* or even of only one of its strophes. His understanding is, at best, a debatable attempt. (Also knowledge of the limited possibilities of an interpretation of the *Gathas* belongs to the conditions under which work on them proceeds.)

It is clear that we will see, in this procedure, that, in all required distinction between description, comprehension and understanding, none of these can be done without reference to the other two. We will see that in the interpretation of data that are difficult to understand these three basic possibilities of religious-scientific perception necessarily supplement one another.

The section of the *Gathas* which will occupy us is the reference to *Yima* in *Yasna* 32,8. Because of the sparse references to mythological tradition in the *Gathas*, this stroph is unusual and consequently noticeable. In *Yasna* 32,8, *Yima* is mentioned, and this is the only place in the *Gathas* where *Yima* is mentioned. (That in the *duš. sastiš Yasna* 45,1 *Yima* is to be seen as a mere supposition.[11])

In *Yasna* 32, *Yima* is placed in a series of blasphemers, and, whoever these blasphemers are[12] and whatever their offense may be[13], the singer of these strophes distances himself from them with vehemence.

Text-critically there are no problems with this stroph, unless one agrees with F. C. Andreas and J. Wackernagel that we must and can reconstruct an original text behind the traditional text (F. C. Andreas and J. Wackernagel, 1913:380f.; 1931:325f.). Whoever rejects that view holds (how could he do anything else) to the probably reliable traditional text that follows:

aēšą̄m aēnaŋhą̄m   vīvaŋhušō srāvī yimascīt̰ yə̄ mašyə̄ng cix-šnušō   ahmākə̄ng gāuš bagā xvārə mnō aēsą̄mcīt̰ ā ahmī   θwah-mī mazdā vīciθ ōi aipī

If we ask now what this text says, we have good reason to hold at first to what we can reliably perceive:

1. In 8a, *Yima*, as son or descendant of *Vīvahvant*, is mentioned 'because of this blasphemy', 'because of such a blasphemy' or 'as one of these blasphemers'.[15]

2. According to 8b, *Yima*[16] sought to 'make' the mortals (the men) 'content', to be there for them, 'to please' them or to 'ingratiate' himself to them.[17]

3. In 8c, *Mazda* is called on, and his 'division', 'separation', 'judgmental decision' or his 'judgment' is referred to.[18]

That is the relatively clear language of this text. In other places the text is less clear for us. The following give cause for special consideration and for different interpretations:

1. The verb in 8a. There is no doubt about the verbal form,[19] but its exact significance is seen in different ways. The mentioning of the judgment in 8c suggests that this concept originated in legal terminology.[20]

2. *gāuš* in 8b. In different ways it has been attempted to see here a transcription of *gəuš* or to postulate a possible variation of the genetive in this form.[21] In a formal sense, it is far more suggested that here, in spite of all difficulties, we have to do with a nominative (H. Humbach, 1959/II:35; W. Hinz, 1961:215).

3. The second participle in 8b: whether *xvārəmnō* may be understood as a causative, perhaps in reference to the Pahlavi translation and some perhaps analogous forms (Chr. Bartholomae, 1961:1866 and 1905.29; H. Reichelt, 1909:100), is very questionable (F. C. Andreas and J. Wackernagel, 1931:325f.; H. Lommel, 1938:242). To interpret this middle participle in the sense of an active is not particularly enlightening (H. Humbach, 1959/II:35). In my opinion, the uses of this middle participle can be considered in the sense of a passive.[22] H. Humbach even considers formerly hardly regarded significances of the basic verb.[23]

4. *bagā* in 8b can mean 'share', 'lot', 'favorable lot' and 'fortune' (Chr. Bartholomae, 1961:921). One should not, however, disregard the use of the same concept for 'God' found in the younger *Avesta*, in ancient Persia and the *Veda*.[24]

5. The syntactical construction in 8b. H. Humbach thinks it is

'especially artfully constructed' and sees *gāuš* in apposition to *yə̄*, and *ahmākə̄ng* as in apposition to *māsyə̄ng* (H. Humbach, 1959/I: 41). This interpretation is not clearly correct, but it probably reckons with a 'preference for the appositional style' (H. Humbach, 1959/I:40).

6. *ahmī* in 8c can be either a verb ('I am') or the Lok. sg. of the pronoun ('in this').

Above all for 8b, clear meanings together with dubious, questionable meanings result in quite different proposals for translation:

— 'To these blasphemers belongs, as known, also Yima, the son of Vivahant, who, to make men content, gave ours the pieces of meat to eat. By you, o Mazdah, I will be separated from them in the future' (Chr. Bartholomae, 1905:29).

— 'As one of these blasphemers was especially known Yomo the son of Vivohont, who sought to please the men belonging to us by eating pieces from the cow. At their punishment I am then, o wise one, among your elect' (F. C. Andreas and J. Wackernagel, 1913:380f.).

— 'Among these sinners, even Yima, son of Vivanghvant, is famed, who, seeking to gratify the vanity of our people, deprecated the Lord of Creation. In Thy final Judgment of such as these, O Mazda, I bow' (D. F. A. Bode and P. Nanavully, 1952:59).

— 'Because of such a blashpemy, even Yima, the son of Vivahvan, was brought to statement,

who wanted to assume the men to himself with gifts of fortune, he wanted to assume us, he, the bull, by making an oath,

just because of such blasphemy − − in this your judgmental decision, o knowing one (H. Humbach, 1959/I:97).

— 'Because of such blasphemy even Yima, son of Vivhvant, was interrogated,

Who − to ingratiate himself with the mortals − ours − the bull! − devoured as parts of sacrifice.

Just because of such blasphemy, I am present at your (judgment −) decision, omniscient one! (W. Hinz, 1961:175f.).

All these translations[25] show that, in relation to the misdeed of *Yima* (or what accompanied it) nothing sure can be found out on the basis of philological analysis. We have to learn more about Yima and his possible misdeed from another source in order to find the way to a reliable translation in 8b. In other words: comprehension must here necessarily supplement description. The ancient Iranian or possibly Indo-Iranian Yima-Tradition must give us information about what Yima did, about his possible misdeed. (Thereby we assume that Zarathustra, when he does refer to a mythological figure, presupposes that this figure is known. He consciously refers to a tradition obviously still familiar in his time.)

What do we know about the *Yima*-Saga in the ancient Iranian or perhaps even Indo-Iranian period?

1. *Yima*, son of *Vivhvant*, corresponds to the ancient Indian *Yama*, son of Vivasvant. Individual aspects of the *Yima/Yama*-Tradition go, therefore, with great probability, back into the Indo-Iranian time.

2. '*Yima*' (or '*Yama*') means 'twin'. (Cf. the French word '*jumeau*' (A. Christensen, 1934:37; G. Widengren, 1965:52) *Rigveda* 10,10 presupposes the idea of a marital union of *Yama* with his twin sister *Yami*, but it attempts, probably for moral reasons, to reject this idea (G. Widengren, 1965:4f.). *Bundahišn* 31,4 speaks of the union of *Yima* with his sister (G. Widengren, 1965:22).

3. The idea of Yima (Yama) as lord of full life probably also goes back into the Indo-Iranian time. *Venidād* 2 speaks of a time of *Yima* which yet knows no cold, no heat, no sickness and no death. Men and animals multiply, therefore, so powerfully that it is necessary to expand the earth (G. Widengren, 1965:14ff.). In the *Mahābhārata* there is an obvious parallel to this tradition.[26]

Immortality is attributed to both *Yima* and *Yama*,[27] — a gift, to be sure, which *Yima*, in other tradition, later lost (A. Christensen, 1934:21). Also in the *Mahābhārata*, *Yama*'s palace is described in the colors of paradise.[28] One can hardly say it differently: the full life is with *Yama*.

4. In India, the lord of the full life develops ever more clearly into the God of the dead. He rules over the kingdom of the dead, and he has men brought to this kingdom by his messengers (A. Christensen, 1934:10).

5. In Iran, *Yima* does not undergo this development into the God of the dead. He is original man and original king of a golden age:

Yima, the shining, herd-rich, the most famous of those born on earth, the one who looks at the sun: in his kingdom he liberated man and beast from death, water and plants from the dryness; nourishment was inexhaustible. Under the rule of brave *Yima* there was neither cold nor heat, neither age nor death, and also no envy was aroused by the counter-gods. Fathers and sons wandered along, both looking outwardly like fifteen-year-old youths...[29]

In the time of the great winter that plagued the world, *Yima* built on the promise of *Ahura Mazda*, a refuge below the earth for men, animals and the seeds of plants.[30]

6. Yima is not only rich in herds and a protector and patron of man and animal. He sacrifices both for *Anāhitā* and *Drvāspā* 100 horses, 1000 cattle and 10,000 sheep.[31] In other places too, he is one who makes sacrifice.[32]

7. A Pahlavi Text shows *Yima* and his sister occasionally united with a demonic wife or husband. From both unions different kinds of animals are born.[33] Accordingly, *Yima* is not only the father of men but also of different animals, and, through, *Yima*, men are related to these animals.[34]

8. But how and why did the time and the kingdom of *Yima* end? Unfortunately, the tradition shows little unanimity on this point. As *Kāūs*, *Yima* lost his immortality through his own mistake (A. Christensen, 1934:21). *Yima* was sawed in two by *Spityura*.[35] *Yima* was the victim of lies and of lying thought. Therefore his glory left him afterwards in the form of a bird.[36] According to Pahlavi texts, *Yima* was deceived by a demon and, through that, became overbearing and was brought away from service for *Ohrmazd*.[37] Or, seduced by a demon, he fell to the joys of the world (A. Christensen, 1934:19).

So much for the essential aspects of the *Yima*-Tradition. What consequences does all of this have for the reference to *Yima* in *Yasna* 32,8? May the difficult line 8b now be better interpreted? In my opinion, the following consequences must be considered:

1. *Yasna* 32,8b was probably hardly understandable already soon

after Zarathustra. If this text had made a clear statement about Yima's blasphemy, the later tradition on this point (we remember the great authority the *Gathas* had in the tradition) would certainly have been clearer and more unified. Somehow one had to explain the end of the happy age, and it was not unusual that this end was brought into connection with a deed or, rather, a misdeed of the original king.[38] But the fact that the tradition has so little to say about the blasphemy of *Yima* shows that a clear and authoritative statement was lacking.

2. Why was Zarathustra's reference to *Yima* hardly understood in later times? Problems with language alone could not have been the chief reason, for the Pahlavi translation shows[39] that later persons made several, probably quite correct, remarks on the wording. Probably the intention of the lines 32,8b caused difficulties.

3. Why does the intention cause difficulties? Certainly Zarathustra used tradition in his reference to *Yima*, the son of *Vivahvant*. However, he probably interpreted this tradition in a special way. Alone the fact that *Yima*, who was otherwise honored as protector of life, original king, original man, as one giving sacrifice, indeed as *ašavan*, as the just one,[40] appears in *Yasna* 32 as blasphemer — alone this fact shows that Zarathustra speaks of *Yima* from a very special point of view. This special point of view probably gave later readers difficulty.

4. *gāuš* in *Yasna* 32,8b is probably not in apposition to *yə̄*, as H. Humbach (1959/II:97) and W. Hinz (1961:175) assume, for *Yima* is never mentioned in the tradition as a bull. *Yima* stands in a manifold relation to animals in the ancient tradition: as protector and patron of man and animal, perhaps even as the father of bears and apes, but in any case as a known follower of the Gods and as a sacrificer of animals. But that he himself is a bull would be a completely new idea. With such an idea, Zarathustra would not only have interpreted the tradition anew, he would also have created new tradition.

5. I find no compulsion to suppose a verbal 'swear' in the root 'xvar' (H. Humbach, 1959/II:35) — and more than a supposition it is not, considering the lack of evidnec. Therefore, I see no reason to

understand *Yima*'s blasphemy as perjury. The significance 'eat, devour', which has found proofs in many ways, lies much closer. One need think only of the 'inexhaustible nourishment' which one ate in *Yima*'s kingdom,[42] of the effort of *Yima* to provide water and nourishment for his beings in refuge,[43] and of the powerful sacrifice of animals which *Yima* offered the Gods.[44]

6. The fact that, in *Yasna* 32,8, *Yima* is consciously mentioned as a blasphemer allows us to suppose that Zarathustra makes the hero an anti-hero, that he interprets a virtue of *Yima* from the point of view of blasphemy. The *Yima* who richly makes animal sacrifices and who, in other places, just for that reason is exemplary, is here, for the same reason, a pronounced blasphemer. In any case, this view of *Yima* and his doings would correspond to one of Zarathustra's most inner interests, namely to his protective attitude toward animals and his opposition to great traditional sacrifices. This may also explain why the later followers of the prophet could not assume this view of *Yima* and his blasphemy. According to all appearances, for them an extensive animal sacrifice was again a great religious virtue.

But how does this supposition relate to the philological situation of the text? In my opinion, it makes for the least amount of difficulty when compared with the interpretations quoted above (see pp. 113–114). We do not need to force *gauš* to be a genetive. For *xvārəmnō* we do not wish to consider new basic significances for which there is no evidence. But *xvārəmnō* can very well be understood as a passive. For *bagā*, the significance 'share', 'lot', 'sacrificial share'[45] lies much closer than 'God', which is nowhere found in the *Gatha*. According to the form, Nom. pl. or Instr. sg., in the sense of an *'Instr. des Grundes'* (cf. H. Reichelt, 1909: § 451:236f.), could be the case. It is probably not accidental that bot *mašyāng* and *ahmāk-āng* are mentioned here. The Pahlavi translation understands the latter as belonging to our kind, that is, the animals (see note 39 above; A. Christensen, 1934:11). In *Yima*, men and animals are often united in a group. *Yima* protects both. Perhaps also because of that *Pahlavi Rivāyat* mentions *Yima*, otherwise father of men, as father of the animals.[46] The *Yima*-tradition yet knows something of an almost related nearness of man and animal. yə̄ in 8b unites an incomplete relative sentence with line 8a and can take here the function of an article or of a demonstrative pronoun (cf. H. Reichelt, 1909: § 749f, 370f.). Therewith we have the following translation of *Yasna* 32,8:

Because of such a wicked deed even *Yima*, the son of *Vivahnt*, was interrogated.

This one wanted to make content the men and those belonging to us (the animals). (Yet) the beast was, as sacrificial shares (or: because of the sacrificial share), devoured.

In your judgment on such a wicked deed, o *Mazdah*, I am thereby.

Finally, we would like to attempt to come a step closer to the understanding of this strophe within the whole of the *Gathas* (it is not to be understood simply in itself). Thereby, we ask about the whence of this statement, about the life that expresses itself in this statement (human life expresses itself in every religious datum), and about the whereto of this verse, about its intention, its aim, about what the verse intends to refer its hearer (every religious datum is a sign for and a reference to a reality which religious life knows as its essential interest.[47]).

The great theme of *Yasna* 32 are the *Daevas* (strophes 1-5) and their wicked followers of all kinds (6-16). In the whole song we hear, therefore, a negative, sometimes mocking (1, 3, 5), sometimes threatening (6, 7) tone. There is no doubt that, in this song, Zarathustra stands over-against his demonic and human enemies.

But why does Zarathustra see himself over-against these enemies? As far as we can understand it (see notes above 12 and 13), the opposition is not an abstract, metaphysical dualism given poetic form in the song. The opposition is concrete. The opponents require the ox as sacrifice (12), they torture it to death in order to win *Haoma* (14).[48] The *Daevas* stand most closely connected with this misdeed: they require what their followers must do (4). They require the sacrifice which their followers make to them. We do not know exactly how these sacrifices were made. However, that Zarathustra speaks of them only with disgust, that he sees in these sacrifices 'murderous drunkenness' and 'coarseness',[49] a 'torture unto death'[50] — that shows how these sacrifices affected him.[51]

With the reference to *Yima*, Zarathustra takes a position on the question about the beginning of these misdeeds. If our interpretation of Y 32:8b is correct, *Yima* appears, on the one hand, as the one who wants to make all living beings content, that is, as the known patron and protector of life. On the other hand, however, the sacrifice of the ox is mentioned in the same line. Is not *Yima* known as a great sacrificer in service to the *Deavas*? As was he not, as the original king, one of the first, if not the first, to have committed this unholy misdeed[52] — holy to the *drǝgvan* and a wicked deed to the *ašavan*? And does not this blasphemy lie doubly heavy on Yima — he who was called to be the keeper and patron of life?[53]

The opposition which characterizes *Yasna* 32 is, certainly, first and foremost Zarathustra's experience: he sees himself placed over-against the service to *Daēva* and challenged by that service. But he looks beyond the actual events in a twofold way. The reference to *Yima* refers, at the same time, back to the beginning of the wrong and, with similar thoughts in strophes 7 and 15, forward to the judgment which those will not escape who adhere to *Daēva*-service, who cultivate the practice of that service and therefore prefer lie to truth.[54] Not even *Yima* can avoid this judgment. And the singer wishes to be there when *Mazdāh* judges the original doer of the wicked deed.

Nothing of the actual opposition is lost through this double broadening — forwards to judgment, backwards to the beginning. The opposition does not become more abstract and more harmless. It becomes only more compelling, more decisive for those who hear Zarathustra's song. The singer places each hearer in the decision between *Mazdah* and *Daēvas*, between the truth and the misdeed. The decision will and must be made — at the latest, in the judgment. Here we have what seems to be one of Zarathustra's most pressing interests: to place men in the opposition which he himself experienced, and in this opposition to show what it means to serve the truth or to choose the lie.

That Zarathustra, with this interest, was already not everywhere understood by his contemporaries, that they, rather, took that to be truth which he took to be lie,[55] and that they considered the sacrifice for the *Daēvas*, that which he took to be a lie, to be a holy duty — all that can hardly cause us to wonder. The decision for the truth in Zarathustra's sense was not self-evident. Just as little do we have reason to wonder at the fact that the later followers of Zarathustra oddly united their greatest respect for him and his *Gathas* with sacrifice and service to the Gods that Zarathustra had vehemently opposed. These later followers hardly had any sense for the mentioned decision; but, therefore, they had all the more a sense for the compromise. Perhaps never has a person been so much honored and so much betrayed at the same time than the singer of the *Gathas*.

After we have now attempted descriptively, comprehensively and understandingly to take up what a short text would like to say, in the following we shall ask about the whence and the whereto, and, therewith, about the meaning of religious texts. The principle of supplementation — as indicated (see above, pp. 102—104) — requires that we now give special attention to the attempt of understanding.

3. RADICAL REALITY

The *bhagavadgītā*, at the beginning of the 7th Chapter, turns emphatically to the reality which is intended in religious reality.[56] Previously, the way to God was the center of interest (the *tapasvin*, the *jñānin*, the *karmin*, the *yogin* and, among these, the *bhakta* — all represent the most elementary possibilities[57]). From the 7th Chapter on, the theme is the 'whereto', 'whence' and 'whereby' of all these ways.

Krishna reveals himself to Arjuna — at first in the form of instruction, then, in Chapter 11, in a frightfully immediate vision. This self-revelation, even as teaching, exceeds in significance and value everything knowable which might be placed beside it, just as ground exceeds what is grounded and meaning exceeds all reflection (*Besinnung*) on it:

Śrī Bhagavān said:
Attaching your mind to me, o son of Pṛthā,
  practicing meditation, orientated to me,
Hear now how (so) you will free of doubt and completely
  perceive me!
  This insight with perception I will proclaim to you
  without remainder.

If you know this, there remains nothing here more
    to perceive. (7:1-2)

'Practicing meditation', naturally does not approach the depth of
significance of the *'yogaṁ yuñjan'*. Perhaps 'realization realizing'
(*Verwirklichung verwirklichend*) more closely corresponds to the
original, and with this translation the doing and the done would be
perceived in the common root and essence. It would also be indicated that the self is bound to the highest reality through Yoga,
even that the self enters into the highest reality. Perhaps it is best,
with *Radhakrishnan* (1949:212) and *Bhaktivedanta*[58], to leave
'Yoga' untranslated.

'This insight with perception' (*jñānaṁ savi jñānam*) is, in this context, an indication of what follows: God wishes to lead to insight
(*jñāna*) through what he teaches about himself, and to perception
(*vijñāna*), experienced knowledge, through the experience of God in
Chapter 11.[59]

In these verses, where God opens his teaching about himself,
the repeated emphasis on the wholeness of the perception to follow
is unmistakable. Perception is now proclaimed which is complete,
which leaves nothing to be perceived. What is to be concluded from
that? It is not that, in the following, everything is said that can ever
be said. Rather, the whole is said. About the whole there remains
afterwards nothing more to say. Not the sum of the real but the
whole of reality is opened without remainder in the self-mediation of
God.

Among thousands of men
    perhaps only one attempts to gain perfection.
Among those who try and (those who) gain perfection,
    perhaps only one perceives me as I really am. (7:3)

As the *lectio difficilior*, *'yatatām api siddhānāṁ'* is probably
to be preferred to the other wording, *'yatatām ca sahasrānām'*
(Radhakrishnan, 1949:213). As Hill has rightly remarked, this leads
immediately to two questions: (1) Can one who has attained perfection at the same time make an attempt? (2) Does not perfection include perception of God? (Douglas and Hill, 1928:165 n.3). In view
of the verse quoted, the second question must be answered in the

negative. Perfection is not identical with actual knowledge of God. The concept of perfection (*siddhi*) is, therefore, to be distinguished from the highest stage of perception of God. That may be done, as in Zaehner, by using the word 'self-perfection' for perfection (R. C. Zaehner, 1969:244). The first question is to be left unanswered. The possible negative answer is given by means of the parentheses in our translation of 7:3.

Also in this third verse, the following self-communication of God is prepared as, again, the goal — the perception of God according to truth (*tattvatah*) — and the value of such knowledge are emphasized. Whoever perceives God in his actuality is eminent even among the many who are eminent. That is reason enough not to hear the following as just any sort of communication.

Earth, water, fire, air
ether, mind and soul,
individuation — this is my
eightfold divided (material) nature.
That is the lesser (nature). Beside that
perceive, however, also my other, higher nature,
which has become life, o strong armed one,
through which the world is preserved. (7:4-5)

One could say that the categories of the *Sāmkhya* mentioned in the fourth verse are the stages of the unfolding of original reality (*Urwirklichkeit*) into the breadth of the real (*des Wirklichen*). One may certainly not, on the basis of that possibility, read out of this simple sketch the whole classical *Sāmkhya* philosophy. Such rudimentary beginnings of the developed system predate the system by several centuries,[60] and the Bhagavadgita never has to do with the truth or, indeed, with the purity of this or that philosophy. (Whoever thinks differently on this second point has to turn to theories that the Bhagavadgītā was later reworked.[61]) The interest of the Gītā is, rather, in the incalculable and unabbreviated wholeness of the reality, which no single philosophical direction can attain and which, at best, is understood in the apparently so contradictory togetherness of all philosophical directions. (And it may be said that what later appear as opposites were, in their *statu nascendi*, as philosophical directions rather easily brought together. Cf. H. V. Glasenapp, 1958: 202f.; E. Lamotte, 1929:29ff). In the Gita, the unity of what is not unity and the togetherness of opposites is probably not misfortune but method.

The relation of God to all areas of the real becomes clear in verses 4 and 5, even if the individual areas are often to be separated only with difficulty. (One thinks of the difficulty in determining how the *jīva-bhūtā* is to be stated![62]) It is also not to be mistaken that God is identical with none of these stages or areas, and that these stages or areas belong, in different ways, to his being.

> These (two natures?) are mother's womb
> for all beings, this is certain.
> I am for the whole world
> the origin as also the destruction.
> There is nothing higher (or deeper) than I,
> o Dhanamjaya.
> All this is strung on me
> like clustered pearls on a thread. (7:6-7)

It is left open whether '*etad*' in verse 6 refers to both or only to the last-named higher nature.[63] '*Parataram*' in verse 7 is probably too abbreviated in the translation 'highest'. It refers to what is more original (*das Ursprünglichere*) and what is later (*das Spätere*), to what is more surpassing (*das Ueberragendere*) and more fundamental (*das Grundlegendere*).

The teaching of God about himself leads here to a double image or comparison (*yoni* and *mani-ganā*)[64], but not to a system which is easily designated with some sort of formula (pantheism or panentheism). How does God relate to the plenitude of the real? — as the mother's womb to the born child, as origin (*Ursprung*) and destruction (*Untergang*) to what arises and passes away (*zum Entstehenden und Vergehenden*), as the thread to the clustered pearls. It is perhaps permissible to speak in another, very similar image of radical reality (*radikaler Wirklichkeit*). '*Radix*' is '*yoni*' in the area of the plant world. Also in this image the relation of God to beings is not bound in a system but simply indicated in a comparison: the reality of God is reality as origin, goal and middle of everything real, as the reality

without which nothing real would be at all, as the reality which
makes the real what it is:

> I am the taste in water, o son of Kunti,
>   I am the light in the moon and in the sun,
> praṇavaḥ (= the syllable OM) in all the Vedas,
>   the sound in the ether, the man-ness in men.
> I am the pure fragrance in the earth
>   and the heat in the fire,
> Life in all things living,
>   the asceticism in the ascetic one.
> Perceive me as the eternal seed
>   of all that lives, o son of Prtha,
> I am the insight of one who has insight,
>   the glory of the glorious am I.
> The power of the powerful am I,
>   free from desire and passion,
> The drive in all that lives, not opposed to the right,
>   I am that, o Prince of Bharatas. (7, 8-11)

Often '*bījam sanātanam*' is translated as 'primeval seed'[65] with reference to the fact that '*sanātana*' does not refer to what is altogether
without time (Zachner, 1969:194). Nevertheless, we remain with the
concept of the 'eternal seed'. 'Primeval' could refer to a first beginning, while here there can be no doubt that the non-temporal original
reality is intended which, ever again and anew, periodically releases
the plenitude of the real out of itself.[66] Therefore, '*sanātana*' is here
more than something originally real in its beginning. Rather, it refers
to what remains as originally real, to the eternally new ground of all
that is real.

But with this new image of the eternal seed, the relation of original reality to the real is, again, not brought into a system. Rather,
again, only an image and not a refined theory refers the real to reality. Here it is an image from the plant world, and one similar to the
image of the *radix* which we have proposed.

As consideration of the concept '*sanātana*' can show, radical reality here does not mean simply what originally gives the ground, but
means the remaining originally real — that which not simply in the

distant past let the real be. Radical reality is what constantly consti-
tutes everything real as such — the waterness[67] of water, the light in
moon and sun, the man-being of man, the heat in the fire, the insight of one who has insight, etc. God is *the reality in the real* which
makes all that is real what it is.

One who allows himself to be led on the course of understanding
through the intention of the datum itself is shown, by the religious
sign in the discussed text, that the sign not only has to do with
a real which is comparable with others, nor only with a distant original reality or super-reality. It refers to incomparable reality, to the
reality in all that is real or, to remain with our image, to radical reality.

We now select a second sign from a completely different time and
culture. It refers us to its reality, and we will follow its own intention
in our interpretation as we let ourselves be directed by it.

Gerhard Tersteegen, in his prayer to the uniquely real God, gives
a sign of incomparable reality. It is a 'peculiar quality of Tersteegen's
to reflect the greatest clarity and make explanatory commentary
unnecessary' (W. Nigg, 1959:357). That is one reason for the choice
of the following sign.

The text we shall quote has numerous parallels in the whole of
Tersteegen's published works. The incomparable reality of God is
contrasted ever again with the disappearing unreality of man.[68]
A search for other correspondences to the selected text will lead the
researcher, as he is guided by aspects in Tersteegen's witness, doubt-
lessly to mysticism.

O God, you necessary and infinite being (*Wesen*), you highest
being, yes, you only being and more than being! Only you can
emphatically say, I am! And this 'I am!' is so unlimited and so
undoubtedly true that no oath can be found which more casts
all doubt away than when this word is spoken by you: I am; I
live! — Yes, Amen! You are! My spirit bows, and what is inmost
in me confesses that you are. How happy (*glückselig*) do I know
myself because you are and because you cannot not be! How
happy I am that I know God is, that I can confess that God is!
All creatures, hear: God is! I concede that you are, God. I am so

pleased that you are. O, how beautiful and good it is that you are, and that you are who you are! I would rather not be and would rather that nothing be, than have you not be.

And yet what am I? And what is everything? Am I well (*wohl*) and is everything well? What is this I and what is this everything? Are we, only because you are and because you will that we should be — we poor beings which in comparison with you and before your being must be called a form, a shadow and not a being at all! My being and the being of all things disappears, as it were, before your being. My being is like a small candle in the bright light of the sun, which, for that great light, is so overcome that it is hardly there at all. Ah, that you might also, therefore, overcome (*überwinden*) me, annihilate (*vernichten*) me; that you, therefore, might overpower and, as it were, extinguish me: your face — my face; your highness — my lowliness; your superb light — yes, my darkness; your pure effectiveness (*Wirken*) — my broken effectiveness; your all — my nothing!

I am only a form, a poor shadow, if you are not in me and if I am (not) in you, if you are not the ground and essence of my essence. All that I know and all that I see is only a self-made dead nothing or yet only an uncertain image, a not enjoyable transitory form and shadow, where you do not enlighten me and where you do not give yourself to my sight, o you only essential truth! All I seek and all I love, all I possess is only shadow and appearance and not being, where I do not seek you and love you and possess you, o you only essential good, joy, you luxury and glory of my soul! All that I do, yes, all movements and effects of my inner and outer powers are only appearance and not being, where you are not their fundamental beginning and mover, o you original, only essential, good and infinitely fruitful life!...

O, that I might no longer be and in myself have neither life nor understanding, nor will, nor thoughts, nor movements, and that you, my God, my Jesus, might be and effect all in me! Let that, o Lord, eternally in me be silent and still which you yourself do not speak into me and effect! Condemn and annihilate everything in me that is not you and not yours! Completely occupy the place where I now am and work in me and through me what pleases you! Let the I no longer be, and let you be only, all in all, and lead me so wholly out of myself and out of all that is mine into you, o my God, my origin and end! Then I shall no longer be nothing and mere appearance, but in being (*im Wesen*) and redeemed from all evil to the eternal glory of your name.[69]

In the language of the mystic and the pietist, Tersteegen thanks his God for his being. This reality of God is for him not only uncontested reality, it is incomparable reality, other than and infinitely superior to all supposedly real outside it. God is 'necessary and infinite being, highest being, yes, only being.' Only he can 'emphatically say: I am!' This reality of God is more certain than the reality of every other being, so certain that no oath can ever effect the certainty of the confession that God is. Before this reality, all creatures 'disappear completely, and all that is in time is, because of its smallness, no longer seen' (G. Tersteegen, 1798/1799[2], I:1,129) or shows itself to be 'poor being', 'shadow and not a being', as a candle in sunlight, as 'nothing' (*Unding*), 'uncertain image', 'transitory form', as nothing (*Nichts*) before God's all, as appearance before his being. This non-being (*Nichtwesen*) is dependent on true being, for what is real, is real, only because and while God is real. What is real is real being (*Sein*) only through participation in God's reality. The second part of the prayer witnesses to the dependence of everything real on this radical reality of God, to the 'we are only because you are.'

In the last part, Tersteegen prays for the realization or for the being-made-being of himself, for the annihilation of all which is not being in him, that is, which does not correspond to the 'only being', and for a complete absorption in the reality of God.

We have said that the whereto of Tersteegen's prayer is *radical reality*. '*Radix*' means root, source, origin, ground and fastness (*Festigkeit*). Radical reality may not be compared with the breadth of the real. He who does compare these two, however, sees all that is real fade into illusion before radical reality. This reality is not only incomparable but also necessary reality — necessary for the breadth of the real. All that is real has only in radical reality its own ground, fastness, existence. Without radical reality, everything real is a paltry papered nothing.

The following witness leads into a completely different world and a completely different world of language. And yet it seems to us that our attempted reflection (*Besinnung*) on the whole of religion finds here a nonidentical correspondence. With poetic power, Chuang Tzŭ is able to be a messenger of the Tao, just as Lao Tzŭ was his life and thought. But, as R. Wilhelm says,

Dschuang Dsi is not a master by whose words one may swear. He is the origin of a movement, and only he has understood him who breaks with his wording and is able to produce the movement which goes forth from his words in himself (1976:12).

He himself describes his method masterfully:

Of my sentences nine in ten are metaphorical: of my illustrations seven in ten are from valued writers. The rest of my words are like the water that daily fills the cup, tempered and harmonised by the Heavenly element in our nature[2].

The nine sentences in ten which are metaphorical are borrowed from extraneous things to assist (the comprehension of) my argument. (When it is said, for instance), 'A father does not act the part of matchmaker for his own son,' (the meaning is that) 'it is better for another man to praise the son than for his father to do so.' The use of such metaphorical language is not my fault, but the fault of men (who would not otherwise readily understand me).

Men assent to views which agree with their own, and oppose those which do not so agree. Those which agree with their own they hold to be right, and those which do not so agree they hold to be wrong. (Chuang Tzŭ, 1962:142).

The language of images puts each on the way which corresponds to him, and it does not make unnecessary one's finding one's own way forwards. Therewith, Tschuang-tse does not at all wish to claim for his way what he has simply borrowed from another and concentrated into image.

The seven out of ten illustrations taken from valued writers are designed to put an end to disputations. Those writers are

the men of hoary eld, my predecessors in time. (Chuang Tzŭ, 1962:142).
Not alone in the following text will we refer particularly to the un-apparent uniqueness, the motioned rest (*bewgte Ruhe*), the concrete infinity and, in all these, the unity and wholeness of Tao which en-compasses the opposites.[70]

Tung-kwo 3ze asked Kwang-3ze, saying, 'Where is what you call the Taô to be found?' Kwang-3ze replied, 'Everywhere.' The other said, 'Specify an instance of it. That will be more satisfactory.' 'It is here in this ant.' 'Give a lower instance.' 'It is in this panic grass.' 'Give me a still lower instance.' 'It is in this earthenware tile.' 'Surely that is the lowest instance?' 'It is in that excrement.' To this Tung-kwo 3ze gave no reply.

Kwang-3ze said, 'Your questions, my master, do not touch the fundamental point (of the Tâo). They remind me of the questions addressed by the superintendents of the market to the inspector about examining the value of a pig by treading on it, and testing its weight as the foot descends lower and lower on the body. You should not specify any particular thing. There is not a single thing without (the Tâo). So it is with the Perfect Tâo. And if we call it the Great (Tâo), it is just the same. There are the three terms, — 'Complete,' 'All-embracing,' 'the Whole.' These names are differ-ent, but the reality (sought in them) is the same; referring to the One thing.

'Suppose we were to try to roam about in the palace of No-where; — when met there, we might discuss (about the subject) without ever coming to an end. Or suppose we were to be together in (the region of) Non-action; — should we say that (the Tâo was) Simplicity and Stillness? or Indifference and Purity? or Harmony and Ease? My will would be aimless. If it went nowhere, I should not know where it had got to; if it went and came again, I should not know where it had stopped; if it went on going and coming, I should not know when the process would end. In vague uncertain-ty should I be in the vastest waste. Though I entered it with the greatest knowledge, I should not know how inexhaustible it was. That which makes things what they are has not the limit which belongs to things, and when we speak of things being limited, we mean that they are so in themselves. (The Tâo) is the limit of the unlimited, and the boundlessness of the unbounded.

'We speak of fulness and emptiness, of withering and decay. It produces fulness and emptiness, but is neither fulness nor emptiness; it produces withering and decay, but is neither withering nor decay. It produces the root and branches, but is neither root nor branch; it produces accumulation and dispersion, but is itself neither accumulated nor dispersed.'[71]

Chuang Tzŭ invites Tung-kwo Tze to a conversation 'without ever coming to an end.' What does that mean? Certainly it means a conversation which is not exhausted in consideration of the finite, which leads beyond the individual and limited and its changes — fullness and emptiness, renewal and ruin, elevation and lowering causes and effects, collection and scattering. The conversation is about 'the Complete,' 'All-embracing' 'the Whole' 'the One thing,' the boundless in all limitation, Tao.

But how can Tao be the object of any sort of conversation? Not in such fashion that the whole is here and there expressed. No here or there is refused to Tao. One must say of Tao that 'there is not a single thing without (the Tâo).' But, just because of that, one must also say, 'You should not specify any particular thing'. One can speak of Tao only in all the signs which refer from the individual to the whole and therewith, from the things to 'that which makes things what they are.' The names 'are different, but the reality (sought in them) is the same; referring to the One thing.'

The conversation 'without ever coming to an end' means, therefore at first, a journey toward the 'palace of No-where' for one who holds to the individual and is orientated to thingness. Is the reflection on Tao, therefore, a losing oneself in the unreal? If being and reality are categories of thingness, Tao is shown to be non-being and non-reality. If however, 'reality' — as 'wholeness, completeness, allness,' or as 'way,' 'meaning,' 'mother,' ground, 'abyss,' — leads from the individual to the whole as signs and names then Tao is reality, and, indeed, reality itself, the reality through which everything real is what it is.

Also this invitation to the conversation 'without ever coming to an end' is shown to be a sign of radical reality, a finger pointing from the individual to the whole, from the real to reality, that is, as thought of the real, not simply as individual, but in its relation to the encompassing and whole, to reality.

Perhaps we find just in the reflection on this conversation the way to a designating essential quality (*eigenart*) of religious data. In what way is the religious datum distinguished in its own intention from a profane datum? It is not through its relation to radical reality, but through its conscious reference to this radical reality. *We name a religious datum something real which in its character as sign makes us aware of the relation in which everything real stands. The religious datum is something real in explicit, expressed relation to reality.* It is something real that makes us aware of, indicates and makes present, indeed, not any sort of reality, such as would be similar to the individual and thing-like, but reality itself, the whole in all individuals, the ground in the dependent, the boundless in the limited, the middle in what is scattered, the reality in the real.

We always find religious data where persons are aware of the real as the real, where the real makes itself known as such, where the relation is expressed in which everything real stands and which makes everything real what it is.

Perhaps we may go a step farther. Perhaps we may say that profanity, as far as it may be called that, would be simply having to do with the real without experiencing the real as somehow real. It would be a using, handling, working of the real apart from its reality. Religion is, in all occupation with the individual, relation to the whole. It is the relation to reality in experiencing, suffering, rejoicing in, perceiving, existing in and living the real.

Considering its character as sign, religion is, therefore, not something separated from life. It is not something special or, indeed, an oddity in the real world. What is peculiar to a religious datum is only its explicit character. It expresses the relation in which everything real stands. Everything real is real in its relation to reality. What is merely profane has the ability, to a great extent, to let us forget this. The religious datum expresses it.

Our short reflection on the three witnesses may, however, never cause us to posit sameness or to find identity, for, as has been said, in history there is nothing identical. Exactly considered, nothing is in two witnesses identical — neither circumstance nor occasion, nor consequence, nor any sort of key word. It would, therefore, be completely false to posit the identity: Tao = God, or Krsna = Tao = God.

And yet, so it seems to us, reflection (*Besinnung*) does lead to non-identical correspondence, that is, to an understanding of the one which, beyond all sameness, leads into an understanding of the other, and vice versa. Both the turn to the radical reality of God and the conversation 'without ever coming to an end', if we once catch a glimpse of its urgency, open the way out of mere discussion of the individual datum (and out of discussing it to death) for our understanding. This openness serves more than our understanding of individual data. 'Non-identical correspondence' means, therefore, not a discovery of sameness but a process in the course of understanding.

The following witness to radical reality leads us, as did the others, on its own particular way. It is unthinkable to turn, in prayer, to what is here intended in the sphere of things. To reflect on what is here witnessed to, means to think all else to the point where there is nothing left to be thought. For only the extinction of what has become opens into this reality.

So I have heard reported:

The elevated one in the Jetahaine near Savatthi, in the Bhikku-heim founded by Anathapindika, once made an instructive, heart-penetrating speech about the nirvana to his Bhikkus. The Bhikkus listened very attentively and noted well the meaning of the speech. In the speech, the elevated one gave these sayings:

'My Bhikkus! There is an empire where there is neither earth nor water, neither fire nor air, neither the area of space-infinity nor of perception-infinity, nor of non-being, nor the boundary area of perception and non-perception, neither this world nor another, neither sun nor moon. I name this neither coming nor going, nor remaining, nor perishing, nor being born again. It is without support, without development, without sensory objects: this is the end of suffering.

It is truly difficult to have insight into the teaching of the not-I, for it is difficult to have insight into the truth. But he who perceives truth has overcome the urge; he who has insight into the truth — for him there is nothing more.

There is a not-born, not-become, not-created, not-built. If this were not, there could be no perception of a way out of the born, become, created, built. But because there is a not-born, not-become, not-created, not-built, therefore there is a way out of the born, become, created and built to be perceived.

Who depends on or is attached to something has unrest; where there is no unrest, there is rest; where rest is, there is no sensory pleasure; where there is no sensory pleasure, there is no coming and going; where there is no coming and going, there is no origin and passing away; where there is no origin and passing away, there is neither this nor that world, nor what lies between both: this is the end of suffering.[72]

Buddhist tradition names this text 'an instructive, heart-penetrating speech about nirvana'. Exactly considered, this is at best as every speech about nirvana is shown to be, an impressive impossibility. Language is orientated to what has become. Nirvana begins where what has become ends. It is no wonder that the 'speech about nirvana' can speak of nirvana only as it discusses the extinction of all that has become. So nirvana appears in the instructive speech neither as an answer to a 'what?' nor to a 'where?' nor, indeed, to a 'who?'. It is, therefore, explicitly indicated as neither infinity nor non-being, nor as 'this' nor 'that world', nor as any kind of occurrence or process. Every statement about nirvana is simply an answer to the question about the way to nirvana and is, therefore, an answer to a 'how?' or 'how no more and what no longer?' Accordingly, it would be completely meaningless to argue about the essence of what is here indicated. For example, the question about whether nirvana is to be interpreted as final nothingness or as highest reality mistakes the sign (cf. G. Mensching, 1933:33ff.). The answers to both parts of the question are indicated in the instructive speech: whoever has insight into the truth — 'for him there is nothing more', not even a 'non-being'; and yet: a 'not-born, not-become, not-created, not-built' is as certain as the 'way out of the born, become, created and built'.

The 'instructive, heart-penetrating speech about nirvana' refers so consistently beyond all that has become and all that can be expressed, that nirvana appears finally only as the radical other to all that has become and to all that can be expressed. One may speak here of radical reality, if it be conceded that the reality of what has become in no way reaches the radical reality of nirvana. Only in the extinction of what has become does what not become appear. Only one who gives up all dependence on what has become and 'attaches himself to nothing' finds the end of suffering, nirvana.

We named a religious sign something real which does not remain by itself but refers to reality, radical reality, reality itself. We have named a religious datum the place where a person assumes, experiences, thinks and interprets the real as real; where he consciously sets the real in relation to reality. As an individual case, this sign can be a prayer, a conversation, a teaching, but also a visible sign, such as the symbol of the heaven or of the sun, as reference of the real to radical reality. In the case of the mentioned visible signs, heaven and sun are not simply things among things but representatives of radical reality in the midst of the manifold of the real. Also, these signs stand, to be sure, only in a relation to each other of non-identical correspondence. Attention to what refers beyond itself in one sign leads into a more consistent interpretation of the other. But 'heaven' in one sign is not equal to 'God' in another, nor is it the same as 'Tao' or 'nirvana' in a third and fourth.

We will now consider this non-identity in all correspondence as we, in addition to the concrete witness, briefly consider the *typical witness*. We speak of a typical witness where a sign not only in its quality of being a sign, but also in the 'how' of this quality does not identically correspond to many other witnesses. It is clear that all talk about typical signs is, at first, only the assumption of a helpful correspondence for one who is trying to understand. This assumption has, then, to validate itself in the course of understanding. Concrete witnesses must, in the way of their reference, show themselves as unequal correspondence. With this reservation, we refer to three typical signs: myth, report of a miracle, and witness of revelation.

Certainly the *myth* belongs to the oldest forms of religious language. But what is myth? Myth is *radical reality present in narrative.* This narrative repeats and forms what the person living in the myth has a presentiment of as ground and goal of the world. In the myth of the beginning everything real returns home to radical reality as its ground. It finds again — in the relation to radical reality, and therewith in relation to its essential determination — what it itself in its inmost essence is. In the myth of the end, all that is real turns to radical reality as its meaning, as is disclosed in its whole provisionality and dependence.[73]

Where radical reality is encountered in a surprising and unrepeatable event, religious language speaks of *miracle (Wunder)*. Miracle is *the unexpected exposing (Aufleuchten) of reality in the real.* Not simply the interruption of what is usual makes an event a miracle, but the presence of radical reality. Without this presence, the event would be, at best, an enigmatic happening (*rätselhaftes Mirakel*) (Cf. G. Mensching, 1957).

Religious sign presents itself often as a witness of *revelation*, where revelation means *that event or process in which radical reality reveals (erschliesst) itself.* Considering the intention of a witness of revelation, revelation does not reveal simply this or that previously unknown part of the real. It reveals a reality incomparable to all other reality accessible to perception, that is, radical reality. But how does this happen? Radical reality reveals itself (Cf. W. F. Otto, 1956; N. Söderblom, 1966).

We have called a religious sign the place where one is conscious of the real as real; that is, where the real does not remain by itself but refers explicitly to reality. But where is this place? Where does the real become a witness to reality? In any case, it is not only in the midst of the broad, vast stream of what is customarily called religious tradition. It may be in a more or less loose connection with the tradition, or it may be, indeed, in that experience and thought which consciously places itself in the greatest possible opposition to the tradition. Both the so-called religious person and the so-called anti-religious or a-religious person signify radical reality. Each gives his sign, of course, according to his own understanding and conviction, and within his own meaning.

Our last quotation leads to Friedrich Nietzsche's interpretation (*Deutung*) of inspiration. The poet seeks, in the last year before his insanity (1888), to account to himself and those near him for the course he has followed ('*Ecce hom*; *Wie man wird, was man ist.*'). To his accounting belong, in decisive passages in the book, Nietzsches's own look back at the history of the origin and at the intention of his works. In his discussion of 'Zarathustra', the poet feels himself driven to speak of what happens in and what encounters him in inspiration:

Has anyone at the end of the nineteenth century a clear idea of what poets of strong ages have called *inspiration*? If not, I will describe it. — If one had the slightest residue of superstition left in one's system, one could hardly reject altogether the idea that one is merely incarnation, merely mouthpiece, merely a medium of overpowering forces. The concept of revelation — in the sense that suddenly, with indescribable certainty and sublety, something becomes *visible*, audible, something that shakes one to the last depths and throws one down — that merely describes the facts. One hears, one does not seek; one accepts, one does not ask who gives; like lightning, a thought flashes up, with necessity, without hesitation regarding its form — I never had any choice.

A rapture whose tremendous tension occasionally discharges itself in a flood of tears — now the pace quickens involuntarily, now it becomes slow; one is altogether beside oneself, with the distinct consciousness of subtle shudders and of one's skin creeping down to one's toes; a depth of happiness in which even what is most painful and gloomy does not seem something opposite but rather conditioned, provoked, a *necessary* color in such a superabundance of light; an instinct for rhythmic relationships that arches over wide spaces of forms — length, the need for a rhythm with wide arches, is almost the measure of the force of inspiration, a kind of compensation for its pressure and tension.

Everything happens involuntarily in the highest degree but as in a gale of a feeling of freedom, of absoluteness, of power, of divinity. — The involuntariness of image and metaphor is strangest of all; one no longer has any notion of what is an image or a metaphor: everything offers itself as the nearest, most obvious, simplest expression. It actually seems, to allude to something Zarathustra says, as if the things themselves approached and offered themselves as metaphors ('Here all things come caressingly to your discourse and flatter you; for they want to ride on your back. On every metaphor you ride to every truth . . . Here the words and word-shrines of all being open up before you; here all being wishes to become word, all becoming wishes to learn from you how to speak').

This is *my* experience of inspiration; I do not doubt that one has to go back thousands of years in order to find anyone who could say to me, 'it is mine as well.' (F. Nietzsche, n.d.:396f., transl. by W. Kaufmann, 1967:300f.)

The question may be raised as to why Nietzsche, in this description of inspiration, again and again uses religious expressions and ideas: 'incarnation,' 'revelation,' 'that shakes one in the last depths,' 'altogether beside oneself,' 'feeling of absoluteness, of power, of divinity.' The way Nietzsche uses these traditionally religious expressions allows the assumption that Nietzsche has a presentiment of the non-identical correspondence of his experience to what happens in the experiences of revelation in the traditional religions. The poet is almost forced to use such language and excuses himself for the fact that every other correspondence to what he describes is lacking. Therefore, there is nothing suggested more than to draw on 'the slightest residue of superstition left in one's system': with traditional religious ideas and expressions, as residue of a world otherwise fundamentally overcome, justice is done to what the poet experiences in inspiration. 'One could hardly reject altogether' these traditional ideas, and they 'merely describe the facts'.

Which 'fact' do they describe? It is a being snatched into a process which not only makes a limitless claim on the subject, but within which all being offers itself to him in word and metaphor. 'On every metaphor you ride to every truth . . . Here the words and word-shrines of all being open up before you; here all being wishes to become word, all becoming wishes to learn from you how to speak.' Inspiration is the event or process in which all being becomes word, opens itself in word and metaphor, and this becoming-word happens in the poet. The poet himself can only allow this self-opening to happen. 'Everything happens involuntarily to the highest degree.' The poet is 'merely incarnation, merely mouthpiece, merely a medium of overpowering forces,' merely the tool of a reality which may not be compared, which is encountered beyond this inspiration, which reminds one, in non-identical correspondence, of the reality which opens itself to the elect in the event of revelation in traditional religions. The 'mouthpiece' and 'medium' is, however, himself transformed in this self-opening and 'becoming-word'. The poet himself takes part in the reality which overcomes him and experiences himself 'as in a gale of feeling of freedom, of absoluteness, of power, of divinity' (F. Nietzsche, transl. by W. Kaufmann, 1967:397).

4. ATTEMPT AT REALIZATION

After having attempted to follow the direction of the sign in several religious data, we now turn to the expression of these signs, for every sign is always more or less clearly both expression of religious thought and life and reference to the reality of religion. We have, therefore, named understanding the course in which one attends to sign and expression and, with attention to both, the course in which one reflects on (*besinnt auf*) the relation of religious life to the reality of religion. This reflection (*Besinnung*), we have said, opens finally into the question: what happens in the relation of religious life to the reality of religion? This is the question, because the meaning of religious data opens itself in this relation. We have called the presence of the reality of religion in religious life the meaning of religion. This has been our guiding idea (*Vor-stellung*).

We may, again, give expression to one reservation before we consider religious expression. Expression is only an intention of the religious datum. It is one of the two elementary intentions of the datum. In attention to the expression, we do not, therefore, grasp for the religious life itself, as we might grasp, for example, for an event in an (so to speak) authentic report. In the expression, religious life expresses itself. *It gives indication of itself (deutet sich an) according to how it sees itself and insofar as it can and wants to let itself be seen.* In expression, therefore, we encounter religious life only in its own intention, thought, striving, experience, feeling and, above all, in its own vision of itself. One cannot speak of a neutral or, indeed, of an objective report about religious life in the expression of religious data. It is only possible objectively to investigate what happens in religious life, if one interprets religious data contrary to the intention of the data. Our wish is to do without such an uncritical so-called objective position, a position which violates the intention of the data. Rather, we wish to reflect on *(besinnen auf)* religious life only as far as it presents and expresses itself and not to assume that we can grasp what it is through any sort of investigation of the expression.

But how, then, does religious life express itself in the data quoted above?

Tersteegen's prayer to the only real God is united with a confession of his own nothingness. 'I am only a form, a poor shadow, if you are not in me and I am not in you, if you are not the ground and essence *(Wesen)* of my essence' (see above p. 127). This confession of his own nothingness in another place in the text, yet more drastic in expression, becomes the confession of his own complete sinfulness:

> Yet what do I say? Without you, I am not only mere appearance and form but also a miserable and frightful monster; and, because I effect things through myself, all is my doing, and as good and holy as this my doing seems, it is ugly, yes, sinful in your sight. It is ugly and sinful not only because it comes from me, who am wholly sinful and corrupt, but also because I, in every beautiful intention and appearance, please and elevate myself and give myself the glory which in all right belongs to you. O, the frightening self! I am terrified and shocked as I regard myself before the bare face of your purity. I am completely saturated with what is my own. I am wholly my own. All my outer and inner movements are my own. All my virtues are my own qualities and impure before you (G. Tersteegen, 1845:463f.).

As his own nothingness stands before God's all, so stands his total sinfulness before God's purity, a sinfulness which in its virtue is especially reprehensible. Over-against this reality, what is religious life in its own intention? It is the way from nothingness to all, the turn from appearance to being, the liberation from being nothing to being, the annihilation of what is one's own and the being fulfilled through the reality of God.

Condemn and annihilate everything in me that is not you and not yours! Completely occupy the place where I now am, and work in me and through me what pleases you! Let the I no longer be and let you be only, all in all, and lead me so wholly out of myself and out of all that is mine into you, o my God, my origin and my end! (See above p. 127—128).

Realization (*Verwirklichung*), *the way from the nothing to the all*, from non-essence to essence, from appearance to being is obviously the greatest interest of this prayer. As we see in the passion of the prayer, the realization is everything but completed. It has, however, begun, for the suppliant recognizes his situation and knows and prays for what is necessary. He knows the way, but he obviously stands at its beginning. He knows himself to be still a captive of 'appearance', and his 'frightening self' still asserts itself, it refuses to yield to the reality of God.

And yet we hear clearly in this prayer the passionate attempt to correspond to the reality of God, to turn to it and to be near it. The nothing turns itself to the all, non-essence to essence, the unreal rejoices because of reality.

Why does nothingness turn to the all? The reason is, certainly, because it has better reason to do that than anything else. If it lost the reality of God, it would lose itself and everything else. Everything far from the reality of God is 'appearance' and 'non-being'. What is, in fact, in question is the being or non-being not only of the own self but of all that is real. He who stands before God, the only reality, and experiences himself as nothing, necessarily seeks realization in God.

To turn now to the completely different world we encountered in Tao, why does one turn from the many to the one, from the individual to the whole? Why does one attempt to go the way of doing nothing; that is, why does one try to distance oneself as much as possible from having to do with the many and wholly go the way of reflection on the one and whole? The following words have been (wrongly) attributed to Khung-Tse:

Fishes breed and grow in the water; man develops in the Tâo. Growing in the water, the fishes cleave the pools, and their nourishment is supplied to them. Developing in the Tâo, men do nothing, and the enjoyment of their life is secured. Hence it is said, 'Fishes forget one another in the rivers and lakes: men forget one another in the arts of the Tâo.' (Chuang Tzû, 1962/I:253).

For man, Tao is what is necessary. The one necessary thing for man to do is to turn to the 'limit of the unlimited and the boundlessness of the unbounded', to that 'which makes things what they are' (Chuang Tzû, 1962/II:67).

In reflection on these statements, religion shows itself to be the *attempt of man to correspond to what he thinks, has presentiment of, experiences and witnesses to as radical reality.* This attempt is never completed in time. It is waylaid by hindrances, inconsistencies, setbacks, difficulties. In part, this attempt even presents itself clearly as a mere beginning — for example, in the pleading prayer for realization in view of one's own nothingness, or in the fact that the conversation about Tao presents itself as invitation.

Yet the imperfection and questionability of the attempt and the inaccessibility of the goal are paired with an incomparable necessity for the one who goes the way of correspondence to reality. Just as the real only becomes what it is out of and in its relation to reality, so the person becomes what he is in relation to what he has presentiment of perceives, experiences and witnesses to as radical reality. The insufficiency of the attempt to correspond to this reality does not contradict the necessity of the attempt. There can be no presentiment of radical reality without a turning to it; it cannot be experienced without a feeling of being personally encountered; it cannot be made present in sign and expression without an attempt to correspond to it. Radical reality, present in the life of a person, always means realization and the attempt, in all insufficiencey of the attempt and in all questionableness and inconsistency, to turn to this reality, to be open to it.

In no two expressions is this necessary and insufficient realization identical. In this innermost and personal relation of the individual of a community to what is, for him or it, radical reality, we have to distance ourselves from every assertion of identity and every cliché. Only in non-identical correspondence do we encounter this unmistakable referal to radical reality in all religious life, this urgently necessary and always insufficient attempt to correspond to radical reality.

Therefore the person gives expression always only to *his* realization, to what is his or his community's own in a completely unexchangeable way. We can never speak, therefore, of the expression of realization as something general. In the expression, we encounter realization never as scheme or as a general act.

The 'instructive, heart-penetrating speech about nirvana' which we quoted above (see p. 135), speaks of a truth difficult to understand. Nirvana is so radically other than all that has become that, finally, no language reaches it and all life which aspires to what has become cannot experience truth. To enter nirvana means to give up all dependence on what has become and, in extinguishing it, to find one's way to what has not become. 'The disappearance of desire, o monks, the disappearance of hate, the disappearance of delusion — that, o monks, one calls nirvana.'[74] In this disappearance and giving-up, all suffering is overcome in its ground. 'Conditioned by all earthly striving, this suffering arises; if, however, all adherence is overcome, suffering can no longer arise.'[75] Exactly considered, this letting-go and giving-free becomes the only necessity because only in it does what has become yield to what has not become and suffering yield to the end of suffering.

Is, then, this realization annihilation? This, too, is scheme and cliché, for with this judgment, being is identified with what has become and the way out of what has become is a way beyond all being. The matter is different, if we do not exclude the possibility that concepts such as 'being' and 'reality' do not end with what is transient, for here radical, highest reality is encountered in the extinction of what has become. Be that as it may, in any case, this attempt at realization leads, in its intention, radically beyond all that has become. Only *in the extinction of the real does reality* come to be.

In order that this manifold of expression, to which no reflection can do justice, not fall prey without resistance to a simplifying scheme, we add yet further data to what we have already mentioned.

Dag Hammarskjöld, in a note from his diary, shows in all clarity what it means for him to correspond to the reality of God.

> Thou who art over us,
> Thou who art one of us,
> Thou who *art* —
> Also within us,
> May all see Thee — in me also,
> May I prepare the way for Thee,
> May I thank Thee for all that shall fall to my lot,
> May I also not forget the needs of others,
> Keep me in Thy love
> As Thou wouldest that all should be kept in mine.
> May everything in this my being be directed to Thy glory
> And may I never despair.
> For I am under Thy hand,
> And in Thee in all power and goodness.
> Give me a pure heart — that I may see Thee,
> A humble heart — that I may hear Thee,
> A heart of love — that I may serve Thee,
> A heart of faith — that I may abide in Thee.
> (D. Hammarskjöld, 1975:93).

The 'Thou' is already through its reality for the one praying a call to realization. It cannot be thought without thinking one's own life along with it. The acknowledgement of this 'Thou' means already a giving of oneself to a process which cannot leave him, to whom and with whom it happens, untouched and unchanged. Realization means here: *to give space to the great 'Thou'* in one's own life and to make a place for him in the world. How does this happen? It happens in the turning to one's fellow man, who needs this turning, and in unshakable thanksgiving for all that happens to him who lives directed toward this 'Thou'. To see Thee, to hear Thee, to serve Thee and abide in Thee — Hammarskjöld calls these his realization, and he lets us perceive that he knows himself to be only at the beginning of being drawn into this process. Therefore, he prays for the fourfold realization.

Another aspect of realization is encountered in one of our last texts. It is not as if what this text places in the center can not be found in another. But not in every expression is just this moment of realization placed so emphatically before us.

Khalîl Djibrân has the prophet Almustafa proclaim his insights to the men of Orphalese during the course of an entire day. He speaks of almost all aspects of life: love, marriage, children, eating and drinking, work, dwelling, clothing, buying and selling, laws, etc. — all are themes of this proclamation. Toward evening the prophet is asked about religion:

And an old priest said, Speak to us of Religion.

And he said:

Have I spoken this day of aught else?

Is not religion all deeds and all reflection,

And that which is neither deed nor reflection, but a wonder and a surprise ever springing in the soul, even while the hands hew the stone or tend the loom?

Who can separate his faith from his actions, or his belief from his occupations?

Who can spread his hours before him, saying, 'This for God and this for myself; This for my soul and this other for my body'?

All your hours are wings that beat through space from self to self.

He who wears his morality but as his best garment were better naked.

The wind and the sun will tear no holes in his skin.

And he who defines his conduct by ethics imprisons his song-bird in a cage.

The freest song comes not through bars and wires.

And he to whom worshipping is a window, to open but also to shut, has not yet visited the house of his soul whose windows are from dawn to dawn.

Your daily life is your temple and your religion.
Whenever you enter into it take with you your all.
Take the plough and the forge and the mallet and the lute,
The things you have fashioned in necessity or for delight.
For in reverie you cannot rise above your achievements nor
fall lower than your failures.
And take with you all men:
For in adoration you cannot fly higher than their hopes nor
humble yourself lower than their despair.

And if you would know God, be not therefore a solver of
riddles.
Rather look about you and you shall see Him playing with
your children.
And look into space; you shall see Him walking in the cloud,
outstretching His arms in the lightning and descending in rain.
You shall see Him smiling in flowers, then rising and waving His
hands in trees. (Kahlîl Gibrân, 1972: 70f.)

In this text we encounter an example of modern nature piety tinted
with pantheism. But what does that mean? Such an ordering is
no more than a vain scheme, if it cuts short reflection (*Besinnung*)
on the whole of religion with the opinion that the essential is stated
in the ordering scheme. Reflection on the whole does not seek such
ordering.

It asks about the intention of such signs and such expressions. It
asks about what happens in such signs and expressions and, therewith, finally about the movement of religious life toward the reality
of religion.

To follow the intention of this text, religious realization is above
all not the matter of particular times, doings, attitudes and spaces.
If that were the case, piety would be no more than clothing that one
would do better to lay aside, it would be nice outwardness. And
the worship of God would not be entrance 'into the house of his
soul'; it would be without a drawing of the whole man into worship.
According to its own intention, religion, as the realization of the
person, wishes to be the fundamental event in human life; an event
in which all that is real turns to reality, finds the way to reality and

experiences its ultimate meaning in reality. Therefore, religion happens 'even as the hands cut stone or work the weaver's loom,' and the plow, the forge, the hammer and the lute, 'the things you form from necessity or pleasure' — all belong in the tempel of life. Is, therefore, everything religion? Religion wants to be all. In its intention, religion is the *movement of all that is real to reality*. Nothing can be fundamentally excluded from this movement. Realization is the fundamental event which, in its intention, penetrates the whole of life.

As we began our short reflection (*Besinnung auf*) on the whole, so do we wish to end it: with a text from the *Bhagavadgītā*. We cannot without limitation agree with Radhakrishnan's judgment that the Gītā 'represents not any sect of Hinduism but Hinduism as a whole, not merely Hinduism but religion as such, in its universality, without limit of time or space, embracing within its synthesis the whole gamut of the human spirit' (S. Radhakrishnan, 1949:12). But it does seem to us that this song can lead, in a special way, to the understanding of what, in the verse, is to be heard as the reality of religion and as religious life.

The following section of the *Bhagavadgītā* immediately follows the text we quoted before (see above p. 121). In celebrative teaching, God opens his own self to Arjuna and, therewith, the way to this his own essence, for radical reality is not thinkable without the attempt at realization, without the attempt to correspond to this radical reality.

Know that (all) states of being —
    what is brought forth by goodness, passion and
    darkness —
arise out of me.
    I am not in them They are in me.
Through these three, the fundamental quality containing
    states of being, deceived,
this whole world perceives me not
    as superior to them, intransient, (and unchangeable).
This my divine, the fundamental-qualities-containing
    Māyā is difficult to transcend.
These, however, who hold themselves to me,
    leave this Māyā behind. (7:12-14)

Here Māyā is clearly 'creative divine power', the 'art work' of the unfolding of the real out of original reality. And yet this power appears already expressed as cause of deception and blindness, as hindrance of the way to God. Not only does the real reveal reality, it also conceals it. The real becomes cause for the person to remain with it and no longer to find the way to reality.

What does this peculiar twofold relation of real and reality mean for the person? He finds himself facing the difficult task of finding the way from the real to reality. How shall he accomplish the task? The Bhagavadgītā would not be what it is, if it only gave the answer: 'in this manner' and 'not that way', Its solution is, and not only with this question: 'also that way and also that way, but this way particularly'. It knows, as ways of realization, impossible, possible, recommendable and preferred ways, but never an exclusive way.

> To me do not come (and do not hold to me)
> the doers of evil, fools, lowly men.
> Their knowledge is swept away by the Māyā,
> they cleave to what is demonic.
> Four kinds of good men
> honor and love me, o Arjuna:
> Those who suffer, those who seek wisdom, those
> who strive for gain, and those who know,
> o Prince of Bharatas.
> Among these the one who knows excels,
> who, always integrated, is devoted to the single
> one in love and honor.
> To the knowing one I am exceedingly dear,
> and he is dear to me. (7:15-17)

The good man (*su-kṛtin*) stands in opposition to the doer of evil (*dus-kṛtin*): the Māyā is fatal for the evil doer, he remains attached to it and so ends in the demonic. (Is not the demonic the mistaking of the real for reality?) The good man seeks and finds the way beyond Māyā to God. But what makes one who knows prominent among good men? He is 'nitya-yukta' and 'eka-bhakti', not devoted to this or that but bound with a single one in love and devotion. One who suffers perhaps seeks through God a lessening of his sufferings; one who is virtuous perhaps seeks through God success; one who seeks wisdom perhaps seeks through God to come to perception. But, in the knowing one, in his seeking and finding God, it is always a question of God. In speaking of the knowing one, one speaks of 'love'. The search beyond the real for the sake of the real is far less than this pure love of reality (cf. Radhakrishnan, 1949:220; R. C. Zaehner, 1969:251).

The knowing one is not simply further progressed in perception. What is said of his concentration, honoring and devotion contradicts the idea of merely advanced perception. The knowing one is, in his whole essential being, the realized one. His self, and not only his knowing, finds the way to (and becomes) God.

Nobel and exalted are all these,
   the knowing one, however, is my own self, so I believe.
For he is, integrated with (my) self,
   come to me, the highest way.
At the end of many births
   comes the knowing one to me (and gives himself up to me).
'Vāsudeva is all' (he perceives).
Such a great soul is very hard to find. (7:18-19)

For Hill, the confession in Verse 19 ('Vāsudeva is all') is the central statement of the Bhagavadgītā (W. Douglas and P. Hill, 1928:18). He sees complete pantheism in the work (ibid:169). Of course, this view is contested. Rāmanuja interprets: 'Vāsudeva is my all'; Mādhva: 'Vāsudeva is the ground of all' (ibid:169 n.2).

It is very clear that this confession is not the assertion of a philosophical equivalency such as all = God. In verse 19, it is not at all a matter of mere perception but of the end of a development, of the goal of a way. If 'vāsudevaḥsarvam' were simply a metaphysical thesis, it would not be understandable why this thesis binds to the divine self, why many births are necessary in order to arrive at this thesis, and why a metaphysical philosophical statement as such distinguishes great souls that are hard to find. Therefore, we have here certainly not a fundamental thesis of a pantheistic metaphysics. 'Pantheism', if we can speak about it at all with regard to this text, can only be the goal of a process whose last (and first) stage is the development forming and transforming the whole self of the person. 'Pantheism' is something like the last distance to be traveled on the way of this realization, on the way to the God of which the Gita sings in Chapter 7. As the knowing one, the person seeks and finds the way beyond the real and does not remain, in demonic mistake, in adherence to the real as ultimately real, and so he seeks and finds ('nitya-yukta' and 'eka-bhakti') the way to reality. Bound to the self, integrated with it ('yukt'ātma'), he becomes one with God's *Ātma*.

5. Understanding of Religion and Science of Religion

The question about what happens in the relation of religious life to the reality of religion stood at the beginning of our short reflection (*Besinnung*) on the meaning (*Sinn*) of religion. The answer to the question may be so expressed: a religious person attempts to correspond to what he has presentiment of, perceives, experiences and witnesses to as radical reality. He attempts to do this in his turning to this reality, in his meditation, his prayer, his following, his obedience, his thankfulness, his devotion, his directing himself toward the chief concern, his asceticism, his active turn toward his fellow man, his doing nothing, his celebration, in his joy in radical reality, in his being open to it, giving space to it, in his service.

But where does such an attempt occur? It occurs where the person not only perceives, overcomes, and forms the real, but also where he has presentiment of, experiences, interprets and knows himself in movement toward reality. If profanity means having to do with the real, then religion is the relation to reality. *Religion is the reality of a person. It is all that refers the personhood of a person not only to what is real but to reality.* For example, it is the experience of the openness of the real and, therefore, the experience that what is real does not stand alone but refers to reality. Or religion is the inability to experience what is real without thinking of reality or simply asking the question about it. Religion is the attempt to find the way beyond the individual thing to the whole. It is the infinitely manifold, continual referal and referring of man to the ground, goal, meaning and middle of all that is real. Religion is his attempt to correspond to this reality. He is not able to correspond only to what is real, because what is real delivers him finally to radical meaninglessness and unreality. Consequently, religion occurs in every human being. A person completely without religion would be a person without reality. But religion never occurs twice in the same way.

Religion often occurs in conscious antithesis to eternity-orientated currents in traditional religion. As such, it is a clearly *inner-worldly realization*, the attempt to correspond to reality not as it was and once will be but in the here and now or in a tomorrow which can be formed. Religion as inner- worldly realization is the attempt to find the ultimate ground and meaning fully in this world.

Religion occurs, also often in antithesis to collectivist tendencies in traditional religion and in modern society, as extremely *individualist self-realization*, as the attempt to correspond, above all, to the radical reality of one's own self and its abilities and possibilities.

Religion occurs in *mass movements* as the attempt to correspond to radical reality with total devotion, for example, as one has a sense of this reality in one's own 'blood' and people.

Religion occurs in *anonymous restraint* toward outward forms of religion in the presentiment of reality in nature, art or personal fate — a religion articulated, at most, to one who is near to such a person, but never publically.

And religion occurs obviously, in *traditional explicitly religious community*, where what binds the community is consciously addressed as religion and where realization is sought in traditional signs and expressions.

To which religion would science of religion turn? For integral science of religion, that is, for a science of religion which asks about the whole of religion, the answer can only be: science of religion should have to do, as much as possible, with every religion. In any case, it cannot deal with only one religion. Religion is far more than traditional explicit religious realization, that is, it is far more than what consciously designates itself as religion.

Where is, however, religiouslessness at all to be found, if all life stands in relation to reality? In integral reflection on (*Besinnung auf*) a religious datum, the concept of religiouslessness is newly defined. On the one hand, according to the intention of religious data, all that is real stands in relation to reality. However, the sign and the expression give us, at the same time, to understand how far they themselves fall short of their innermost intention. This falling short, this failure in the own intention is, actually, religiouslessness. Therefore, the lives of those who belong to no explicit religion are not religiousless. Religiouslessness is not at all beyond or in contradiction to religious thought and experience. Religiouslessness is the *against-itself* (*das Gegen-Teil*) *of religion*; that is, that in religion which contradicts religion, the over-against-itself (*das Gegenüber*) that every religion carries in itself.

Religiouslessness is not something other, something foreign to the attempt at realization. It is, rather, failure in this attempt, falling short, losing itself. Therefore, there is no one single religiouslessness. Every realization carries, rather, its *own* contradictory against-itself (*Gegen-Teil*) in itself. In the attempt to enter reality in the extinction of all that is real, religiouslessness is the ever new, penetrating adherence to what is real. In the attempt to give space to radical reality in service to fellow men and in love, religiouslessness is the ever new fall into lovelessness and egoism. Just as little as we can speak of religion as a single form of realization, so we cannot speak of a single form of religiouslessness. In a religion of conscious reflection on (*Besinnung auf*) the one, religiouslessness is the ever losing-oneself in the many. But in the attempt of inner-worldly, world-forming and world-changing realization, religiouslessness is a becoming fatigued within the real and an attempting to grasp reality in a new inward, spiritual way. *Every realization*, just as it expresses itself in intentions, *bears within itself the seed of its against-itself.* The reality of persons is, especially as religion, never clearly univocal. Enthusiasm is bound with lameness, hope with failure, joy with boredom, perception with mistake, love with hate. The task of an integral science of religion is, in thinking the whole of every religion, also to think its religiouslessness. The reflection on the elementary intentions of every religious datum cannot overlook what contradicts its intention. This attention to the against-itself, the contradiction, belongs necessarily to a reflection on (*Besinnung auf*) the whole of religion, just because sign and expression are only intentions, no more and no less. If the against-itself, the failure, the falling short of the intention is overlooked, religion appears in an idealism, a simplicity and consistency which is never found in human reality. *In this encompassing sense, including intentions and the against-itself, the reality of persons is the object of integral science of religion.*

But why does religion occur at all and, consequently, also religiouslessness? In conclusion we risk briefly considering this question, which stands at the outer edge of every integral reflection. Religious signs and expressions often refer to a twofold ground. First, what is real refers ever anew to reality. Because what is real exists reality exists and because a person is real, he sees himself constantly referred to reality through the openness of the real. Second, a person does not seem to be able to endure what is merely real. Dealing merely with what is real without asking about reality lies beyond every person's possibilities. The real with relation to reality would result in complete meaninglessness, to radical chaos. We are, according to one's point of view, either damned or chosen to live toward or in reality. To be a person means, as task and as gift, to be a real person. But to be a real person is not without seeking, asking about or having a presentiment of reality.

The openness of the real and the referal (*Angewiesensein*) of the person to reality are, however, only in superficial consideration two different reasons for religion. Religious witness sees them as one. Not only is the person pressed toward living in or toward reality, and not only does what is real refer to reality; rather, in both, radical reality refers to itself, sets itself in relation to the person in human seeking, having presentiment of, hoping and experiencing.

In this chapter, we have tried to draw the consequences from our previous integral reflection (*Besinnung*) for the understanding of science of religion. This attempt was unavoidable for what integral reflection yields for the understanding of science of religion. Not only does Methodology have, as reflection (*Bedenken*) on its course, consequences for further movement on this course, but the entrance onto this course also has its consequences for methodological reflection.

EXCURSUS III. ON THE DISTINCTION BETWEEN RELIGION AND RELIGIOUSLESSNESS

What religiouslessness as the against-itself (*das Gegen-Teil oder vielmehr den Gegen-Teil*) of religion means can perhaps be better clarified by a discussion with U. Tworuschka's work, 'Integral Religionswissenschaft — Methode der Zukunft?' (1974:239-243). The author critically discusses my earlier attempt in the direction of an integral science of religion, *Interessant und Heilig, Auf dem Weg zur integralen Religionswissenschaft* (1971). Tworuschka not only emphasizes the actuality and necessity of an integral science of religion, he also attempts to widen the area of questioning into the discussion of fundamental categories (*Grundlagen*) in church history and pedagogy of religion. Just as emphatically as he wishes to have an integral science of religion, he refuses my attempt in my earlier book. He does not refuse my question but my results and the 'radical consequences' of the book. Concretely, he reproaches me for 'leveling the boundaries between religion and religiouslessness' (U. Tworuschka, 1974:243). I think the opposite is the case. The sketch in my earlier book shows that religion also happens in the midst of so-called secular life. Tworuschka has, indeed, no objection to this insight. He himself speaks of religion being possible and real outside the 'positive' religions. His concept of the 'religions outside of religion' is also correct, as is his struggle against the 'traditional dogma' in science of religion which identifies religion with 'positive' religion. If Tworuschka agrees with me in all this, and if he more clearly expresses what I tried to say, what is the basis of his objection? It seems to me that he is inconsistent. After he concedes the possibility and reality of 'religion outside of religion' and of 'secondary history of religion', he sees religiouslessness somehow yet as secular life and experience, and he wants to have this more clearly distinguished from religion. But may one yet speak in such a way of 'religiousless-ness' once the identity of religion and traditional religion has been broken? May one continue to speak as if all that is not 'positive' religion is yet somehow religiousless? Certainly the distinction between 'religion outside religion' and 'positive' religion is correct. Tworuschka proposes that we speak not of secular religion but of the 'outer- and non-religious transport of religious content' (1974:243). Wholly apart from the fact that this formulation somehow wakens the idea of an only fragmentary religion and, therein, unconsciously devaluates secular religion over-against traditional religion (our own attempt at distinction seems to us far less disqualifying), one cannot confuse the distinction between explicit religion and secular religion with the distinction between religion and religiouslessness. Secular life and experience is only fictively religiousless. As soon as the too-narrow view of modern science of religion is significantly widened and the mentioned 'dogma' (that religion is explicit religion) falls, integral science of religion turns from fictive to real religiouslessness, to the religiouslessness which belongs to the whole of religon or, as we expressed in the first book, to the 'against-itself' (*Gegen-Teil*) which all religion carries in itself (U. Tworuschka, 1971:196). What is real religiouslessness? It is not the half-religious or fragmentary religion which one thinks he finds in secular life but, as we have said above, it is what is diametrically opposed to religion (*Gegen-Teil*). If religion is experience of meaning, religiouslessness is losing oneself in meaninglessness. If religion is participation in the mystery of reality, the religiouslessness is wallowing in mysticism; it means unreal, construed dealing with mysteries and thoughtless liturgical activity. If religion is the attempt to correspond to radical reality, then religiouslessness is the failure of this attempt and the counter attempt to deceive oneself about radical reality with insignificant theories. Real religiouslessness is a much too serious matter and a much too significant happening to be brought exclusively in connection with secular life. For where does religiouslessness happen? It does not happen far away from all explicit religion but exactly where religion happens. Precisely because all religion, both explicit and secular, is always only an attempt, failure, self-deception and loss of self are not foreign to it. Religiouslessness belongs to the whole of religion as the over-against which religion carries in itself, as the alien part of itself (*das Gegen-Teil oder den Gegen-Teil*) which constantly accompanies religion. To correspond to radical reality means also to miss or fail this reality. And to orientate oneself to the meaning of all that is real means ever again to lose oneself in what is of limited meaning and in what is meaningless.

5

The Identity

1. SELF-EVIDENT PARALLELS

We have understood methodology as the attempt of science of religion to clarify what the science does. That means that methodology asks about the task, premises and methods of work in science of religion, and, last but not least, about the verification (*Bewährung*) of what methodology has perceived as principles of integral science of religion. All in all, this attempt to clarify is certainly nothing other than a piece of systematic self-discovery. As the encompassing goal of integral science of religion is insight into the whole of religion, so the encompassing goal of methodology in science of religion is a most possibly clear and encompassing knowledge of the task, preconditions and methods of the science; that is, in short, of its own identity.

Therefore, the theme which we take up in this last chapter is not at all new. It was a matter of debate in every previous chapter. Nevertheless, the need to take up this theme again seems to me to be unavoidable. In all our previous discussions, one circumstance has not been directly brought into focus, and yet it cannot be overlooked in reflection on the identity of modern science of religion. This circumstance is the phenomenon of self-evident parallels.

We name self-evident parallels those endeavors for a research of religion which, as long as there is a science of religion, accompany the work of the science as supplement, confirmation, correction and contradiction, but which are never to be identified straightway with science of religion. We call these parallels 'self-evident', first, because they are self-evidently there, because their contradiction of and their supplement to science of religion belong clearly to the historical situation of modern science of religion. It may be vexing to science of religion that it does not have the only claim to perception of religion and to interpretation of religious reality. But if it finds the matter vexing, its judgment of the situation is wrong. Science of religion does not have a monopoly on research of religion. It never has had a monopoly and it never will have it. Whether it wishes it or not, the most contradictory accompaniment belongs to it as it follows its course.

We call these parallels 'self-evident', second, because science of religion can really only be evident to itself when it is also clear about its relation to these parallels. It cannot be the task of a methodology in science of religion to outdo these parallels, to contest their right to have to do with religion. But it is very much the task of science of religion to consider these parallels so thoroughly that no doubt can exist about the unexchangeable self, the identity, of science of religion.

Self evident parallels are, in the sense we have indicated, certainly not exclusively but, in their significance, chiefly: theology and criticism of religion.

2. THEOLOGY AND SCIENCE OF RELIGION

As long as there has been science of religion, it has seen itself constantly accompanied, supplemented, placed in question and challenged by the partly so similar, partly so contradictory efforts of theology. Therefore, science of religion can do no other than be aware of this accompaniment and reflect on its relation to this contradictory parallel. It can clarify itself only if its relation to theology is clarified. And one can say the same about theology. It must also disturb theology that such a different sort of undertaking wishes to understand the whole of its subject matter.[76]

How, therefore, is science of religion related to theology? Our consideration will begin with the different possibilities of theology and will lead, then, into the different possibilities of science of religion. According to what 'theology' and 'science of religion' are taken to be, their mutual relation will also take shape.

1. In the most elementary sense of the word, theology is reflection

(*Nachdenken*) on or teaching about God, or, even more basically, it is reflection on the reality of religion. So understood, theology is an expression of every religious life. Just as there is no human life without some form of reflection, so there is no religious life without some form of reflection. In religious life, theology is the reflection or thought of belief, the 'fides quaerens intellectum' (cf. K. Barth, 1958:14ff.). Theology is *realization as reflection* and, therewith, at least in its beginnings, an aspect of every religious life.

As an aspect of religious life, however, theology is clearly an object of integral science of religion, for religious reality in all its aspects is the object of the research of science of religion. In its attempt to understand religious reality, integral science of religion reflects, yea even, on theology. Long before theology emerges as contradictory accompaniment to science of religion, it is already the object of integral science of religion. Or, to remain with the image implied with the word 'accompaniment', science of religion has theology primarily not of its side but already in front of itself as its object.

2. Theology first becomes parallel to science of religion where theology finds the way to systematic reflection, that is, to a method-conscious and, in its method, consequent reflection on its own religious reality. Theology reflects in a way very similar to science. That does not mean that it, with its reflection, is automatically science. We have called 'science' the systematic research of a definite area of the real. Therefore, systematic procedure in its method of perception does not make theology science. It is essential to the designation of theology as science that it understand itself only as research of a definite area of the real, for example, as research of its own religious tradition.

It is clear that theology, in any case Christian theology, in wide areas, does not understand itself as science in the way we have defined it; that it seeks nothing other than systematic research of its own religious reality and tradition, for example, consistent description, comprehension and understanding of the New Testament or of the data of church history. So understood, theology is nothing other than *science of religion of Christianity*. As such, theology is not simply the object but also a part of integral science of religion. As one's own religion belongs essentially to the whole of religious reality, so theology as science belongs to integral science of religion.

In the elementary sense of realization as reflection (*Nachdenken*), as the thought of religious life on itself and the reality of religion, theology is, therefore, to be distinguished very clearly from theology as integral science of one's own religion. In the first sense, which, as a rule, is completely unsystematic and pre-scientific, theology is the object of integral science of religion; in the second sense, it is a part of science of religion.

3. Between pre-scientific and scientific theology yet a third typical possibility of theology introduces itself, namely *pseudo-scientific theology*. This theology unites scientific method, that is, systematic procedure, with everything but scientific premises and intentions. In a certain sense, it unites also elements of pre-scientific theology with elements of scientific theology.

The following three tendencies seem to us characteristic of this half-scientific theology. From case to case *one or another of these tendencies* may be more prominent.

(a) Pseudo-scientific theology shows a tendency to *speculation*. We call 'speculation' the attempt to make scientific statements about the reality of religion. This attempt seems to us to be a self-contradiction. Science is systematic research of a definite area of the real. Only religious reality, however, is the area in religion which is scientifically researchable. The religious reality is the object of religious-scientific research. The reality of religion — the ground, goal and middle of all that is real — is never the area of scientific research of what is real. Every statement about the reality of religion is religious witness, not scientific or scientific-theological perception. Science of religion can express itself about the reality of religion only in its interpretation of a religious sign. It can never state what the reality of religion is; it can only attempt to understand what is witnessed to as the reality of religion. In its direct statements about the reality of religion, speculative theology is itself religious witness, yet it pretends to be science. Science of religion and, with it, scientific theology seek to understand religious witness without being witness, because the task of understanding requires this reserve. As religious witness, how could science of religion do justice to the whole manifold of religious witnesses in its description, comprehension and understnanding? Would it not, in its research of other witnesses, at best only understand itself? As itself religious witness, science of religion violates itself as science and the religious witness it seeks to understand.

(b) As religious witness, speculative theology constantly obscures the boundaries between personal truth and scientific perception. We call personal truth the presence of the reality of religion in our own lives, our personal relation to the reality of religion. The perception of science of religion is knowledge of foreign religious reality — that of other persons, times cultures — as well as one's own. If we speak of the reality of religion in our own lives, we speak in a confessional way. If, however, we constantly obscure the boundary between personal witness and the insight of science of religion, the witness loses its character as witness and the perception loses its character as perception, and both become now hardly distinguishable, personal, general witness-like and scientific *propaganda*. A second designating mark of this pseudo-scientific theology is this propagandistic character. Propaganda means — in distinction from personal witness — science used for the purpose of confession in the disguise of science. Self-evidently, the theologian (and the scientist of religion) can and may also represent personal truth. No one can prohibit him from doing so. But personal witness is to be made recognizable as such. Scientific theology gives notice that personal witness is personal witness. Pseudo-scientific theology obscures the limits between personal truth and the perception of science of religion.

(c) A third characteristic of pseudo-scientific theology is its tendency to be *ideology*. If science seeks systematic perception, system of method and of its course of procedure, ideology ends with a system of the perceived, a system of reality. A theology which abandons its own systematic task — the systematic description, comprehension and understanding of religious reality — in favor of speculative reflection is always in danger of systematizing its seemingly scientific perception of the reality of religion. It is clear that these ideological tendencies hinder rather than help the task of understanding. For ideology, what is really understandable is only what fits into the system of the perceived.

It is not to be mistaken that pseudo-scientific theology also belongs to the religious reality of many religions. And consequently, as religious reality, it deserves the interest of the scientist of religion. It is to be comprehended and as much as possible to be understood. But it is impossible for theology as religious speculation, propaganda and ideology to be a part of integral science of religion. As a sort of parallel, such theology is, at best, the antithesis of science of religion, for it neither seeks the understanding of other religious reality nor helps it. Rather, it hinders understanding. Theology in all its forms is the object of integral science of religion. As scientific theology, it is also a part of integral science of religion. As pseudo-scientific, it is in contradiction to integral science of religion.

Perhaps the following scheme (see opposite page) is a good way of presenting a summary of what we have said about theology.

4. As we now attempt to discuss more thoroughly the relation of science of religion and scientific theology, we need to say that it is clear that the two are not related simply as parts of a whole. Rather, one sees often a quite contradictory and tense unity of them. That is not surprising if we consider that both easily lose sight of their integral interest, both often do not nearly do justice to the whole of their subject matter and exhaust themselves in the presentation of special problems and aspects. This falling short of the own interest and intention of both cannot be without consequence for their mutual relation.

According to their goals, integral science of religion and integral theology are without doubt one. Both seek the encompassing perception of their respective subject matters. Even the, at the moment, most obvious difference between them — integral theology asks only about the whole of Christian belief, integral science of religion asks also about the whole of other, non-Christian religions — is only provisional. The understanding of one's own belief cannot remain by itself but seeks also the understanding of persons beyond its own religious tradition. Christian theology cannot have its end in understanding what belongs to Christianity.[77] If it so limits itself,

Theology

pre-scientific	pseudo-scientific	scientific
reflection in every religious life, realization as reflection	religious witness in scientific disguise, tendency to speculation, propaganda and ideology	systematic research of one's own religious reality, e.g. integral science of the Christian religion

unsystematic	systematic procedure	
religious witness		Interpretation of religious witness
	opposition to integral science of religion	part of integral science of religion

Object of Integral Science of Religion

it only shows that it does not yet have a real understanding of Christianity. Integral science of religion and integral theology not only have a common subject matter, but also seek a most encompassing and thorough description, comprehension and understanding of this common subject matter. Purely on the basis of their interests, there could never be contradiction or even tension in their relation. Contradiction and tension result from the inability of the two to do justice to their common interests. Integral perspective and method is intended by both, but neither is actually capable of overcoming its limitations in order to be fully integral. True integral science of religion would be true theology and vice versa. There would be no reason to see them as different, the mutual objection to the other would not exist. But the more they fall short of their interest and intention, the more uncritically each insists that its own limited perception is perception of the whole, the more unavoidable and, therefore, necessary will be the clear distinction of the two and their contradictions of each other.

An heretical — for example, a purely descriptive and comprehensive — science of religion, even if it does not wish to acknowledge it, needs the opposition of an understanding theology, otherwise its short-sightedness becomes dogma. Science of religion must let itself be referred to the reality of religion as the middle and ground of all religious reality. It must let itself be told that, he who refuses to understand, is not fair to the whole of religion.

An heretical — for example, a purely doctrinaire — theology, which understands itself simply as scientific penetration of given truths of belief, must let itself be referred to the fact that the whole of belief is never identical with the sum of the truths of belief which it considers given. It must let itself be told that he most surely misses the whole who renounces asking about the whole in the opinion that he already has it. All real understanding begins with questioning. Therefore, it cannot be surprising that a self-assured doctrinaire theology has always been challenged and contradicted by modern science of religion. Modern science of religion has attempted to expose assumptions of possession of all insight, and it has done that with every possible means — from reference to the questionableness of the history on which the self-secure doctrine is based to the demonstration of inner contradicitons and inconsistencies. Indeed, such criticism has, in part, not borne much fruit. Once heresy has become a tradition, it is not so easily moved by arguments. Nevertheless, the criticism was as necessary as the constantly repeated reference to the reality of religion in theology's criticism of merely descriptive or comprehensive science of religion. And this criticism, too, has not always been fruitful. The heresies of science of religion will soon be as old and holy as those of theology.

What would happen if heretical theology and science of religion were no longer contradicted? What would happen if the unfolding of presently true belief were simply taken to be perception of the whole of religion? *As much as theology and science of religion are one in their goals, just as much are they dependent on one another as they move on their respective courses* — even when it is difficult for each to listen to the other. Their accompaniment of each other is completely unfruitful only in one case. This case is not where one has difficulty accepting the objection of the other, but where the objection of the other is never given because both err into the same one-sidedness. Here theology and science of religion are not at all capable of helping each other but, at most, mutually strengthen their common error. A purely descriptive theology and a purely descriptive science of religion no longer have anything to say to one another, to object to in the other. At one in their short-sightedness, they cannot fulfill even their first service to one another, which is to correct and to contradict. It may be concluded that the *integral interest is never wholly fulfilled, but it is never wholly lost as long as theology and science of religion are in contention.*

EXCURSUS IV. ON ULRICH MANN'S SYNOPTIC METHOD

1. Forword

Ulrich Mann[78] recommends a procedure, develops a style of work and presents interpretations — all with the intent of replacing an often still relationless beside-one-another of science of religion and systematic theology with a conscious correlation of theology, science of religion, philosophy of religion and psychology of religion. We would like to examine his view of the matter and his procedure.

We encounter four difficulties.

1. Mann's publications are stages on a way or phases of a development. Not only has his field of vision widened constantly — to the limits where one individual is hardly able to sight the whole field;[79] but also his perspectives have significantly changed since his first publications.[80] His procedure itself has also never been presented conclusively. Rather, he has changed it and added to it with the com-

pletion of each new phase. All is still in movement. Therefore, we can only indicate tendencies or follow the way he has gone. It is not possible for us to concentrate Mann's work into a finished program.

2. Mann often uses both imagery to make comparisons as well as associations when he explains his way or method. This not only makes interpretation easier in his own entry into the synoptic procedure, it also makes it more difficult where the interpreter begins to ask about details. The interpreter is in danger of interpreting the image too widely or of taking it too literally.

3. As stimulating as his work on the whole is, it rests ever more clearly in the course of his publications on metaphysical, theological and depth-psychological principles which no critical reader can simply assume. We mean here above all Mann's strong leaning on the depth-psychology of C. G. Jung and on the theology of religion which is visible behind his models and in his projections.[81] How can a critic do justice to a work when he does not share its premises, implications and consequences?

4. Exactly considered, 'synopsis' and 'synoptic' designate for Mann neither simply a method nor simply a procedure and its results.[82] His use of the concepts of synoptic and synopsis has become, in his last works, increasingly multifarious (1975:30-54; 1976: 19-37). All in all considered, the two concepts seem to have the following meanings:

— a *task* which all sciences having to do with religion should assume,

— a *method* for mastering this task,

— a *theory*, a view of the whole which as a guiding presentation (*Vorstellung*) determines the method and which is visible as result in the model.

We wish to examine briefly all these aspects in the following — at first without stating our own position. In the final part, we shall ask about the relation of synoptic work to integral science of religion and venture a judgment.

2. *Synopsis as Task*

Insofar as theology pursues its task, so to speak, self-sufficiently, it has for a long time treated its theme exhaustively . . . That may be most clearly exemplified in the systematic discipline: for a long time now there have not been many smaller or larger projections in this discipline which were not at some earlier time, and then often better, represented (1976:22). Basically, a systematist cannot get around admitting that everything has already been said and, indeed, usually better than it could be said again. If he wants to insist on the independence of his work, he is left only with the work of interpreting the great old themes, for example the doctrine of the two natures, into today's categories of understanding. But 'basically' one has to repeat the concept so deploringly often. 'Basically' Christology, as a central theme — again to use this example, has been exhausted to the point that there is really nothing more to teach or assert that has not, at some time or other, already been taught or asserted (1973d:137).

What follows from this pessimistic judgment of the situation of systematic theology?[83]

Genuine tasks of research which open frontiers are coming in new and overpowering fullness upon theology. Theology only has to recognize them. It recognizes them when it thinks about the unity of science which is coming into being. That is the 'new' that promises a future (1973d:137).

Nevertheless, wherever . . . systematic projections or these represent something that really leads further, it is a matter of projections or these that result from the critical encounter (*Ausinandersetzung*) with neighboring sciences, and, therefore, it is a matter of results of synoptic work (1976:22).

Synopsis is the future task of theology. Where theological work in our time is rich in yield, that work is done on the new, the synoptic level. Hereby, it is a matter of work which trespasses boundaries. At first the nearest disciplines should be questioned, above all science of religion and psychology of religion, then those disciplines which are further away until finally the whole of science can become the theme of theology (1973d:138).

The situation of systematic theology is found in milder form in all other disciplines:

> Basically this is also true, and actually above all, of the theological disciplines which work strictly historically. One thinks, to cite an example, of the impulse which Qumran-research mediated for New Testament science: here it is clearly a matter of impulses from archeology, history of literature and research in history of religions; and, therefore, it is clearly a matter of synoptic working-together. . . . In any case, in the whole breadth of its historical range of research, theology works synoptically. There is no fundamental difference in method in the analysis of texts of Epictetus and those of the Apostle Paul, of Babylonian Marduk-hymns and pre-exile Psalms of the King; and the same is true of research in the history of the church and theology (1976: 22).

In comparison with systematic theology, therefore, historical theology is in a better situation, because for a long time it has proceeded synoptically. If it does not proceed synoptically, then it must face the fact that 'at least since Bultmann the *self-sufficient* theological themes of the historical disciplines are finished' (1973d:137).

Considering the boundless breadth of religious reality, one would expect the independent work of science of religion to be just as unlimited, but that may not be the case:

> Is not also for this field of research a comparatively closed body of facts conceivable? . . . In the age of the computer such an 'idealization' . . . need not necessarily be regarded as a mere wish, even if it might come about only in the distant future (1976:20).

All scientific disciplines which have to do with religion are, therefore, dependent on one another if perceptions are still to be won which lead further. Thereby, systematic theology is especially called to cooperation with science of religion and psychology of religion. Previously, where it has chosen to cultivate a conversation with another discipline at all, it has done that almost exclusively with philosophy. In the debate about secularization, this one-sidedness led to unrealistic theories. Especially systematic theology is now called to take up conversation with the discipline which, according to its subject matter, stands closest to systematic theology, and that is science of religion.[84]

3. Synopsis as Method

How does one have to go about synoptic work in actual practice?

The answer is simple: one does research in such a way that different areas overlap. The scientist working synoptically does not simply engage in conversation with the representative of a neighboring science at symposia, as important as this may be. He himself researches in the area of that science! It is self-evident that this can only happen within certain limits, just as it is self-evident that the danger of dilattantism threatens here (U. Mann, 1976:34).

Is specialized research in one's own field replaced through this 'overlapping'? By no means. In spite of the previously mentioned pessimism, much is expected of specialized research.[85]

Therefore, synopsis cannot simply wish to dissolve special research. On the other hand, synopsis is certainly more than a mere take-over of methods. Both taking and giving, it rather enters in some way into the whole of the neighboring science; it actively takes part, therefore, in the basic problems of that science. And this is what is really new (U. Mann, 1976:23).

But how does synoptic work enter into the whole of the neighboring science? In Mann's newer works, the expression 'bundling of aspects' appears almost as a stereotype (1971a:99; 1970b:68; 1970a:69). We 'want to bundle all pertinent directions of vision into synopsis' (1970a:42).

In the narrow sense, however, we bundle above all four disciplines into the synoptic aspect of the perception of religion: philosophy of religion, science of religion, psychology of religion, theology (1975:17).

The four sciences of interpretation (*Deutungswissenschaften*) bring namely their own partial perspectives regarding antique-oriental and western history of religion and spirit, and these perspectives seem to differ widely among themselves. We want to try to bundle these perspectives (1970a:185).

It was a matter of synoptically bundling the view of history of religion and spirit into a unified perspective, and that depended on bringing the four sciences of interpretation (*Deutungswissenschaft*) into agreement (1970a:192).

Almost as frequently, synoptic work is compared with a conversation (1973a:235; 1973b:125; 1970a:96; 1976:27) or with a musical quartet or orchestra (1971a:41; 1970a:118; 1973a:237). Therein conversation is not considered a dispute without result. Rather, conversation leads to an approximation or, indeed, to a unification of standpoints.

> One can even assert that in synopsis finally a congruence of the four partners will result. So one could also say finally that synopsis is both theology and depth-psychology etc. Then we can actually no longer need the concept theology. Nevertheless, we use the concept in connection with the concept synopsis, because we wish to indicate that we, with our questioning, come from theology, from specialized, traditional theology as a particular discipline of research. Therefore, we distinguish between specialized and synoptic theology (1971a:42).

As synoptic, therefore, theology becomes congruent with its three conversation partners. In an orchestra or quartet, individual tones are distinguishable, but it is above all their togetherness that is heard:

> Thereby, this or that instrument can certainly carry the melody or even play a solo part; but the other instruments must always be ready, or at least be perceivable as ready to participate, in a given case, in that playing of all four parts which gives the whole its harmonic support (1975:34).

Therefore, synopsis leads to a harmonic togetherness. Or, to refer to two other images Mann uses: here (separating) ditches are filled (1973d:136) and 'connecting threads bound with one another' (1970a:98).

4. Synopsis as Theory

Because religion is a whole relation to the whole, it must itself basically be synopsis! Religion is actually nothing other than the synopsis in all synopses. That is finally true of all functions of perception, for man is a synoptic essence. As we stand before a significant work of art, we begin, without being conscious of it, to see at once with numerous eyes. The two eyes which mediate the outward work of art to us are inwardly multiplied, for here within we observe with a thousand-faceted optic to which belong all aspects of feeling, intuiting and thinking perception. In religion where we, as Tillich says, have to do with what 'ultimately concerns' us, out synopsis is raised to a higher power. In view of this synopsis in the synopses, it is a modest requirement when we require, for research-work in religion, at least a four-fold bundled synopsis from scientific disciplines, especially because also within empirical research synopsis has long since been practiced. The unity of the science is coming of necessity. (1975:37).

Therefore, synoptic work not only corresponds to the trend of other sciences, especially natural science (1975:37) but also corresponds most deeply to its object, religion. Religion itself is synopsis, a whole relation to the whole. But because, in any case, every person has religion (1971a:73ff.; 1970a:46ff.), this movement from the many to the one, from the individual to the whole, belongs to the human being of man. Man is a synoptic essence. Because every individual finally turns to the whole, it is valid to perceive the religion in the religions, and the way to this religion in the religions begins with reflection on Poseidonios of Apameia and the 'thought of cosmic all-sympathy, of the micro-macrocosmy' (1975:24).

The movement from the individual to the whole and from the many to the one becomes a particular interest of our time:

In the area of art, as in the area of non-theological science, it is ever more strongly felt that in every individual utterance and discipline a centrifugal tendency is effective which threatens to lead, with explosive dynamism, finally to the atomization of the whole. The ideal of the unity of art and science, which at the turn of the 19th Century was still valid as self-evident reality, has lost its binding power. But even as something that is lost to sight, it still has a strong enough effect to have us ask about the unifying middle without which a real meaning of artistic formation and scientific research can not be won. We have on all sides reached limits where the theological question comes up. That should not mean that on all sides the way into theological thought is also opened. That is by no means the case and it is not to be expected. But the theological question cannot be escaped as soon as certain limits are reached, and today that is largely the case. It is the question about the unity in the depth, about the single meaningfulness within the superficial manifold of meaning and often contradiction of meaning in the fullness of appearance (1969:470).

Because the manifold of meaning belongs to the superficial, and because science cannot be contented with limitation to the superficial and thereby, with the absolutizing of the superficial (1969:471), a 'new beginning of phenomenological thought' comes into being (1969:470):

The thought which became effective in phenomenological thought and everywhere leads to theological questions is characterized by a double tendency: on the one hand, it seeks, with new courage, to enlighten the dark depths of being; but, on the other hand, it does this in decisive adherence to the bright surface of things, which is for us the given place for all research — a research which, since the 19th Century, even in the so-called *Geisteswissenschaften* can never fully disregard the empirical. As the spirit of our time inexorably dictates, perception of the depth of being, as it announces itself in the most different places, must be projected on that screen which is found on the ground of the superficially given' (1969:471).

In the depths is unity. The many and the individual belong to the surface of the real. What does that mean theologically? It means, at first, an understanding of the revelation that knows no bounds:

One must think the concept of revelation as realistically and as universally as possible — both at the same time. All is revelation, and God reveals himself in all (1969:469f.).

As vision of the essence of the one and as turning to the one, the unity in the depths, phenomenology not only partly overlaps with natural theology, it often completely overlaps natural theology (1969:477). Exactly seen, in its turn to the one, all of the four mentioned *Deutungswissenschaften* become congruent. Theology becomes science of religion, psychology of religion and philosophy of religion and vice versa:

> We can exchange the names, if that is called for . . . . As special, traditional disciplines they are thoroughly different from one another; however, insofar as their object forces them to a complex, synoptic vision, in this dimension they all tend to congruence (1970a:124).

The perception of the one becomes, the more closely it comes to the one, all the more clearly one itself. History of religion is, at once in its whole breadth, history of revelation. In it, God has subjected himself to 'a process of becoming': 'History of religion, to be perceived as the history of the perception of God, is at the same time to be grasped as process of theogony' (1970a:184, cf. 21).

5. Synopsis as Model

'Today, the religious can also only be conceived as unity' (1975:10). This corresponds to the understanding, sketched above, of the real and to the interest of a world experienced ever more as unity (1975: 10f.). But *how* can the religious be conceived as unity? *How* does synoptic science of religion or synoptic theology (or however one wishes to designate this research) find the way to the one and the whole of religion?

> . . . in the wholeness lies the unity. But this unity is at first concealed. It is concealed behind a great abundance of phenomena which are so strewn in this wide world of the religious wholeness that they often enough appear to us to be non-unifiable. Nevertheless, science of religion has its point of departure in the fact that its object of research is a unity. If it did not do so, it would have to give up its name. That encourages us to make an attempt which aims at projecting a model — a model which promises an orientation in this confusing fullness of individual appearances and which can be helpful in the search for unity. We do not need to point out that such an attempt is a risk. But we wish . . . to do no more than project a model to which other models may

be opposed or which other models may supplement. This model should serve us in the search for a new dimension. This dimension is the one in which the common middle of all religion would have to be perceptible, if it is at all: the religion in the religions (1975:11).

Synoptic research, therefore, seeks to come nearer to the whole of religion by projecting a model. Ulrich Mann has previously presented two detailed models. In the one (1970a) he proceeds 'diachronically'; he develops a model of the phases of development of religion with special regard to the ancient orient and to the Mediterranean area, and in this way he arrives at the scheme of seven successive days. In the other (1975:cf. 8ff.) he tries to develop a model 'synchronistically'; he projects — including now Buddhism, Hinduism and Islam, and using the above-mentioned model of concentric circles (see above p. 72) from Friedrich Heiler — a new circular model which places us 'before four equal fundamental religious types' (1975:139).

> Thereby, to be sure, we have to take regard of the fact that every living religion is orientated somehow to all four goals and never simply to one, which would result in the death of religion. But, basically, the heart of every really living religion beats . . . in the middle of our wind rose, which I would like to designate as the 'centrum numinosum' (1973b:148 n.2).

The 'timeless-unhistorical' scheme of F. Heiler has, therewith, made a place for a model which also takes account of genetics, that is, psychogenesis (1973b:150; 1975:138ff.). Not accidentally, the circular image becomes the *Mandala*.[86]

6. Synopsis and Integral Science of Religion

As we now attempt to judge synopsis as task, method theory and model, we first concede that no judgment can be universally valid. Each judgment corresponds merely to the view and standpoint of the one who makes the judgment. Therewith, every judgment is indirectly also a judgment about the position and the view which the critic himself represents. And that means, in our case, it is a judgment about integral science of religion.

One can praise synoptic work for a great deal — for example, for the courage it shows in representing an unusual, strange and untimely insight, or for the wide horizon this work opens, or for its unavoidable call to conversation among neighboring sciences — a conversation which, when it is an open and genuine conversation, promises stimulation, criticism and perception.

One can deplore and reject synoptic work for just as much — for example, for the imprecision or, indeed short-sightedness in its judgment of many particulars,[87] for the pantheisizing metaphysics which underlies this work, for the far too uncritical use of the depth-psychology of C. G. Jung, for the pessimism in view of the present and future possibilities of the various sciences, for the tendency to speculation which becomes visible in the striving for a view of the whole and which identifies history of religion, history of revelation and psychogenesis, and for the schematism which is especially expressed in the diachronic model.[88]

With all this praise and criticism, the decisive judgment is only indicated. Ulrich Mann himself has referred to the only criterion which can lead to a judgment which does justice to the subject matter:

> In the case that the unity of religion may be asserted, it will always only be a result of synoptic work. With the little word 'only' we naturally do not mean that in synopsis the empirical enlightenment of facts in science of religion is judged of little value — on the contrary. Synoptic interpretation (*Deutung*) presupposes empirical research completely and fully, and it includes this research. It also never does violence to the facts in order to force a thesis. Therefore it can never bend or, indeed, arbitrarily reconstruct historical material as Sigmund Freud did, who today is so emphatically praised as a strictly empirical researcher. Freud was absurdly arbitrary in his most decisive conclusions in psychology of religion. Synoptic *Deutung* interprets the factically given, but it does not construct it. In this interpretation, whether or not it is just toward the most possibly complete state of the facts to be considered — this alone is the criterion for its success as judged from the empirical side (1975:37).

How is synoptic work to be judged when we measure it by its own measure? We can cite an (admittedly fairly crass) example of how the synopsis of theology and depth-psychology, and the identification of revelation-history and psychogenesis which corresponds to that synopsis do justice to a New Testament text:

I represent the position that all the parables of Jesus have to be understood at first as witnesses of his own inner experience. If that is so, then the Nazarene characterized himself in the image of the lost son, and he perceived and taught this experience as paradigmatic for human being generally. What is the essential thing in the image? It is that the one returning home, in distinction from the one who remained at home, first gives the father the possibility of becoming *father* in the deepest sense of the word, namely to *give birth to* the reconciliation of the opposites. Is not every person basically the reconciliation of the opposites of father and mother?

Yet to give birth, two are needed. . . . Where is the mother-pole of this spiritual birth?

It is a spiritual pole, self-evidently; and it lies *in the son!* The mother-element received the son as it worked *in him* as spiritual pole: as that trust, namely, that the return home without claim is in the meaning of the father — therefore, as that psychic attitude of the son which let him *repent. Teschuwa, metanoia* — we translate these concepts with *repentance.* And repentance and faith are one; therefore, we name the new attitude faith — in the widest, most inclusive sense of the word.

This faith makes the father father, and yet more: it is itself the conception and the mother in one.

We may go further. Faith is also the bride which is led by the son into the father's house. As the bridegroom, Jesus celebrates the royal marriage. Uppermost in the synoptic conversation, psychology of religion has now therewith priority. We may anticipate: Jesus, as the son who returns home, has realized just what we described as essential for the new theological thought of the image of God of our time. As person he has taken over the responsibility for God, he has practiced the care of God. He has made God God. (1973b:157f.).

With this 'interpretation' of the parable of the lost son, Mann wants to show that Jesus 'makes God a valid father' (1973b:157), that Jesus' father-image has a 'new, yet at the same time originally old, initial meaning'.[89] The interpreter does not have a difficult time showing this, for his interpretation is so obviously a reading of his own ideas into Jesus, his synopsis is so obviously an assimilation of theological and depth-psychological perspectives, that the religious datum — the text of the parable with its own statement and its reference — are not allowed to speak. The New Testament text becomes an experimental field for theories in depth-psychology. But why, in the synopsis, does such misinterpretation, misformation, even violation of religious data occur?

In its nature and goal, synopsis is primarily *overlapping synthesis*. Synopsis begins where specific research, the individual discipline, is finished with its theme, where specific research can only repeat itself instead of winning new perception. Here it attempts the conversation among the neighboring sciences. But what kind of conversation is it? It is, from the beginning, a matter of synthesis. Mann speaks of 'synthesis' before he takes up the concept of 'synopsis' (1962:46; 1965b:195). This conversation is not an open one with an end that is also open. Rather, all is directed toward congruence, unification, even coincidence (1970a:139). The synoptic conversation is to lead to a 'picture of the whole' (1970a:94f.), to a 'total perspective' (1971a:99; 1970a:192), to a 'synthetic' (1970a:22; 1965b:195) or 'synoptic' view (1965b:69). Synopsis is synthesis in interdisciplinary conversation.

Secondarily — in its execution — synopsis becomes integrating systematic. As every 'picture of the whole' that is sought and found in the overlapping of the individual, so also the 'synthetic view' cannot have its success without forcing the religious data to fit with each other, without their misinterpretation and schematization (cf. p. 58f.). *The overlapping is forced to become, in different places, an open transgression.* The synoptic view is forced to become an ordering into a schematic model.

In our view of the matter, integral science of religion stands in greatest opposition to this integrating systematic. Or, more precisely:

when integral science of religion degenerates into integrating systematic, it has lost its most essential task. Its task is to ask about the meaning of individual religious data. However, this understanding is not to be separated from corresponding description and comprehension. Integral science of religion does not begin where specific research is exhausted. It is also not an overlapping summary of individual specifically researching disciplines. On the contrary, exactly considered, integral and specific science of religion happen in every discipline in science of religion. The former is the direction towards the whole and the question about the meaning, the latter is the orientation to the individual, the description and comprehension of concrete religious data. With or without interdisciplinary conversation, integral and specific science of religion occur in every discipline in science of religion (see above p. 29).

The whole of religion toward which our integral reflection moves is, therefore, never a picture of the whole or a model, and it is certainly not a synthetic view into which the individual only has to be integrated. We encounter the whole, in an ever unchangeable way, in the sign and statement of every religious datum. It is never so that the whole intended by one sign or statement is identical with that intended by another sign or statement, nor can the whole intended by one be brought together into a system with the whole intended by another. Rather, it refers in unequal correspondence to these other signs or statements.

An overlapping synthesis, widening itself into an integrating system, is a possibility which certainly lies close to every integral reflection. But this possibility must ever anew be opposed in order that integral science of religion, whose interests Ulrich Mann represents in large parts of his works, does not unconsciously become integrating science of religion.

3. CRITICISM OF RELIGION AND SCIENCE OF RELIGION

Just as self-evident for science of religion as the accompaniment of theology on its right, is the accompaniment of criticism of religion

(*Religionskritik*) on its left. In a certain sense, these two stand diametrically opposed. In the one, believing thought, the reflection of
religious life is encountered; in the other, consciously unbelieving
thought is encountered, as far as a given form of religion is concerned. Here is a thought which, in order to unmask a given witness
and expression, seeks to expose the witness in its nothingness, limitation, danger or nonsense. If theology, in the elementary sense of
the word, is reflected realization (*reflektierte Verwirklichung*), so
is criticism of religion the attempt to see this realization as abandonment to the unreal. In all that, however, just as with theology, one
cannot speak of only *one* form of criticism of religion. Correspon-
dingly manifold is also the relation of science of religion to criticism
of religion. At least three typical forms of criticism of religion are to
be distinguished.

1. Traditional-religious criticism of religion

Criticism of religious signs and expressions was and is an essential
aspect of the traditional religions. Prophecy is directed against the
tempel-cult; the insight of the *jnanin* is directed against exclusive
sacrifice-piety; the redeemed and enlightened one unmasks the futili-
ty of other ways of salvation The one bound directly with God unmasks the representatives of religious institutions; convinced belief
in one God opposes polytheism; the mystic knows the worthlessness
of mechanical piety; the attempt to be obedient to revelation becomes radical criticism of so-called religion. In one of its essential
aspects, religious history is ever again criticism of religion. Therefore, in the most original and most elementary sense, 'criticism of
religion' has the sense of the genetive subjective as well as the geni-
tive objective (religious criticism of religion). As an essential aspect
of religious reality, criticism of religion is also an essential object
of integral science of religion. Here is also true what was said about
theology: integral science of religion has criticism of religion as an
object of research, and it has this criticism only secondarily as a chal-
lenging parallel.

2. Secular-religious criticism of religion

Both modern individual religiosity and secular-religious mass movements often distance themselves very critically from all traditional,
explicit religions. Often, radical criticism of all explicit so-called
religions is nearly the most obvious characteristic of these new
worldly forms of religiosity. Individual religiosity is profiled in its
contradiction of religious convention. Inner-wordly realization explains itself in its protest against all search for and all dreaming-
oneself-into a world beyond. Why does traditional religion lose itself in the unreal beyond? Because radical reality is only to be encountered in the real world this side of such a beyond. The rejection
of traditional religion arises from a subjectively better, secular-
religious conviction. Or, in the words of Jewgenij Winokurow:

> History of religion is an arsenal
> of gigantic and empty fabrications,
> altogether a spun web
> where flimsy threads of thought run along together!
> What affairs and prognoses are not to be found there,
> What billows of smoke are not puffed out!
> Here there is a Zebaoth and Lucifer the evil one,
> golden Baal and bad shamans.
> The priests lament wet with sweat
> and witness to chimeras to the end.
> The bees, however, with instinct and good sense
> of direction, reach, at first attempt, and infallibly,
> their goal. (F. P. Ingold and I. Rakusa, 1972:20)

'History of religion' in these lines very clearly means a jumble of
traditional religious institutions and ideas. But why is traditional
religious realization an absurd loss of self to what is unreal, an abandonment of self to 'empty fabrications', 'spun webs', 'flimsy threads
of thought', 'chimeras'? The poet of this verse gives these lines the
title 'Nature'. In the sense of this title the author, in the last lines,
likens traditional-religious loss of self to the instinct of bees. It
reaches its 'goal' at 'first attempt, infallibly'. Nature finds the reality
it seeks. Realization is possible, also for men, but not in traditional

religiosity. But where then? The poem leaves the question open. The example of the bee only indicates that reliable, perhaps even infallible realization is possible. Other verses of this poet refer to science as a reliable alternative to irrational religion (F. P. Ingold and I. Rakusa, 1972:20).

In a way similar to pseudo-scientific theology, secular-religious criticism of religion often shows a tendency to ideology, to propaganda and to speculation. We have called speculation the attempt to make scientific statements about the reality of religion. Just such speculation is risked by secular-religious criticism of religion when it states what the reality of religion is — for example, when it says that the reality of religion is nothing more than pure fantasy. Therewith, secular-religious criticism of religion places itself in clear opposition to integral science of religion. Science of religion is never able to state what the reality of religion is; rather, it only attempts to understand what religion witnesses to, experiences, confesses, has presentiment of, seeks and makes present. The statement that history of religion is 'an arsenal of gigantic and empty fabrications' is itself an expression of secular-religious, probably scientistic conviction, but it is not a judgment of science of religion.

3. The criticism of religion by science of religion

In its premises and methods, integral science of religion implies already a certain criticism of all religion, of explicit and implicit religion, as it accepts data as such and describes, comprehends and understands religious reality. It would often correspond much better to religious and secular-religious conviction, if one's personal witness were not taken to be only one religious sign beside others, but as truth beside error — as what is incomparable beside what is hardly worthy of consideration, and perhaps as what is not even religious but scientific or revealed beside the degradation of multifarious religion. Integral science of religion criticizes religious and secular-religious experience neither in their value nor in their lack of value and not at all with reference to the scientist's own experience of radical reality. But it does criticize religious experience in its monomania, in its conviction of being not religious or secular-religious experience but something wholly other than and totally opposite mere religion or secular religion. Integral science of religion need not loudly and shrilly denounce this monomania. It is not called to struggle against the monomania of traditional religions or secular religions. It takes note of such claims to special status as an aspect of religious reality and attempts to understand them. But it does not acknowledge this claim where monomania would force the science to give itself up and no longer be integral science of religion. In this fashion, integral science of religion researches both the religious witness which lifts itself above all that is religious and the secular-religious conviction which contrasts itself as scientific perception with all that is religious. Wherever human life has not only to do with what is real but is referred to reality, there science of religion — in spite of the frequency of monomania — recognizes its task. It is not the task of this science to change religious and secular-religious experience, to drive out the monomania which obstructs an integral research of religious reality. The science is not called to be the prophet or reformer of contemporary religious history. However, integral science of religion cannot allow its task to be limited or, indeed, prohibited by religious or secular-religious claims. *Integral science of religion is criticism of religion just as it recognizes religious reality as religious reality.*

Notes

NOTES TO 'INTRODUCTION'

1. In 1954, K. Goldammer (p.231) wrote that 'a serious effort at method-criticism and -betterment rules in the old schools of science of religion in Germany and in all the world'. If one had that impression in 1954, one has it much more strongly today. The literature on methodology of science of religion encompasses innumerable titles. J. Waardenburg has published an extensive bibliography of this literature, excluding only the most recent, in *Classical Approaches to the Study of Religion*, Vol. 2: *Bibliography* (The Hague-Paris, 1974). Shorter bibliographic listings have been published by C. H. Ratschow, 'Methodik der Religionswissenschaft', *Enzyklopädie der geisteswissenschaftlichen Arbeitsmethoden*, 9th Instalment (München-Vienna, 1973a), pp. 397-400, and in G. Lanczkowski (ed.), *Selbstverständnis und Wesen der Religionswissenschaft* (Darmstadt, 1974), pp. 395-399. On the history of science of religion see: P. Meinhold, 'Entwicklung der Religionswissenschaft im Mittelalter und zur Reformationszeit', in: *Theologie und Religionswissenschaft*, ed. by U. Mann (Darmstadt, 1973a), pp. 357-380; P. Meinhold, 'Entwicklung der Religionswissenschaft in der Neuzeit und in Gegenwart', in: *Theologie und Religionswissenschaft*, pp. 381-412; K. Goldammer, *Religionen, Religion und christliche Offenbarung. Ein Forschungsbericht zur Religionswissenschaft* (Stuttgart, 1965). For the most recent state of research see: 'The History of Religion: An International Survey', special issue of *Religion, Journal of Religion and Religions*, on the occasion of the 13th Congress of the International Association for the History of Religions (IAHR) August 1975. The following works on methodology emphasize its importance for contemporary science of religion: M. Eliade and J. M. Kitagawa, eds. *The History of Religions. Essays in Methodology* (Chicago, 1959; German Salzburg 1963) J. Waardenburg, *Classical Approaches to the Study of Religion*, Vol 1: *Introduction and Anthology* (The Hague-Paris, 1973); G. Lanczkowski, ed. *Selbstverständnis und Wesen der Religionswissenschaft* (Darmstadt, 1974). No less characteristic of the great interest in methodology today is the space and time the IAHR devoted to methodology in its meetings: the study conference, held in 1973 at Turku, on the theme 'Method in Science of Religion', the papers of this congress are published by Lauri Honko, ed. in The Hague-Paris-New York, Mouton Publishers ('Religion and Reason', Vol. 13), 1977; at the 13th Congress of the IAHR in 1975, one section occupied itself exclusively with methodological questions. H. R. Schlette, has said that science of religion is at its end, if it does not reflect

on its methods an intentions far more critically ('Ist die Religionswissenschaft am Ende?' *ZM* 54 [1970], p. 199), In view of that statement, past and present intensive occupation with methodological questions in science of religion justifies the hope that within the end already a new beginning is being born.

2. Cf. also N. Micklem (1948:11f.):
    The scientific or comparative study of religions is made the more formidable by the recent accumulation of an immense mass of information regarding the religious ideas, rites and habits prevalent today and in the past. Such collections may be found, for instance in Hastings' *Encyclopedia of Religion and Ethics* or the volumes of Frazer's *Golden Bough*, suggest that most of what we call religion is a confused jumble of ideas and practices almost infinitely various, almost equally irrational, and often repellent and obscene. Most of the observable religion of 'savages' is, indeed the pitiful and arbitrary crossed occasionally by the sublime; even the developed religions, such as Christianity, Judaism, Hinduism, Buddhism and Islam, empirically regarded, offer in each case a congeries of diverse and often contradictory beliefs and practices.

NOTES TO 'CHAPTER I: THE TASK'

1. A truly delightful example of theological sugared exoticism is to be found at the very beginnings of modern science of religion: 'Abraham Rogers *Offne Thür zu dem verborgenen Heydenthum: Oder/Warhaftige Vorweisung dess Lebens/und der Sitten/samt der Religion/und dem Gottesdienst der Bramines, auf der Cust Chormandel, und denen herumliegenden Ländern: Mit kurzen Anmerkungen/Aus dem Niederländischen übersetzt Samt Christolph Arnolds Auserlessenen Zugaben/Von den Asiatischen/Afrikanischen/und Americanischen Religions-sachen/so in XL Capitel verfasst. Alles mit einem nothwendigen Register.* Nürnberg/ In Verlegung/ Johann Andreas Endters/ und Wolffgang dess Jüng.Seel. Erben M.DC.LXIII.'

2. Traditional religion is, in the first place, what traditionally has been called religion, what traditionally has been addressed as religion or has so designated itself. Traditional religion is, therefore, in this way distinguished from secular religion, which only in modern times has been recognized and understood as such. See below, Chapter 2.2.

3. Meinhold refers to the fact that rationalistic understanding of religion, for example, is hardly able to enter into 'transcendental and transsubjective moments in religion' (1973:382f.).

4. K. Goldammer mentions two processes which led 'to the broadening of the concept of religion' and, therewith, to modern science of religion: 'the criticism and disintegrating and transforming work of man on his own traditional religion, and increasing acquaintance with foreign, wholly different religion, which presents itself in overpowering diversity.' That need be supplemented only with the statement that these two processes influenced one another.

5. G. Rozenkranz (1951) understands the concept of Religionskunde differ-

ently. For him it is, in the first place, 'theological interpretation', which is to say evangelical theology of religion. Cf. also G. Rosenkranz (1955:225-253), where Religionskunde unites a science of religion with a theological task.

6. In view of what is said below in Chapter 5, we refer here to another possible understanding of philosophy of religion — an understanding which, in our opinion, has to do with an essential aspect of work in science of religion. Philosophy of religion is that part of an integral science of religion which is attentive to theology and criticism of religion as essential aspects of religious reality. Because these aspects of religious reality require a special measure of reflection and because 'philosophy of religion' in itself shows a special measure of reflection, we understand philosophy of religion to be the science of religion of theology and of criticism of religion. That is, it is the science of religion which has to do with those aspects of religious reality which, as task and as self-evident parallels, challenge science of religion in a very special way.

7. In the following, all that is referred to the whole or orientated to the whole is called 'integral'. Therefore, we can speak of integral effort, integral reflection and consideration (*Besinnung*), and integral questionability as that effort, reflection and questioning in science of religion which aims not at individual religious data but at the whole of religion. Integral is therefore contrasted with specific, which is orientated only to the individual religious datum or data.

8. Cf. the list of different ways one can arrive at a definition of the essence of religion in S. Holm (1960:173ff.).

NOTES TO 'CHAPTER II: THE PREMISES'

1. C. H. Ratschow emphasizes this when he speaks of the twofold reflection of God in man and in the cult or word. Instead of three dimensions of religion, he speaks of three levels in which it can be asked: 1. can we inquire about myths, rites and other religious material in order, through comparison, to lift out the essential of a religious world; 2. in all materials, can we ask about the person whose world- and self-understanding expresses itself in them . . . ; 3. can one, from the religious saga and action, attempt to draw a conclusion about the divinity. Ultimately, the epiphany of the divinity stands behind all language and action of a religious kind. To grasp the peculiarity of these divinities can, therefore, only be the ultimate meaning of the research of science of religion. (Ratschow, 1973a:361).

But how can we, in science of religion, ask about God, if God can never be the object of the research of science of religion? In the same article (p. 353), Ratschow writes,

'If one wishes to know what is essential in a religion, then one must ask about its Gods. These remain closed to science of religion, however, even if we do have to ask about them. That is the central dilemma (*Aporie*) of all science of religion.'

Men encounter God in their being referred to him, and this takes place only

in myth, rite, dogmas prayer, amulet, etc. – all of which refer to the referal
of man to God (p. 353):
Science of religion, therefore, sees the sanctum of the religions, God, twice
reflected: first in the person, and second in his cult or word or religion.
In my opinion, Ratschow has, in principle, presented the 'central dilemma
of all science of religion'. We would disagree with his concept of the three
levels in a threefold regard. (1) The whence, ground and middle of all religious reality is not everywhere and exclusively God or the Gods. G.
Stephenson has called this 'not allowed concretizing (*Konkretisierung*)':
(1975:201). (2) We would not simply identify the second level, which reflects itself in the first, with man, the *homo religiosus*. Also the first level,
the dimension of the data themselves, belongs to human reality. Therefore,
we call the second dimension religious experience, that is, the feeling,
thinking, willing that expresses itself in the religious datum. (3) May we,
simply through comparison on the first level, 'lift out the essential of a
religious world'? Does this correspond to the statements of Ratschow
about the necessity of understanding? Is Ratschow's in principle so convincing method weakened and shaken by an over-estimation of comparison?
on the subject, see G. Stephenson, p. 202.

2. U. Tworuschka (1974:243). The designation itself of the subject matter in
   question causes difficulty. U. Tworuschka speaks also of 'outer- and non-
   religious transport of religious content' (*ibid.*, 234); K. Goldammer (1969:
   126) speaks of 'non-religion': J. Waardenburg (1972:332) speaks of 'non-
   religion and half-religion'; G. Stephenson (1976:193, 213) speaks of 'para-
   religious phenomena'; K. Beth speaks, 'with more or less confidence', of
   'religionoid formations' (*Bildungen*), and he understands by that the most
   different currents in the border area of what, in the strictest sense of the
   word, can still be addressed as religion ('Religion: IV A. Wesen der Religion',
   RGG[2] IV, 1878).

3. It no longer seems meaningful to me to make the radical distinction between 'modern' and 'new' science of religion which I tried to make in *Interessant und Heilig* (Schmid, 1971:9-20). Even if modern science of religion
   (the science of religion of the modern period) is everything but a closed,
   unchangeable whole, it would be an over-estimation of the obvious changes
   in situation, question and methods of this science in the last decades, if one
   were to separate modern science of religion from a contemporary 'post-
   modern' science of religion. Contemporary science of religion also stands in
   a very obvious tradition and is, therewith, also modern science of religion.

4. Cf. the Introduction to W. Gruehn (1960:7) where Gruehn remarks about
   the unsure self-understanding of the religions and precision and reliability
   of empirical science. On the understanding of psychology of religion as
   empirical science, cf. W. Keilbach (1962:13-30); W. Keilbach (1964: 15-
   42).

5. P. van Buren (1966), Van Buren wishes to find and finds only what corresponds to his axioms.

6. As an example, we can use E. Troeltsch's relation to positivistic theory of
   religion and his alternative. In view of the positivistic theory, Troeltsch

writes: 'The idea of religion must have a freer range. In that theory, one knows from the beginning what religion is.' (1906:463). Over-against the positivistic theory, Troeltsch acknowledges 'the possibility of qualitatively peculiar spiritual dispositions and life-contents'. (*Ibid.* 463f.) This view of the matter leads Troeltsch to the following consequences.

One does not simply know what it (religion) is. We have first to win a perception of what it really is from the analysis of it. And what it is may, first, only be perceived out of itself, out of the research and comparison of its own statements about itself, out of the relation it gives itself to other elements of culture which these elements give it. Then one is not, from the beginning, bound to know what religion cannot be, especially that it cannot be what it wants to be. Analysis is not obligated to a completed basic view of things — which already regulates the whole idea on the basis of completed basic views; but it can take from the object itself the object's inner essence or, in any case, this essence as the object knows it. It is only the second question about how this own essence of the object relates itself to other reality; whether it, in such relations, is able to assert itself at all or not, which modifications it suffers or must suffer in these regulations. (*Ibid.*:464)

In Troeltsch's argument, we see an exemplary attempt to break up an 'integrating' view in favor of a broader view which is adequate to its object.

7. Cf. G. Widengren, 1974a:87-113; W. Baetke, 1974:138f.; E. O. James, 1954: 93ff.; U. Bianchi, 1964:5-8. For an example of a relatively early criticism of the search for origin, see M. Rade:2198.

8. G. van der Leeuw refers to the limits of the idea of development in both natural and spiritual history (*Geistesgeschichte*) for the history of religions: G. van der Leeuw:1875-1877.

9. F. Max Müller, 1878:14, 21. On the problem of determining essence, see also M. Rade: 2199:

It is impossible simply to read a concept of the essence of religion out of the many-sidedness of the religions. In such an attempt, one falls ever again to the mistake of suppressing that religion which offers the least for the formation of such a concept, for the one that has gaps, the one that has remained behind, the one that has degenerated has to fit into the concept. Away with this Procrustean bed!

For a more detailed discussion of the problem of determining an essence of religion, see K. Beth, 1878:1877-1888.

10. On the last two relations and the position of recent research, compare Joachim Matthes, 1967/1969.

11. E. Durkheim, 1968:65f., n. 1, also quoted in J. Waardenburg, 1973c: p. 323, n. 18. We would have, of course, to ask whether the later definition was not too formal, too much like a cliché (E. Durkheim, 1968:65):

A religion is a unified system of beliefs and practices relative to sacred things, that is to say, things set apart and forbidden — beliefs and practises which unite into one single moral community called a Church, all those who adhere to them.

(Also quoted by J. Waardenburg, 1973c:316.) The use of the designation

'Church' for religious community generally and the reference to an 'absolute' (E. Durkheim, 1968:53) opposition of holy and profane reminds one very strongly of a schematic construction.

12. For a more detailed discussion of this, see below, pp. 89ff.

13. Heiler, 1961:18-21. Also J. Wach (1923:33-55) uses the image of the 'center' as illustration; recently reprinted in G. Lanczkowski, ed., 1974:30-56.

NOTES TO 'CHAPTER III: THE METHODS'

1. E. Hardy (1898) as quoted in: G. Lanczkowski, ed. (1974:7). No less impressively does W. Keilbach (1964:19) insist on a necessary manifold of methods in psychology of religion: 'because of the manifold forms and reality (*Wirklichkeitsgeladenheit*) of the experience under discussion, basically only a plurality of methods working together can lead to the goal. 'Within specific limits, every method has its use' (*Ibid.*:28).

2. Cf. E. Hirschmann (1940). G. Widengren (1974b:257-271); C. J. Bleeker (1974:225-242); K. Rudolph (1971:241-250); R. Pettazzoni (1954:215-219). On the whole problem of phenomenology and religion, see H. Duméry (1957:135-177); see also the corresponding discussions by J. Daniélou, SJ (1963:147-174); J. D. J. Waardenburg (1972:315-335); J. D. J. Waardenburg (1973b:304-325); J. D. J. Waardenburg (1973a:109-136). On the use of phenomenological method in theology, see K. Schwarzwäller (1966).

3. That is, the exclusion of the subjective, the theoretical, the tradition, disregard for existence and for all that is non-essential in the object: I. M. Bochenski (1971:23f.).

4. As an example, we remind the reader of the debate about the religious apriori. (Kurt Leese gives a survey of the debate, 1954:147-181). Even if different interests were combined in this postulate of the religious apriori, one essential aspect was the fact that religion cannot be derived from something else: 'Religion is itself present at its commencement' (*Religion fängt mit sich selber an*), said Rudolph Otto (1923:160). 'Unableitbarkeit' and Apriorität' may not be separated from one another (Otto, 1963:160).

The numinous is of the latter kind. It issues from the deepest foundation of cognitive apprehension that the soul possesses, and, though it of course comes into being in and amid the sensory data and empirical material of the natural world and cannot anticipate or dispense with those, yet it does not arise *out of* them, but only *by their means.* (Otto, 1923:117).

The holy shows itself to be a priori category over-against all other moments of human reality:

We conclude, then, that not only the rational but also the non-rational elements of the complex category of 'holiness' are *a priori* elements and each in the same degree. Religion is not in vassalage either to morality or teleology, '*ethos*' or '*telos*', and it does not draw its life from postulates; and its non-rational content has, no less than its rational, its own independent roots in the hidden depths of the spirit itself. (Otto, 1923:140).

From this position, Otto rejects all explanations of religion which derive religion from something other than itself:

The justification of the 'evolutionist' theory of to-day stands or falls with its claim to 'explain' the phenomenon of religion. That is in truth the real task of the psychology of religion. But in order to explain we must have the data from which an explanation may be forthcoming; out of nothing, nothing can be explained. Nature can only be explained by an investigation into the ultimate fundamental forces of nature and their laws: it is meaningless to propose to go further and explain these laws themselves, for in terms of what are they to be explained? But in the domain of spirit the corresponding principle from which an explanation is derived is just the spirit itself, the reasonable spirit of man, with its predispositions, capacities, and its own inherent laws. This has to be presupposed: it cannot itself be explained. None can say how mind or spirit 'is made'. (Otto, 1923:118)

Therefore, religion may only be explained on the basis of the religious apriori. With this view, Otto can, *mutatis mutandis*, refer to Schleiermacher's *On Religion* (London, 1893:124):

Man is born with the religious capacity as with every other. If only his sense for the profoundest depths of his own nature is not crushed out, if only all fellowship between himself and the Primal Source is not quite shut off, religion would, after its own fashion, infallibly be developed.

5. What Jane R. Martin calls 'external understanding' would, in our conception, correspond to comprehension (*Begreifen*). What we here name 'understanding' is near her concept of 'internal understanding' (1969:56f.).

6. Not accidentally, G. van der Leeuw names '. . . such experience, it is true, being more an art than a science' (1963:675). Th.P. van Baaren thinks that van der Leeuw's concept of understanding is 'too subjective to be used as a valid argument in scientific research'. (1973:49).

7. When, in our diagram, the reality of religion appears as something over-against (*als Gegenüber zum*) religious life, this corresponds to some but not all forms of religous reality. It corresponds especially to the emphatically personal forms; it especially does not correspond to the mystical forms of religious reality. In mysticism, the reality of religion is experienced less as something over-against than as the depth of one's own self and awareness. In a diagram of mystical forms, datum, life and the reality of religion would have to be related to one another as follows.

religious datum

religious life

reality of religion

This reference to the relation between religious life and the reality of religion in mysticism shows that every diagrammatic scheme, including this one, soon arrives at a limit where, without essential modification, it is no longer correct. But this does not hinder us from referring to the diagram, for even if the 'how' of the relation of datum, life and the reality of religion never fit into a diagram, a diagram can emphatically refer to the 'that' of their relation to one another.

8. J. Waardenburg, 1972:315-335; 1973b:304-325; 1973a:109-136). Waardenburg refers to the fact that already J. Wach consciously used the concept of intention (J. Waardenburg, 1972:321). We can add to that, that also G. Mensching has 'understanding science of religion' ask 'about what is meant in all religious phenomena' and, hence, about their 'intention' (1959:13).

9. Cf. also the remarks of G. Mensching (1959:13):
   Modern science of religion asks about *what is meant* (*nach dem Gemeinten*) in all forms of religious appearance. If one does not ask this question, as happened in earlier research, then one falls easily in danger of ascertaining basic differences where differences exist only in the phenomenal and not in the religious intention.

10. An attempt to move from the merely similar to what corresponds is also to be found in the distinction between the analogous and the homologous. R. Otto took over this distinciton from the 'developmental history of living things' (1917:150). H. Frick took up the distinction: analogy designates the same function with non-identical origin (*Herkunft*), homology designates identical origin (1928:16) G. Mensching works with this Distinction (1938:12, 21ff.). Because the distinction originates in morphology, it is certainly only of limited use with regard to religious phenomena. Nevertheless, as Mensching's example shows, it contributes to the prevention of hasty identification or hastily drawn parallel in cases of outer similarity, and it contributes to science of religion's asking 'about what is religiously meant' (1938:22).

11. Therewith, the category in science of religion is given a new function. It is no longer a *result* of perception in science of religion, but a *chance* for this perception. It is no longer a goal or a result, but an aspect of being under way. It is no longer *similarity as ascertainment*, but *correspondence as a help to understanding*.

NOTES TO 'CHAPTER IV: THE VERIFICATION'

1. Fundamentally, it is methodology which asks about the conditions of perception in science of religion. In fact, however, every concrete research in science of religion does so. The first task, methodology, does not release one from the second, because concrete research always proceeds under ever new conditions.

2. On the difficulties that one encounters in the understanding of the *Avesta* in general and of the *Gathas* in particular, cf. G. Lanczkowski (1956:77f.):
   One can say that the Avesta is the most difficult of all religious documents to understand, that every attempt at translation to a high degree implies interpretation, that nowhere as here the word '*traduttore-traditore*' has its own validity. It is certainly only a small exaggeration when one asserts that in many places in the *Avesta* we have not progressed beyond mere

spelling and that many translations are not essentially more understandable than the original text.

Cf. also A. Meillet (1925:33):

L'Avesta n'est ni un livre, ni un recueil de livres ou de pièces complètes. C'est une suite de fragments, à vri dire, un champ de ruines.

Cf. also F. Altheim (1944/1949:257): 'Just because of the understanding of their language, the *Gathas* belong to the most inaccessible works of antique literature.'

3. A. Meillet (1925:21-32); W. B. Henning, 1970:150-156); F. Altheim (1970: 170); W. Hinz (1961:23ff).

4. M. Boyce (1975:189). Cf. also W. Hinz, (1961:22ff.); Chr. Bartholomae (1970:7ff.); H. H. Schaeder (1970:102); W. B. Henning (1970:157ff).

5. On M. Molé, who also sees this aspect of the tradition in doubt (cf. 1970: 312f., 314-319, 320-335).

6. In Yasna 33,6, Zarathustra designates himself as zaotar. On the informative reference to the reward he has as priest in Yasna 44,18 and 19, and in 46, 19, cf. Hermann Lommel, (1970a:199-207).

7. Yasna 46, 1-2.

8. Yasna 51,12.

9. On the predecessors and the family names, cf. Yasna 46,13, 51,12, 53,1, 46,15. On the relatives and followers, cf. 53,2f., 28,7, 46,14, 51,16, 28,8, 46,16, 51,17, 46,17, 49,9, 51,18f., 46,12. On the opponents, cf. 49,1f., possibly 32,12ff., 51,12.

10. In my opinion, the works of H. Humbach, which have been innovating in many regards (above all H. Humbach, 1959), see the *Gathas* too exclusively from this perspective.

11. Only the second instance of this word in Y 32:9, shortly after the reference to Yima, speaks for this supposition. H. Humbach (1959/II:61).

12. Cf. the difficult $gr\bar{\vartheta}hma$ in strophes 12-14.

13. Cf. the contested interpretation of 10c: H. Lommel (1970b:360-376); H. H. Schaeder (1970:103f.); H. Humbach (1959/I:98).

14. vīvaŋhušō, Chr. Bartholomae (1961:1451).

15. aēnah as substantive or adjective; cf. Chr. Bartholomae (1961:21f.); the relation to strophe 7 suggests a partitive genetive.

16. $y\bar{\vartheta}$ is most probably referred to Yima.

17. mašyāng cixšnušō.

18. vīciϑōi, Lok.sg.

19. 3 .sg.aor.pass.

20. vīciϑōi in 8c; cf. the use of this concept in *Yasna* 46.18; H. Humbach (1957: 365); W. Hinz (1961:215).

21. Chr. Bartholomae (1961:58); H. Reichelt (1909:186); F. C. Andreas and J. Wackernagel (1913:318).

22. Analogous to sārəmnō Y 32,2. Cf. also A. V. W. Jackson (1968:188 §680, 5).

23. With reference to German words ('Schwur', 'Schwäre'), Humbach (1959/II: 35); Humbach (1957:157, 366f.).

24. Cf. P. Thieme (1970:401f.); M. Boyce (1975:23,196); Dastur F. A. Bode and P. Nanavutty (1952:59).
25. We have not mentioned translations which deviate essentially from the philological state of the matter (*Befund*) mentioned above, for example: Ces pécheurs avaient pourtant entendu Jima, fils de Vivahvant, qui enseigna aux hommes à nous donner une part de la viande qu'ils mangent.' Darmsteter, as quoted by A. Christensen (1934:11).
26. *Vana Parva* 141; A. Christensen (1934:6ff).
27. RV 1,83,5; *Menoki i Xrat* 8,27; A. Christensen (1934:6,24).
28. *Sabha Parva* 8; A. Christensen (1934:9).
29. Y 9,3-5 in the translation of W. Hinz (1961:32).
30. *Venidad* 2,20-43; A. Christensen (1934:16ff.). On the interpretation of the *vara*: G. Widengren (1965:53); on the whole of tradition: O. Paul (1938: 176-203).
31. Yt. 5,25, Yt. 9,8; A. Christensen (1934:8, 12).
32. Yt. 15,15, Yt. 17,28; A. Christensen (1934:13).
33. *Pahlavi Rivayat*; A. Christensen (1934:28f).
34. On the significance of animals in the old Iranian feast: G. Widengren (1965:49).
35. Yt. 19,46; Bundahisn 31,5; A. Christensen (1934:14, 22).
36. Yt. 19,33ff.; A. Christensen (1934:13f).
37. *Datastan i Denik* 39,16; A. Christensen (1934:23).
38. Cf. A. Christensen (1934:50):
    La chute est la conséquence logique de l'idée de l'âge d'or. Si l'âge d'or a pris fin, sin l'immortalité a cessé d'exister sur la terre . . . . l'explication qui de présente d'elle même à la réflection est celle-ci, que la race de l'âge d'or et en premier lieu le chef de cette race ont détruit leur bonheur par leurs péchés.
39. A. Christensen (1934:11):
    Parmi ces devs il y avait un pécheur méchant, à savoir Jim, fils de Vivanghan, le fameux, qui enseigna aux hommes ainsi: 'Mangez par morceaux la chair des êtres de notre espéce'.
40. Yt. 13,130.
41. *Pahlavi Rivayat*; A. Christensen (1934:29). That this Rivayat works over very old traditions is demonstrated by the incest motif, which is to be connected with the birth of the animals as the progeny of Yima (or of his sister).
42. Y 9,4; as quoted by K. F. Geldner (1926:25).
43. = *vara*; *Venidād* 2, 25ff.; A. Christensen (1934:17f.).
44. Yt. 5,25; Yt. 9,8; A. Christensen (1934:12).
45. W. Hinz (1961:175), chooses 'sacrificial share' (*Opferanteil*).
46. *Pahlavi Rivayat*; A. Christensen (1934:28f.).
47. This last part of our chapter on Y 32,8 will be shorter than the others because here great caution is required of understanding. The danger of an overinterpretation of such a short and dark reference is much too present. We shall discuss understanding in greater detail in the next two chapters, where we shall have to do with it in relation to other data.
48. On the connection between animal sacrifice and *Haoma*. cf. H. Lommel (1938:252ff.).

49. Yasna 29,1 (Humbach, 1959/II:8, 80). Cf. also Y 44,20, Y 49,5, Y 51,14.
50. Y 32,14.
51. When M. Boyce finds no opposition to blood sacrifice in Zarathustra, she orientates herself, in my opinion, too uncritically to later tradition (M. Boyce, 1975/I:214-216).
52. Cf. in addition to the Pahlavi translation of Y 32,8, which sees *Yima* as a teacher. A. Christensen (1934:11). If one considers the close connection between *Haoma* preparation and animal sacrifice, one also has to consider that Vivahvant, the father of *Yima*, was, according to *Yasna* 9,4, the first to prepare the *Haoma*.
53. Probably the opponents of Zarathustra found here no contradiction. The sacrifice of the bull serves the maintenance and furtherance of life, not its destruction.
54. Cf. Y 32,12c.
55. Cf. Y 43,15.
56. Ramanuja's division of the work, in which the first six chapters are dedicated to the perception of the own self as immortal and the next six chapters, to the perception of God, is valid only *grosso modo*. (R. C. Zaehner, 1969:243). Nevertheless, one should not mistake the fact that a new section is begun with chapter 7:1ff. of the work.
57. 6,46-47.
58. A. C. Bhaktivedanta Swami Prabhupada (1974:406). also in 'Sir Edwin Arnold's Translation of the Bhagavad Gita' (1952:123); T. R. Ananthараman (1961:55).
59. On the discussion of *jñāna* and *vijñāna*, cf. W. Douglas and P. Hill, (1928: 135 n.2).
60. On the question about the early *Sāṃkhya*, cf. H. v. Glasenapp (1958: 197ff.); E. Lamotte (1929:3ff.).
61. A short survey of different theories about the redaction of the work is given in *Radharkrishnan* (1949:14f.).
62. On the contested interpretation of the concept of the *jīva-bhūtā*, cf. Zaehner (1969:245f.).
63. Cf. Edgerton, 73, 183. Edgerton prefers the singular but he sees the plural as a possibility.
64. On the pre-history (*Vorgeschichte*) of this last comparison, see Zaehner, p. 247.
65. Zaehner (1969:247, 194); Hill (1928:167); Bjaktivedanta (1974:421); differently: Edgerton (1952/I:75); Radhakrishnan (1949:216); Robert Boxberger (1955:54); Leopold von Schroeder (1965:53). Arnold translates: 'the root undying', Edgerton (1952/II:123).
66. cf. also 9,18 and 10,39.
67. 'rasa' is more than taste. It also means liquidity, water, the essence of liquidity.
68. Cf. G. Tersteegen (1798/1799[2]: I, 1, 66f.; 128f.; I, 2, 432ff.; II, 3, 466; II, 4, 302ff; Addition to the 2nd ed., 27).
69. Gerhard Tersteegen (1845:462-464). Walter Nigg has published a text which differs from Gebauer's edition (1966:15-17). A complete critical edition of Tersteegen has, I am sad to say, never been published.

70. Tao Te Ching 14, 25, 34, 35, 37, 41; (1951:76ff., 98f., 106, 116ff., 130f., 155ff. On the early taoist literature and the historical-critical problems connected with it, cf. W. Eichhorn (1973:78-87, 104ff., 179f). On the later understanding of Tao, cf. Philip Rawson and Laszlo Legeza (n.d.).
71. Chuang Tzŭ XXII, 6; *The Texts of Taoism*, Part II, pp. 66f.; cf. Tao Te Ching (1951:152ff.); cf. also Dschuang Dsi (R. Wilhelm, (1976:230f.).
72. Udana VIII:1-4, in: Gustav Mensching, *Buddhistische Geisteswelt*, (n.d.: 213ff.).
73. Cf. M. Eliade (1964:9-34; 1954:438-490); P. Grimal (1967:12-27); K. Hoffman (1965); R. Pettazonni (1954b:24ff.).
74. Samyutta-Nikaya XLIII, 34, in G. Mensching (n.d.:104).
75. Udana III, 10, in G. Mensching (n.d.:60).

NOTES TO 'CHAPTER V: THE IDENTITY'

76. Cf. G. Rosenkranz (1964:11-36); P. Meinhold (1973b: 381-412); C. H. Ratschow (1973b:413-424). On the theme 'science of religion and theology' and 'theology of religion' cf. moreover: C. J. Bleeker (1954:142-143); Kees W. Bolle (1967b:43-53); G. Rosenkranz (1967); K. Goldammer (1967b'181-198); K. Goldammer (1969:105-135); E. Benz (1968:8-22); E. Fahlbusch (1969:73-86); P. Beyerhaus (1969:87-104); U. Mann (1971a).
77. At best, religious apologetic is the attempt to make one's own belief understandable to one outside this belief. Theology is more, namely the readiness to understand the other in understanding its own reality. Cf. above pp. 14.
78. S. Grossman has compiled a detailed 'Bibliographie Ulrich Mann', (1975: 263-271). Especially informative for our question about the synoptic method are, among Mann's larger works:
Das Christentum als absolute Religion (Darmstadt, 1971a). *Theogonische Tage. Die Entwicklungsphasen des Gottesbewusstseins in der altorientalischen und biblischen Religion* (Stuttgart, 1970a). *Einführung in die Religionsphilosophie* (Darmstadt, 1970b). *Einführung in die Religionspsychologie* (Darmstadt, 1973b). *Die Religion in den Religionen* (Stuttgart, 1975). I am indebted to Prof. W. Neidhardt, Basel, for the reference to significant works of Mann which pertain to my thesis.
79. In his publications, Mann writes on themes of the history of theology and the church as well as of *Geistesgeschichte* (Luther, Hamann, Hölderlin, byzantine image controversy, the Order of St. John, eastern churches, Paul Tillich, etc.), on methodological questions (philosophy of religion, psychology of religion, theology and neighboring sciences, hermeneutic), on the depth-psychology of C. G. Jung and his school, on themes in social and individual ethics (military service, ethos of mountain climbing, the Christian Democratic Union in Germany), on themes from cultural and religious history in the widest sense (Hellas, Egypt, ancient Iran, Elam, Sumer, Mesopotamia, Mitanni, Hatti, India, Tibet, Buddhism, prehistoric religion, etc.), and on different questions of systematic theology (dimensions, original revelation, relation of theology and church, essence of protestantism, theological anthropology, etc). For individual titles, see S. Grossmann (1975).

80. Accents or perspectives have shifted, for example in the understanding of non-Biblical revelation, in the judgment of secularization and in the understanding of Christianity as religion. On the *first*: the close connection of theology and proclamation (*Gottes Nein und Ja.* Hamburg, 1959:12-15) is later supplemented by an attempt clearly to separate and distinguish between theology and proclamation ('Hermeneutische Entsagung', 1965a: 34f.). Theology, now defined with K. Girgensohn as the 'scientific self-presentation of the Christian religion' (1970c:183; 1971b:254) and often elsewhere can still acknowledge only a minimal tie to the church (1970c: 182). It is not church science; the church is now only the 'sociological place of theology' (1971b:253).

   On the *second*: at first the accent lies clearly on the 'delimitation against natural theology' (1959:34-37); the reference to the creator and, therewith, to the meaning of all beings in general revelation has its ground in the cross of Jesus (1961:53). Later, Mann consciously goes beyond this position (1964:250 n. 3), projects a far more encompassing and detailed theology of religion (1964:259-261), and finally arrives at a point of view bringing together history of religion, history of perception of God, and the process of theogony (1970a:21f., 184).

   On the *third*: the agreeing reference to F. Gogarten's understanding of secularization (1961:54) yields later to bitter remarks 'on the yawning boredom, on the rootless and therefore nauseating flavorlessness of secular reality!' (1970a:174).

   On the *fourth*: while at first Christianity is not 'religion' — 'but "what is Christian" belongs in the field of the religious' — (1961:59), later Mann speaks almost self-evidently of Christianity as religion: 'No scientist of religion can and will remove Christianity from the circle of the religions' (1971a:2).

81. On the intensive discussion of Ulrich Mann with the work and the school of C. G. Jung (cf. 1965b:118-196; 1967:331-336; 1969:469-478; 1971c: 494; 1972:446f.; 1973c:446f.; 1974:599f.; 1973a:222-238; 1973b). On the theological position that is visible in the models and projections of Mann's more recent works, (cf. 1970a:15-199; 1971a: 1975:8-135).

82. Mann refers explicitly to these two aspects of the use of the word in his 'Glossar häufig verwendeter Grundbegriffe', (1970a:708).

83. With this prognosis or these about the end of theology, Mann refers to analogous discussions on the situation of physics by W. Heisenberg: (1973d: 134f.; 1976:19ff.).

84. At the same time, systematic theology is required to open itself to a faith which includes experience and, therewith, to the empirical:

   Through the awakening of an inclusive faith which is able to relate every experience of life to the religious, an activation and amplification of the religious soul-potential is attained which is very difficult in current belief, which is narrow and small. We find this judgment confirmed with every look into the exegetical and dogmatic literature of dialectical theology. That literature seems to have nothing more important to say than to warn nervously in a stereotyped way against psychologism, experience-piety and inward religion. Its result is in accordance with that. Christian faith thus becomes an 'empty space', a mere readiness for the Kerygma coming perpendicularly from above which happens only momentarily and can never be described or experienced or lived out. Accordingly, dogmatics becomes a series of purely abstract theorems which today no longer interests anyone. That is why all sorts of adventurous ersatz-projections are spread around, beginning with the 'death of God' theology and extending to the 'theology of revolution', only again to change surprisingly into sentimental ejaculations calling themselves 'post-theistic' theology — but all without real effort of the theological concept!   . . . Theology has to open itself decisively to the empirical. (1973b:152).

The tendency in Man is clear which leads to the diastase of systematic theology and science of religion back to the 'powerful influence of dialectic theology, which placed the concept and the subject matter of religion under the verdict of theology' (1973a:VII, cf. also 254ff.; 1971a:7ff.). W. Trillhaas has objected to that idea, in my opinion correctly:

The diastase of theology and science of religion is not at all an effect of the Barthian school alone. Already in this school among its students, it was a coarsening (*Vergröberung*). But the authority of the concept of religion was broken with the end of the 'religion of German idealism', and the Ritschlian school contributed its full measure of causes. The whole business is itself a problem of science of religion! (W. Trillhaas, 1974).

85. It depends on the insight of the specialists, for actually they are the source of new results of research in every scientific area. Above all and firstly, they would have to be won for the requirement of synoptic work. They would actually have to be the ones who perceive most clearly that a new epoch has begun in which science has to accomplish a two-fold task. First, and here one must remain unyielding, there must be solid special research of the traditional kind, which alone is able to produce new results. Second, science must go beyond this special research and burden the researcher with additional tasks — it is synoptic work beyond the limits. (1973d:138).

The remark that only special research and not synoptic work can bring new results stands in singular contradiction to the preceeding statement that new insights are opened only in synoptic work because the self-sufficient theological themes, for example in the historical disciplines of theology, are finished (1973d:137). Probably such contradictory statements are to be explained by the fact that here different things are said with the same concepts. On the one hand, the special research which wants to produce something new, works already synoptically, for example in the historical disciplines of theology, as Mann insists (1973d). On the other hand, he says that special research is the first task of theology, and that the second task, the synoptic, is clearly to be distinguished from it (1973d:138).

86. 1975:138, cf. 288ff.; C. G. Jung (1962:8-125) 'Geschichte und Psychologie eines natürlichen Symbols'.

87. e.g. the thoroughly unified view of prehistoric religion (1975:140; 1970a: 203ff.). The theory of original monotheism is taken over directly (1970a:

222f.). The discoveries in the dragon's den (*Drachenloch*) are interpreted, without discussion, as sacrifices (1970a:222). In the discussion of ancient Iranian religion, Zarathustra is dated, without commentary, according to W. Hinz (1970a:468; 1971a:143). These statements of Mann are either unguarded in particulars or too general, and that is probably not to be avoided where a vision of everything altogether — in the proportions of Mann's projections — is strived for. Mann pays dearly for his very good, perhaps ever great over-view of religion with numerous unguarded particular judgments.

88. Cf. the scheme of the seven days, 1970a:203-641.
89. 1973b; cf. on the whole interpretation also C. G. Jung (1962:44-77), 'Dogma und natürliche Symbole'; C. G. Jung (1961).

Bibliography

ABBREVIATIONS

RGG   = Die Religion in Geschichte und Gegenwart.
Kud   = Kerygma und Dogma
NC   = La Nouvelle Clio
ZDMG   = Zeitschrift der Deutschen Morgenländischen Gesellschaft
ZMR   = Zeitschrift für Missionkunde und Religionswissenschaft
ZthK   = Zeitschrift für Theologie und Kirche
ThLZ   = Theologische Literaturzeitung
ZM   = Zeitschrift für Missionskunde
ZRGG   = Zeitschrift für Religions- und Geistesgeschichte
NZSTh = Neue Zeitschrift für Systematische Theologie. Berlin.

Achelis, Th. (1904), *Abriss der vergleichenden Religionswissenschaft*. Leipzig.
Altheim, F. (1944/1949), *Zarathustra als Dichter*, Paideuma 3.
– (1970), 'Zarathustra', *Zarathustra*, B. Schlerath, ed. Darmstadt.
Anantharaman, T. R. (1961), *Die Bhagavadgita*.
Andreas, F. C. and Wackernagel, J. (1913), 'Die erste, zweite und fünfte Ghatha des Zuraxthustro', *Nachrichten van der Königlichen Gesellschaft der Wissenschaften zu Göttingen*, Heft 3.
– (1931), 'Die erste, zweite und fünfte Ghatha des Zurathustro, Anmerkungen', *Nachrichten von der Königlichen Gesellschaft der Wissenschaften zu Göttingen*.
Arnold (1952), 'The root undying', in: F. Edgerton, ed., *The Bhagavad Gita* II.
d'Aviella, Goblet (1887), *Introduction à l'histoire général des religions*. Brussels.
Baaren, Th. P. van and Drijvers, H. J. W., eds. (1973), *Religion, Culture and Methodology*. The Hague-Paris, Mouton ('Religion and Reason', Vol. 8).
Baetke, W. (1974), 'Aufgabe und Struktur der Religionswissenschaft', in: G. Lanczkowski, ed., *Selbstverständnis und Wesen der Religionswissenschaft*. Darmstadt.
Barth, Karl (1958), *Fides quaerens intellectum*. Zollikon.
Bartholomae, Chr. (1905), *Die Gathas des Awesta*. Strassbourg.
– (1961), *Altiranisches Wörterbuch*. Berlin.
– (1970), 'Zarathustras Leben und Lehre', *Zarathustra*, B. Schlerath, ed. Darmstadt.
Benz, E. (1959), 'Über das Verstehen fremder Religionen', in: *Grundfragen der Religionswissenschaft*, M. Eliade and J. M. Kitagawa, eds. Salzburg.

Benz, E. (1968), 'Die Bedeutung der Religionswissenschaft für die Koexistenz der Weltreligionen heute', in: *Proceedings of the XIth International Congress of the International Association for the History of Religions*. Leiden.
Beth, K. (1878), 'Religion: IV A. Wesen der Religion', *RGG*², IV.
Beyerhaus, P. (1969), 'Zur Theologie der Religionen im Protestantismus', *KuD* 15.
Bhaktivedanta Swami Prabhupada, A. C. (1974), *Bhagavad-gita, Wie Sie Ist.*
— (1952), 'Sir Edwin Arnold's Translation of the Bhagavad Gita', in: F. Edgerton, ed., *The Bhagavad Gita* II.
Bianchi, U. (1964), *Probleme der Religionsgeschichte*. Göttingen.
Bleeker, C. J. (1954), 'The relation of the History of Religions to kindred religious Sciences', *Numen* 1.
— (1974), 'Die phänomenologische Methode', in: G. Lanczkowski, ed., *Selbstverständnis und Wesen der Religionswissenschaft*. Darmstadt.
Bochenski, I. M. (1971), *Die zeitgenössischen Denkmethoden*. Munich.
Bode, Dastur F. A. and Nanavutty, P. (1952), *Songs of Zarathustra*. London.
Bolle, Kees W. (1967a), 'History of Religions with a hermeneutic oriented toward Christian theology?', in: *The History of Religions: Essay on the Problem of Understanding*, ed. by Joseph M. Kitagawa with the collaboration of Mircea Eliade and Charles H. Long. (Essay in Divinity, Vol. I). Chicago-London, The University of Chicago Press.
— (1967b), 'Religionsgeschichtliche Forschung und theologische Impulse?', *Kairos* 9.
Boxberger, Robert (1955), *Bhagavadgita*. Stuttgart.
Boyce M. (1975), *A History of Zoroastrianism*, I. Leiden-Cologne.
Buren, P. van (1966), *Reden von Gott in der Sprache der Welt*. Zürich.
Chantepie de la Saussays, P. D. (1891), *Manual of the Science of Religion*. 1st ed., London-New York.
Cherbury, E. Herbert von (1663), *Die religione gentilium errorumque apud eos causis*. Amsterdam.
Christensen, A. (1934), *Le premier homme et le premier roi dans l'histoire légendaire des Iraniens*, II. Leiden.
Chuang Tzû (1962), *The Texts of Taoism*, Translated by James Legge, Part I and II, the Sacred Books of the East, Vol, XL. New York.
Daniélou, J. SJ (1963), 'Die Phänonmenologi der Religionen und die Religionsphilosophie', *Grudfragen der Religionswissenschaft*, M. Eliade and J. M. Kitagawa, eds. Salzburg.
Douglas, W. and P. Hill, (1928), *The Ghagavadgita*. London.
Duchesne-Guillemin, J. (1948), *Zoroastre*. Paris.
— (1951), 'L'originalité de Zoroastre', *L'âme de l'Iran*. Paris.
— (1953), 'L'ordre des Gathas', *NC* 5.
Duméry, H. (1957), *Critique et religion, Problèmes de las methode en philosophie de la religion*. Paris.
Durkheim, Emile (1899), *'de la definition des phénomènes religieux'*, L'Année Sociologique, II. Paris. German translation by J. Matthes, I/1967 and II/1969.
— (1968), *Les formes élémentaires de la vie religieuse*. Paris (1. ed. 1912).
Edgerton, F., ed. (1952), *The Bhagavad Gita*, Vol. I and II.

Eichhorn, W. (1973), *Die Religion Chinas*. Stuttgart.
Eliade, M. and Kitagawa, J. M., eds. (1959), *The History of Religions. Essays in Methodology*. Chicago. German: 1963. Salzburg.
Eliade M. (1954), *Die Religionen und das Heilige*. Salzburg.
— (1963), *Patterns in Comparative Religion*. Cleveland-New York.
— (1964), 'Gefüge und Funktion der Schöpfungsmythen', In: *Quellen des alten Orients, Schöpfungsmythen I*. Einsiedeln.
Emmet, D., The Nature of Metaphysical Thinking.
Fahlbusch, E. (1969), 'Theologie der Religionen, Uberblick zu einem Thema römisch-katholischer Theologie', *KuD* 15.
Flournoy, Th. (1911), *La Philosophie de William James*. Saint Blaise.
— (1919), *Métaphysique et Psychologie*. Geneva-Paris.
Frick, Heinrich (1928), *Vergleichende Religionswissenschaft*. Berlin-Leipzig.
Geldner, K. F. (1926), 'Die zoroastriche Religion', *Religionsgeschichtliches Lesebuch*, I. Tübingen.
Gibrân, K. (1972), *The Prophet*. London.
Glasenapp, H. v. (1958), *Die Philosophie der Inder*. Stuttgart.
Goldammer, Kurt (1954), 'Aufgabe, Grenzen und Möglichkeiten religionswissenschaftlicher Forschung', *Studium Generale* 7.
— (1960), *Die Formenwelt des Religiösen*. Stuttgart.
— (1965), Religionen, *Religion und christliche Offenbarung. Ein Forschungsbericht zur Religionswissenschaft*. Stuttgart.
— (1967a), 'Faktum, Interpretation und Varstehen', *Religion und Religionen, Festschrift für Gustav Mensching zu seinem 65. Geburtstag*. Bonn.
— (1967b), 'Die Frühentwicklung der allgemeinem Religionswissenschaft und die Anfäge einer Theologie der Religionen', *Saeculum* 18.
— (1969), 'Die Gedankenwelt der Religionswissenschaft und die Theologie der Religionen', *KuD* 15.
Grimal, P. (1967), 'Der Mensch und der Mythos', in: *Mythen der Völker*. Frankfurt.
Grossmann, S. (1975), 'Bibliographi Ulrich Mann', in: *Synopse, Beiträge zum Gespräch der Theologie mit ihren Nachbarwissenschaften*, Festschrift für Ulrich Mann zum 11. August 1975. Darmstadt.
Gruehn, W. (1960), *Die Frömmigkeit der Gegenwart*. Konstanz.
Hammarskjöld, Dag (1975), *Markings*. London.
Hardy, E. (1898), 'Was ist Religionswissenschaft?', *Archiv für Religionswissenschaft* 1. 1974 in: G. Lanczkowski, ed., *Sebstverständnis und Wesen der Religionswissenschaft*, 7. Darmstadt.
Heiler, Friedrich (1961), *Erscheinungformen und Wesen der Religion*. Stuttgart.
Henning, W. B. (1970), 'Zoroaster', *Zarathustra*, B. Schlerath, ed. Darmstadt., trans. by B. Creighton and revised by W. Sorrell, Penguin Books.
Hesse, Hermann (1963), *Steppenwolf*.
Hinz, W. (1961), *Zarathustra*. Stuttgart.
Hirschmann, E. (1940), *Phänomenologie der Religion*.
Hörmann, M. (1968), *Religion der Athleton*. Stuttgart-Berlin.
Hoffmann, K., ed. (1965), *Die Wirklichkeit des Mythos*. Munich.
Holm, S. (1960), *Religionsphilosophy*. Stuttgart.
Holsten, W. Religionswissenschaft, *RGG*^{3}, V.

Honko Lauri, ed. (1978), *Studies in the Methodology of the Sciences of Religion*, Proceedings of the Study Conference of the International Association for the History of Religion, held in Turku, Finland, August 1973. The Hague-Paris-New York, Mouton Publishers ('Religion and Reason', 13).

Humbach, H. (1957), 'Zur altiranischen Mythologie', *ZDMG* 107.

— (1959), *Die Gathas des Zarathustra*, Band I/II. Heidelberg.

Ingold, F. P. and Rakusa, I., eds. (1972), *Gedichte an Gott sind Gebete, Gott in der neuesten sowjetischen Poesie*. Zürich.

Jackson, A. V. W. (1968), *An Avestan Grammar*. Darmstadt.

James, E. O. (1954), 'The History, Science and Comparative Study of Religion', *Numen*, I.

Jung, C. G. (1962), 'Dogma und natürliche Symbole', 'Geschichte und Psychologie eines natürlichen Symbols', *Psychologie und Religion*. Zürich-Stuttgart.

Keibach, W. (1962), 'Die empirische Religionspsychologie als Zweig der Religionswissenschaft', *Archiv für Religionspsychologie*, 7 Göttingen.

— (1964), 'Der immer noch umstrittene Gegenstand der Religionspsychologie'. *Archiv für Religionspsychologie*, 8. Göttingen.

Khalîl Djibrân, (1975), *Der Prophet*, Olten-Freiburg i.B.

Klostermaier, K. (1965), *Hinduismus*. Köln.

Kobbert, M. (1910), *De verborum religion atque religiosus usu apud Romanos*. Königsberg.

König, Gisbert (1973), 'Methodologie', in: Gerhard Sauter, ed., *Wissenschaftstheoretische Kritik der Theologie. Die Theologie und die neuere wissenschaftstheoretische Diskution*. Munich.

Kortzfleisch, S. von (1967), *Religion im Säkularismus*. Stuttgart-Berlin.

Kristensen, W. B. (1960), *The Meaning of Religion*. The Hague.

Lamotte, E. (1929), *Notes sur la Bhagavadgita*. Paris.

Lanczkowski, G. (1956), *Heilige Schriften*. Stuttgart.

Lanczkowski, G., ed. (1974), *Selbstverständnis und Wesesn der Religionswissenschaft*. Darmstadt.

Leese, K. (1954), *Recht und Grenze der natürlichen Religion*. Zürich.

Leeuw, Gerhard van der, 'Religion: III. Religionsgeschichtliche Entwicklung', *RGG*[2], IV.

— (1956), *Phänomenologie der Religion*. Tübingen.

— (1963), *Religion in Essence and Manifestation: A Study in Phenomenology*, Vol. 2. Translated by J. E. Turner with Appendices to the Torchbook edition incorporating the additions of the second German edition by Hans H. Penner. New York-Evanston, Harper & Row (Harper Torchbook 101).

Lommel, H. (1930), *Die Religion Zarathustras*. Tübingen.

— (1938), 'Yasna 32', in *Wörter und Sachen* 19, Neue Folge I.

— (1970a), 'Zarathustras Priesterlohn', *Zarathustra*, B. Schlerath, ed. Darmstadt.

— (1970b), 'Die Sonne des Schlechteste?', *Zarathustra*, B. Schlerath, ed. Darmstadt.

Mann, Ulrich (1959), *Gottes Nein und Ja*. Hamburg.

— (1961), *Theologische Religionsphilosophie im Grundriss*. Hamburg.

— (1962), 'Sybillinische Offenbarung', *Lutherische Monatshefte(1*.

— (1964), 'Theologie und Religionsgeschichte', *Lutherische Monatshefte 3*.

- (1965a), 'Hermeneutische Entsagung', in: *Seelsorge als Lebenshilfe*, H. Harsch, ed., Festschrift Walter Uhsadel yum 65. Geburtstag. Heidelberg.
- (1965b), 'Tiefenpsychologie und Theologie', *Lutherische Monatshefte* 14.
- (1967), 'Quaternität bei C. G. Jung', *Theologische Literaturzeitung* 92.
- (1969), 'Seinstiefe und Oberfläche', *Zeitwende* 40.
- (1970a), *Theogonische Tage. Die Entwicklungsphasen des Gottesbewusstseins in der altorientalischen und beblischen Religion*. Stuttgart.
- (1970b), *Einführung in die Religionsphilosophie*. Darmstadt.
- (1970c), 'Theologie in oder neben der Kirche', *Universitas* 25.
- (1971a), *Das Christentum als absolute Religion*. Darmstadt.
- (1971b), 'Wahreit in Wissenschaft, Theologie und Religion', *Zeitwende* 42.
- (1971c), 'Aesthetische Philosophie', *Lutherische Monatshefte* 10.
- (1972), 'Erkennen des Menschen', *Lutherische Monatshefte* 11.
- (1973a), ed., *Theologie und Religionswissenschaft*. Darmstadt.
- (1973b), *Einführung in die Religionspsychologie*. Darmstadt.
- (1973c), 'Gleichartige Erkenntnis', *Lutherische Monatshefte* 11.
- (1973d), 'Abschluss der Theologie? Forschung muss in Zukunft "synoptisch" arbeiten', *Lutherische Monatshefte* 12.
- (1974), 'Der erfahrene Gott', *Lutherische Monatshefte* 13.
- (1975), *Die Religion in den Religionen*. Stuttgart.
- (1976), 'Zur synoptischen Methode in der Religionspsychologie', *Archiv für Religionspsychologie* 12. Göttingen.
Martin, Jane R. (1969), 'Another Look at the Doctrine of Verstehen', *British Journal of the Philosophy of Sciences*, 20.
Matthes, Joachim (I/1967 and II/1969), *Religion und Gesellschaft, Einführung in die Religionssoziologie*. Reinbeck by Hamburg.
Meillet, A. (1925), *Trois conférences sur les Gâthâ de l'Avesta*. Paris.
Meinhold, P. (1973a), 'Entwicklung der Religionswissenschaft im Mittelalter und zur Reformationszeit', pp. 357-380 in: U. Mann, ed, *Theologie und Religionswissenschaft*. Darmstadt.
- (1973b), 'Entwicklung der Religionswissenschaft in der Neuzeit und in der Gegenwart', pp. 381-412 in U. Mann, ed., see above.
Mensching, Gustav (n.d.), *Buddhistische Geisteswelt*. Baden-Baden.
- (1933), 'Zum Streit um die Deutung des buddhistischen Nirvana', *ZMR*.
- (1938), *Vergleichende Religionswissenschaft*. Leipzig.
- (1957), *Das Wunder im Glauben und Aberglauben der Völker*. Leiden.
- (1959), *Die Religion*. Stuttgart.
MIcklem, N. (1948), *Religion*. London-New York-Toronto.
Molé, M. (1970), 'Antwort an J. Duchesne-Guillemin', *Zarathustra*, B. Schlerath, ed. Darmstadt.
Müller, F. Max (1878), *Lectures on the Origin and Growth of Religion*. London.
Nietzsche, Friedrich (n.d.), *Ecce homo*, in: *Schriften aus dem Jahre 1888, Nietszches Werke*, Klassiker Ausgabe VIII. Leipzig. Translated by Walter Kaufmann (1967), *F. Nietzsche, The Genealogy of Morals; Ecce Homo*. (Vintage Books, Random House) New York.
Nigg, Walter (1959), *Heimliche Weisheit, Mystisches Erleben in der Evangeli-*

schen Christenheit. Zürich-Stuttgart.
- (1966), *Für alle Tage.* Zürich-Stuttgart.
Nyberg, H. S. (1970), 'Die altiranische soyiale Religion II: Die Gathagemeinde',
   Zarathustra, B. Schlerath, ed. Darmstadt.
Otto, Rudolf (1917), 'Das Gesetz der Parallelen in der Religionsgeschichte',
   Vishnu-Narayana. Jena.
- (1923), *The Idea of the Holy.* London.
- (1963), *Das Heilige.* Munich.
Otto, W. F. (1956), *Theophania.* Hamburg.
Paul, O. (1938), 'Exegetische Beiträge yum Awesta', *Wörter und Sachen*, Neue
   Folge I.
Penner, H. H. (1971), 'The Poverty of Functionalism', *History of Religions*, 11.
Pettazzoni, R. (1954a), '"History" and "Phenomenology" in the Science of
   Religion", *Essays on the History of Religion.* Leiden.
- (1954b), 'Myths of Beginnings and Creation-Myths', in: *Essays on the History
   of Religions.* Leiden.
*Proceedings of the Sixth Annual Meeting of the Congress of Religion, Boston
   1900,* (1900) Chicago.
Pruyser, Paul W. (1972), *Die Wurzeln des Glaubens.* Bern-Munich-Vienna.
Rade, M., 'Religionsgeschichte und Religionsgeschichtliche Schule', *RGG* 1, IV.
Radhakrishnan, S. (1949), *The Bhagavadgita.* London.
Ratschow, C. H. (1973a), 'Methodik der Religionswissenschaft', in: *Enzyklo-
   pädie der geisteswissenschaftlichen Arbeitsmethoden*, 9th Instalment. Munich-
   Vienna. Also published in: *Selbstverständnis und Wesen der Religionswissen-
   schaft,* G. Lanczkowski, ed. (1974). Darmstadt.
- (1973b), 'Systematische Theologie', in: U. Mann, ed., *Theologie und Re-
   ligionswissenschaft*, Darmstadt.
Rawson, Philip and Legeza, Laszlo, *Tao, Die Philosophie von Sein und Werden.*
   (Droemer-Knaur, n.d.).
Reichelt, H. (1909), *Awestisches Elementarbuch.* Heidelberg.
Religion, Journal of Religion and Religions (1975), special issue: 'The History
   of Religion: An International Survey, on the occasion of the XIIIth Congress
   of the International Association for the History of Religions, August 1975.
Rosenkranz, G. (1951), *Evangelische Religionskunde, Einfürung in eine theo-
   logische Schau der Religionen.* Tübingen.
- (1955), 'Wege und Grenzen des religionswissenschaftlichen Erkennens',
   ZThK, 52.
- (1964), 'Wege und Grenzen des Religionswissenschaftlichen Erkennens',
   Religionswissenschaft und Theologie. Munich.
- (1967), *Der christliche Glaube angesichts der Weltreligionen.* Bern.
Rudolph, K. (1970), 'Zarathustra — Priester und Prophet', *Zarathustra*, B.
   Schlerath, ed. Darmstadt.
- (1971), 'Religionsgeschichte und Religionsphänomenologie', *ThLZ* 96.
Sauter, Gerhard, ed. (1973), *Wissenschaftstheoretische Kritik der Theologie.
   Die Theologie und die neure wissenschaftstheoretische Diskussion.* Munich.
Schaeder, H. H. (1940), 'Ein indogermanischer Liedtypus in den Gathas', *ZDMG*
   94.

– (1970), 'Zarathustras Botschaft von der rechten Ordnung', *Zarathustra*, B. Schlerath, ed. Darmstadt.

Schleiermacher (1893), *On Religion*. London.

Schlerath, B. ed. (1970), 'Die Gathas des Zarathustra', *Zarathustra*, Darmstadt.

Schlette, H. R. (1970), 'Ist die Religionswissenschaft am Ende', *ZM* 54.

Schmid, Georg (1971), *Interessant und Heilig*. Zürich.

Schroeder, Leopold von (1965), *Bhagavadgita*.

Schwarzwäller, K. (1966), *Theologie oder Phänomenologie*. Munich.

Soderblom, N. (1966), *Der lebendige Gott im Zeugnis der Religionsgeschichte*. Munich.

Spencer, John (1669), *Dissertatio de Urim et Thummim*. Cambridge.

– (1685), *De legibus Hebraeorum ritualisbus at earum nationibus libri tres*. Cambridge.

Stephenson, G. (1975), 'Kritische Bemerkungen zu C. H. Ratschows Methodenlehre', *ZMR* 59.

– (1976), 'Zum Religionsverständnis der Gegenwart', *ZM* 60.

Tao Te Ching (1951), *Reden und Gleichnisse des Tschuang-Tse*, Deutsche Auswahl von Martin Buber. Zürich.

Tersteegen, Gerhard (1798/1799[2]), *Geistliche und erbauliche Briefe über das inwendige Leben und wahre Wesen des Christenthums*, I and II.

– (1845), *Erbauliches und Beschauliches*, ausgewählt und herausgegeben von D. August Gebauer. Stuttgart.

Thieme, P. (1970), 'Die vedischen Aditya und die zarathustrischen Am sa Sp nta', *Zarathustra*, B. Schlerath, ed. Darmstadt.

Tiele, Cornelius Petrus (1897), *Elements of the Science of Religion*, I. Edinburgh.

– (1904), *Grudzüge der Religionswissenschaft*. Tübingen-Leipzig.

Tillich, Paul (1963), *Christianity and the Encounter of the World Religions*. New York-London.

Transactions of the third International Congress for the History of the World Religions (1908), II, 'Die Hilfswissenschaften der vergleichenden Religionsgeschichte', Oxford.

Trillhaas, W. (1974), 'Versuchter Brüchenschlag', *Lutherische Monatshefte* 13.

Troeltsch, Ernst (1906), 'Wesen der Religion und der Religionswissenschaft', In: *Die christliche Religion*. Berlin-Leipzig. Also published in: *Die Kultur der Gegenwart*, Part I/IV (1906). Berlin-Leipzig.

Tworuschka, U. (1971), *Interessant und Heilig, Auf dem Weg zur integralen Religionswissenschaft*. Zürich.

Tworuschka, U. (1972), 'Integral Religionswissenschaft – Methode der Zukunft?', *ZRGG* XXVI, 3.

Waardenburg, Jacques (1972), 'Grundsätzliches yur Religionsphänomenologie', *NZSTh* 15/3.

– (1973a), 'Research on Meaning in Religion', in: Th. P. van Baaren and H. J. W. Drijvers, eds., *Religion, Culture and Methodology*. The Hague-Paris, Mouton ('Religion and Reason', 8).

– (1973b), 'Religionen der Gegenwart im Blickfeld phänomenologischer Forschung', *NZSTh* 15.

– (1973c), *Classical Approaches to the study of Religion. Aims, Methods and*

Theories of Research, Vol. I: Introduction and Anthology, The Hague-Paris, Mouton ('Religion and Reason', 3).

— (1974), *Classical Approaches to the Study of Religion. Aims, Methods and Theories of Research,* Vol. II: *Bibliography.* The Hague-Paris, Mouton ('Religion and Reason', 4).

Wach, Joachim (n.d.), 'Understanding is not mirroring (Abspiegeln)' *RGG*², V.

— (1923), 'Zur Methodologie der allgemeinen Religionswissenschaft', *ZMR* 38. Reprinted in G. Lanczkowski, 1974.

— (1924), *Religionswissenschaft — Prolegomena zu ihrer wissenschaftstheoretischen Grundlegung.* Leipzig, J. G. Hinrichs.

— (1931), 'Verstehen', *RGG*², V.

— (1954), 'Religionswissenschaft', *RGG*², IV.

— (1961), *The Comparative Study of Religions,* ed. with an Introduction by Joseph M. Kitagawa, New York-London (paperback ed.).

Werblowsky, Zwi R. J. (1959), 'On the Role of Comparative Religion in Promoting Mutual Understanding', *Hibbert Journal,* 58.

Wilhelm, R. (1976), in: Dschuang Dsi, *Das wahre Buch vom südlichen Blütenland.* Zürich.

Widengren, G. (1974a), 'Evolutionistische Theorien auf dem Gebiet der vergleichenden Religionswissenschaft', in: G. Lanczkowski, ed., *Selbstverständnis und Wesen der Religionswissenschaft.* Darmstadt.

— (1974b), 'Die Methoden der Phänomenologie der Religion', in: G. Lanczkowski, ed., *Selbstverständnis und Wesen der Religionswissenschaft.* Darmstadt.

— (1965), *Die Religionen Irans.* Stuttgart.

Zaehner, R. C. (1969). *The Bhagavad-gita.* Oxford.

Index of Names

Index of Subjects

apologia religiosa, 48, 49

biologism, 47
Buddhism, Buddhist, 49, 134, 174, 184

Christian, Christianity, 14, 40, 49, 85,
    159, 184, 194, 195
Christian theology, 14, 39, 159
Christology, 167
Communism, 42, 46, 47

depth-psychology, 170, 175—177
Deutungswissenschaften, 169, 170, 173
Dharma, 90

enlightenment, 9

Fascism, 42, 46
fundus animae, 54

God, 57, 59, 61, 88, 101, 122—128,
    133, 141, 144—146, 148—150, 173,
    179, 185, 193, 195

Hinduism, 147, 174, 184

incarnation, 137—139
inspiration, 137, 138
Islam, 15, 40, 49, 174, 184

Joga, 122
Judaism, 15, 40, 184

Kerygma, 195

Mandola, 174

Marxism, 47
miracle, 135, 136
mystic, the, 41
myth, 135, 136

Neoplatonism, 14
nirvāna, 134, 135, 143

pantheism, 124, 149, 150
perfection, 123
philosophy, 168
pseudo-religion, 42, 46, 47
psychogenesis, 174, 176
psychology, 46
psychology, depth, 170, 175—177
psychopathology, 46

quasi-religion, 42

racism, 47
Rationalism, 9
rationalistic philosophy of religion, 15
revelation, 135—139, 172, 173

secular religion, 41—44, 46, 50
scientism 45, 49, 50, 86
sociology, 46
siddhi, 123
statism, 47

theogony, 173
theosophy, 39, 40
truth, 123
tattvatah, 123